# textile

# ARCHITECTURE

## TEXTILE ARCHITEKTUR

SYLVIE KRÜGER

# textile ARCHITECTURE

## TEXTILE ARCHITEKTUR

jovis

© 2009 by jovis Verlag GmbH

Texts by kind permission of the author.
Pictures by kind permission of the photographers/holders of the picture rights.
Das Copyright für die Texte liegt bei der Autorin.
Das Copyright für die Abbildungen liegt bei den Fotografen/Inhabern der
Bildrechte.

Cover/Umschlagfoto: Inside Outside
Concept and Editing/Konzept und Redaktion: Sylvie Krüger, Munich
Editing/Lektorat: Oliver G. Hamm, Berlin
Translation/Übersetzung: Rachel Hill, Berlin; Alexander Hamann, Berlin (p.12–15)
Design and setting/Gestaltung und Satz: Heike Henig, Munich
Lithography/Lithografie: Adelgund Janik, Munich
Printing and binding/Druck und Bindung: fgb freiburger graphische betriebe

Bibliographic information published by Die Deutsche Bibliothek
Die Deutsche Bibliothek lists this publication in the Deutsche Nationalbibliografie;
detailed bibliographic data are available on the Internet at http://dnb.ddb.de

Bibliografische Information der Deutschen Bibliothek
Die Deutsche Bibliothek verzeichnet diese Publikation in der Deutschen Nationalbibliografie; detaillierte bibliografische Daten sind im Internet über
http://dnb.ddb.de abrufbar.

jovis Verlag GmbH
Kurfürstenstraße 15/16
10785 Berlin

www.jovis.de

ISBN 978-3-86859-017-3

# INTRODUCTION
## *EINLEITUNG*

Textiles are light, flexible, transparent, opaque, thick, fine, bulky, delicate, and much more. They provide protection from heat and cold, absorb noise, and give control of the amount of light entering and the view. Their manifold characteristics and application potentials make textiles a highly interesting architectural material. Textiles further possess very special, sensually tangible, often poetic aesthetics. And classical textiles are transient–a factor that is also reflected in their contemporary application.

Textile materials have always been used for weather and visual protection. They did, however, begin to lose in significance as people became increasingly settled and erected more solid dwellings. The question arose as to what extent textiles would be needed in architecture after the invention of heating, air-conditioning, and improved methods of insulation. Yet multifarious past applications certainly provide inspiration for contemporary tasks: for example the retractable roofs that now cover our sports stadiums were preceded by *vela* structures that protected visitors to Roman amphitheatres and arenas from the sun. Traditional textile structures continue to be used in various corners of the earth today: examples of such include retractable textile coverings over streets and squares in Spain, North Africa, South America, or Japan, as well as the tents of North-African and Arabic nomads.

Textiles also remain of interest from an energy-saving point of view. Just as they protected from heat or cold generation in the past, textiles are now increasingly being used to reduce the amount of energy required to increase or decrease room temperatures.

Yet, what exactly is meant by the term "textile" in this context? Classical textile materials comprise fabrics made of organic cotton, linen or wool fibres, of inorganic metal or glass fibres, and of synthetic polyester or polyamide fibres. This book also looks at membrane materials; although the classical definition of textiles no longer applies to them, they do exhibit "textile" characteristics and they can take on "textile" functions. The *shoj* paper-covered movable partitions that are commonly used in Japan, or flexible bast mats that are used for visual and sun protection on house façades, are not textiles in the classical sense, just as plastic films are not. However, in their own areas of application, they represent a further development of traditional textile membrane materials.

The manifold application potentials of textile architecture, presented and placed in relation to one another in this book, originate from very different areas. We are surrounded by "textile architecture" in our everyday lives. Everyone has slept in a tent or used an umbrella to protect themselves from rain. Whether building-site protection, awning or festival tent: textile structures fulfill a wide range of functions in our everyday environments without us really noticing them. And it is often precisely such quotidian applications that, alongside the highly complex structures developed by engineers, constitute the special allure of textile architecture. Textiles were long avoided by architects in interior spaces or, if used, were robbed of their sensual qualities. The reason behind that was most likely–apart from transformed outlooks on architecture in the first decades of the twentieth century–modernism's obsession with hygiene. Richly draperied nineteenth century spatial textiles were considered to be "dust catchers."

In the mid-twentieth century, lively involvement began in the area of self-supporting membrane structures; this was fundamentally influenced by the work of Frei Otto. New textile protective roofs and tent constructions were created that found application at world fairs, over open-air theatres and sports complexes. Textile construction conquered novel fields of action, taking on a permanence, as an alternative to classical architecture, which it had never seen before. This was enabled by the increased post-1945 development of synthetic fibres as well as modern finishing technologies.

A euphoric future-oriented phase between the nineteen-fifties and seventies saw much experiment with pneumatic structures in the most diverse areas. However, technical shortcomings and the large amounts of energy needed to maintain such air-supported structures led to decreased use of that technology. A return to or revival of the architectural application of textiles can be observed in recent years. Innovative structures are now being created that are characterised by their new experimental use of textiles. The spectrum reaches from designs by renowned architectural practices, through high-tech applications developed by engineers, to the work of young architects and designers who are currently sounding out the temporary potentials of textile architecture.

Textilien sind leicht, flexibel, transparent, blickdicht, dick, dünn, voluminös, zart und vieles mehr. Sie bieten Schutz vor Wärme oder Kälte, dämpfen Geräusche und ermöglichen es, den Lichteinfall und die Sicht zu steuern. Ihre vielfältigen Eigenschaften und Anwendungsmöglichkeiten machen Textilien zu einem hochinteressanten architektonischen Material. Zudem ist dem textilen Material eine ganz besondere, sinnlich erfahrbare, oft poetische Ästhetik eigen. Und klassische Textilien sind vergänglich – ein Merkmal, das sich im temporären Gebrauch widerspiegelt.

Seit jeher werden textile Materialien verwendet, um sich vor Witterungseinflüssen sowie vor Einblick zu schützen. Zwar verloren sie mit der beginnenden Sesshaftigkeit und dem Bau massiver Behausungen an Bedeutung, und man könnte die Frage stellen, wozu man nach der Erfindung von Heizung, Klimaanlage und verbesserter Möglichkeiten der Isolierung noch Textilien in der Architektur braucht. Aber die vielfältigen Beispiele der Vergangenheit bieten durchaus Inspiration für aktuelle Aufgabenstellungen: Die wandelbaren Dächer, die unsere Sportstadien überspannen, finden ihre Vorläufer beispielsweise in der Konstruktion der *Vela*, die die Besucher römischer Amphitheater und Arenen vor der Sonne schützten. Und bis heute sind in verschiedenen Teilen der Erde traditionsreiche textile Konstruktionen in Verwendung; Beispiele dafür sind die wandelbaren textilen Überdachungen über Straßen und Plätzen in Spanien, Nordafrika, Südamerika oder Japan sowie die Zelte der nordafrikanischen und arabischen Nomaden.

Auch unter dem Aspekt der Energieeinsparung ist die Anwendung von Textilien heutzutage durchaus von Interesse. Genauso wie Textilien in der Vergangenheit vor zu hoher Wärme- oder Kälteentwicklung schützten, werden sie auch heute wieder vermehrt zu diesem Zweck eingesetzt, um den Energieaufwand für das Kühlen oder Erwärmen der Raumtemperatur gering zu halten.

Aber was ist in diesem Zusammenhang überhaupt unter dem Begriff „Textilien" zu verstehen? Klassische textile Materialien sind beispielsweise Gewebe aus organischen Baumwoll-, Leinen- oder Wollfasern, aus anorganischen Metall- oder Glasfasern sowie aus synthetischen Polyester- oder Polyamidfasern. In diesem Buch werden außerdem auch Membranmaterialien vorgestellt, auf die die klassische Definition von Textilien nicht zutrifft, die aber gleichwohl „textile" Eigenschaften besitzen und „textile" Funktionen übernehmen können: So sind etwa die in Japan gebräuchlichen, mit Papier überzogenen beweglichen Raumteiler, die *Shoji*, oder die flexiblen Bastmatten als Sicht- und Lichtschutz an Hausfassaden keine Textilien im klassischen Sinn, ebensowenig wie Kunststofffolien. Sie stellen jedoch in einigen Einsatzbereichen eine Weiterentwicklung der traditionellen textilen Membranmaterialien dar.

Aus ganz unterschiedlichen Bereichen stammen die zahlreichen Anwendungsmöglichkeiten textiler Architektur, die in diesem Buch vorgestellt und miteinander in Beziehung gesetzt werden. Im Alltag sind wir umgeben von „textiler Architektur". Jeder hat schon einmal in einem Campingzelt übernachtet oder sich mit einem Schirm gegen Regen geschützt. Ob als Baustellenschutz, Markise oder Festzelt: Textile Konstruktionen erfüllen mannigfaltige Funktionen in unserem Alltag, ohne dass wir uns dessen wirklich bewusst sind. Und oft sind es gerade die alltäglichen Anwendungen, die neben hochkomplexen, von Ingenieuren entwickelten Konstruktionen den besonderen Reiz textiler Architektur ausmachen. Von Architekten wurde der Werkstoff Textil im Innenraum lange vermieden oder seiner besonderen sinnlichen Qualität beraubt. Grund dafür mag – neben dem Wandel in der Architekturauffassung in den ersten Jahrzehnten des 20. Jahrhunderts – die Hygieneobsession der Moderne gewesen sein: Die reich drapierten Raumtextilien des 19. Jahrhunderts wurden als „Staubfänger" angesehen. Wesentlich beeinflusst durch die Arbeit Frei Ottos begann Mitte des 20. Jahrhunderts eine rege Auseinandersetzung mit der Thematik der freigespannten Membrankonstruktionen. Es entstanden neue textile Schutzdächer und Zeltkonstruktionen, die auf Weltausstellungen, über Freilichttheatern und über Sportstätten zum Einsatz kamen. Das textile Bauen eroberte neue Aufgabenfelder, indem es als Alternative zur klassischen Architektur eine Dauerhaftigkeit beanspruchte, die früher nicht gegeben war. Ermöglicht wurde dies durch die verstärkt nach 1945 einsetzende Entwicklung synthetisch hergestellter Fasern sowie moderner Veredlungstechnologien.

In der euphorischen, zukunftsorientierten Phase der 50er bis 70er Jahre wurde mit pneumatischen Konstruktionen in den verschiedensten Einsatzgebieten experimentiert. Technische Mängel und der hohe Energieaufwand zur Aufrechterhaltung dieser luftgestützten Konstruktionen führten jedoch zu einem nachlassenden Einsatz dieser Technik.

In den letzten Jahren ist eine Rückbesinnung bzw. Wiederbelebung des architektonischen Einsatzes von Textilien zu beobachten. Es entstehen innovative Konstruktionen, die sich durch einen neuen, experimentellen Umgang mit dem textilen Material auszeichnen. Die Bandbreite reicht von Entwürfen renommierter Architekturbüros über von Ingenieuren entwickelten Hightech-Anwendungen bis hin zu Arbeiten junger Architekten und Designer, die den temporären Aspekt textiler Architektur ausloten.

**Interview with Petra Blaisse**
by Sylvie Krüger

# " THE EMANCIPATION OF THE CURTAIN "

How do you use textiles to change the atmosphere of interior space?

First of all, space is affected by organizing points of view, allowing one to experience another space: interior or exterior, close by or far away. We add movement and flexibility to space: the movement of an object itself, of its materiality, and of the users as they manipulate the object or are steered in a certain direction by its positioning or shape.

And then we often use colour, which, needless to say, has an enormous influence on space. You can change the entire visual rhythm and atmosphere of architecture using layers of curtains of various degrees of transparency and of different colours. A curtain, with its own composition and form, can also change the division of planes within a space. For instance, we did not like the architectural division of the glass façade of a private apartment that we were working on in London;

we used a curtain to neutralize the vertical structure by installing a thick, horizontal seam over the entire width of the circular space. This gave the room a different quality in an architectural sense. We use curtain tracks to define paths, to choreograph the movement of an object, to regulate its trajectory. Such tracks can be shaped independently of architecture to create a space within a space, thus escaping architectural logic. Architectural rules can be disabled using round corners or curves and a shift in volume can be used to break a given logic; we did so in the Haus der Kunst in Munich, moving from symmetrical to asymmetrical.

And finally, the acoustics of a space can also be completely changed; as in the Haus der Kunst and in many other projects, where the acoustic quality and flexibility of spaces – like in the concert halls and rehearsal studios of Casa da Música in Porto – play an important role.

What are the potentials of textile structures and where are their limits?

You can't guarantee textiles for twenty-five or fifty years. There certainly is a limit. They decompose and that is the beauty of them. From the moment you start to use textiles, they begin to disintegrate slowly. The new range of weaves that is now available, from metals and pvc to charcoal and glass fibres, should last much longer, if not forever. Yet, textile, in the classical sense, is, of course, temporary. As far as construction goes, woven and non-woven cloths do hold much potential, however they are limited in relation to stretch and weight and it is still impossible to erect a textile building without the help of a stiff structure of some kind. Yet, a weave can be integrated into a fluid and hardening material, as in space technology and for product wrapping purposes; the life span of both materials combined can become limitless.

The special charm of your work results precisely from that combination of functionality and aesthetics. Technical demands such as light, climate, acoustics, and changing spatial situations are solved through sensitive application of the individual features of textiles. You highlight the material characteristics and processing technologies of different textiles, bringing their poetic qualities to the fore. Each choice of material and type of textile structure comes in direct response to a specific situation.

Do you prefer to come up with your own solutions or do you also use prefabricated industrial textiles? Do you work with new developments and technologies?

We generally use existing weaves or non-wovens. We are a bit like Louis Kahn, who said, "What do you want, Brick?" A material does dictate its unique potentials and limitations. It is a joy to learn to "read" each material's "message" by playing around endlessly with it. We hardly ever use existing industrial – already created and ready-for-use – solutions, but we usually work with existing base materials. We are perpetually in search of materials that are flame retardant, do not melt, are not poisonous when heated, are not smelly, etc. There is an endless list of demands and restrictions in public buildings. It is interesting because it means that you can only work with a limited range of materials; you start manipulating them into something more intriguing than what they are if left alone. You challenge and test them to discover what their limits and qualities are or could become; so limitations are actually very inspiring.

Textiles are very flexible. In contrast to the static character of buildings, they can adapt to the permanently changing needs of human beings. How do you deal with such contrasting characteristics?

The contradiction makes them very easy to combine. It is often a very charming combination: hard and soft. However, it is extremely important to develop your idea of how to apply textiles to a building while it is being designed. It is easier to understand the implications and the potentials of textiles if you also understand the whole architectural concept; including the structural concept, because textiles can be quite weighty. Textiles often require a certain weight and fullness for acoustic reasons; the whole structure of a building sometimes needs to be adjusted to accommodate this mass of cloth. You also have to store the cloth somewhere when it is not in use. In that sense, it is beautiful to work with architects to discover the compatibility of the various mediums used to form an interior; and to achieve a composition in which invisible storage and motor space can be made, so that the disappearance and appearance of the curtain becomes a choreography in its own right.

Textiles have the potential to create varying spatial situations without permanently changing the architecture; they inherently accommodate temporality and modification. Is the "non-architectural" of textiles of benefit and how do you use it?

I'm just wondering why we don't make permanent structures. So far, the essence of our work has been that it is not permanent. I often think that I must have some kind of claustrophobia; that anything permanent or not transparent or porous in some way or another is an almost suffocating limitation to me.

You work with flexible and adaptable materials such as textiles and plants. Is that a coincidence or a conscious decision?

I have discovered that when working on gardens for instance you are confronted with a time issue that is op-posite to the one that occurs in the use of textiles. While textile starts to decompose the moment it is used, gardens need time – twenty, fifty, a hundred years – to grow into what you envision in your design. Within the timeline of its development, the garden goes through yearly cycles of seasonal change from being dormant and seemingly dead, to rejuvenation – when it starts to bud and grow again. As it goes through this sequence of death and birth time and again, a garden strengthens and settles, finding its own path. A textile object, on the contrary, is born during one continuous process of creation and manipulation. It reaches its final form in a relatively short time; ready to be installed, used and enjoyed as planned! Then disintegration starts; the bare spots appear, the bleached and thinning areas, the restoration marks, the loosened yarn and all those signs of history and temporality that make a cloth so beautiful …

until it is no longer; or until, in some cases, it is saved by curatorial thoroughness and stored in the darkest drawer of a museum.

Contemporary architecture is often rather reduced and cool. Do you feel that textiles have the capacity and duty to add a human dimension to it?

That was once the general interpretation. Modernist buildings often used to be described as harsh and minimalist. The application of rich, soft materials such as silk and velour provided a welcome contrast. However, that is too simple. Textiles have taken on many more roles than that; they have many functions and respond to many needs that architecture cannot always manage by itself. We have called this the "emancipation of the curtain." The curtain, as we apply it, has become almost competitive.

Textiles are often added later – after a building has been designed or even built – to solve "problems" such as visual or sun protection. You are increasingly consulted during the conceptual design phase. How does such early collaboration influence the outcome and quality of a building?

Last year Herman Herzberger, who was working on a new university building in Utrecht at the time, caught me on my bike and said, "I want to build an outside lecture theatre. It is situated on the corner of the building on the second floor and has a concrete, cantilevering roof. Can I make an outside curtain there and what do I need to consider?" We had a whole conversation, in which I outlined the basic essentials to him: that he could integrate the track into the concrete roof, and that the fixing technique, the shape, and the choice of track depends on the quality, size, and weight of the curtain; that the occurring wind, rain, and sun intensity, its degree of "free movement" and its storage position should be considered, etc. We never heard from him again, but he most probably did something with it!

I don't dare to state that our consultations and interventions always positively influence the quality of a building, but they do add another way of looking at things; they occasionally open up hidden potentials and set off experiences; and our work does allow architects to count on us when it comes to solving issues, it gives them more freedom in the use of thin and transparent skins. Think of the thin roof of the glass pavilion from Sejima & Nishizawa in Toledo; or the glass façades in the concert halls of the Casa da Música by OMA.

Within your work you directly react to existing or planned architectural contexts and you develop complementary interventions. Are you attracted by the idea of creating a whole building made of textiles? Or is relating to existing architecture the main challenge?

Yes, so far it has always been the main challenge. Working closely with different architects with totally different points of view is also interesting.

To actually create a building ourselves is not my personal aim, because I think our work is already a from of architecture. Curtains do not only create or regulate space; they are space in themselves. Their scale, shape, structure, pleats, and folds and technical implications become part of the architecture that they are serving. It is true that we are in a perpetual search for textile as a self-supporting structure … emancipating it from walls, ceilings, or other stiff structures. But we haven't found the answer quite yet!

For centuries, textiles were used in architectural contexts as a result of their special functional and aesthetic characteristics. As technological progress was made regarding the climatic regulation of buildings and as perceptions of architecture changed in the early twentieth century, textiles – with a few exceptions – became less relevant in architecture. They are being rediscovered as architecture appears to be becoming increasingly "emotional." What do you think of such developments and how significant do you feel textiles to be in contemporary architecture?

Although the curtain was censored for a time, textiles never disappeared. They secretly continued to be used, even in modern architecture. Architects like Le Corbusier and Mies van der Rohe did use them, although intellectually they might have denied them. The "white-washed wall" was declared a curtain in itself, so I think the curtain as a phenomenon never really disappeared either. Its role may have been temporarily replaced by carpets, rugs or screens but it is now coming back in its classical form; as curtain, wall covering and temporary enclosure. In Japan, architects are very interested in using textiles again; both inside and out screen. In the West, textiles are being re-introduced as a form of decoration in a lush, bourgeois, baroque manner, especially in the private domain and – of course – in theatres. Even fashion designers like Issey Miyake have been invited to design theatre curtains lately … which is a good development!

However, I think that the way we have started working with textiles in the last few years has more to do with the so-called "blob-architecture" movement that started in the eighties. Since then, buildings have been designed digitally meaning that supposedly soft and fluid forms – that are actually not flexible at all, but that look like soft material frozen in time – can now be developed. Although their shapes may be compelling and complex, they are seldom functional, if I may say that. Anyhow, such very "organic" structures, with their three-dimensional and decorative finishes, clearly take away the wish to use textile as one more soft, rich material in their interiors! What is interesting here is that on the contrary, these folded, pleated, and twisted shapes, together with their often thin, weightless or transparent façades and roof claddings require sturdy and functional additions to regulate unsolved issues like the ones you already mentioned: climate, sound, light, and the programming of spaces – yet in new ways. We have found that we can fulfill that role with textiles; we are all the more excited by this because the work is starting to become much more subtle and relatively invisible, even more integrated than before. Our interventions, super present as they are at times, start to trigger subconscious experiences and effects, pulling our interior work more in the direction of the natural, biological world that we also like to work with. So yes: the importance of textiles in contemporary architecture is clearly growing; and not necessarily only in the decorative sense.

Dutch designer **Petra Blaisse** works in a multitude of creative areas, including textile, landscape, and exhibition design. She founded **Inside Outside** in Amsterdam in 1991.

*Interview mit Petra Blaisse*
*von Sylvie Krüger*

# „ DIE EMANZIPATION DES VORHANGS "

Wie setzen Sie Textilien ein, um die Atmosphäre eines Raums zu verändern?

Zunächst einmal wird die Atmosphäre eines Raums dadurch beeinflusst, wie das Blickfeld organisiert ist. So kann man jeweils andere Räume erleben: Innen- oder Außenräume, nahe oder ferne. Darüber hinaus setzen wir auf Bewegung und Flexibilität: Das betrifft die Bewegung des Objektes selbst, seines Materials und die der Benutzer, die mit dem Objekt umgehen oder durch seine Ausrichtung bzw. seine Form in eine bestimmte Richtung gelenkt werden. Und wir machen oft von den Möglichkeiten der Farbe Gebrauch, die natürlich die Raumwahrnehmung enorm beeinflusst. Durch hintereinander geschichtete Vorhänge in verschiedenen Transparenzstufen und verschiedenen Farben kann man den visuellen Rhythmus und die gesamte Atmosphäre der Architektur verändern. Mit speziell gestalteten Vorhängen lassen sich Flächen

auch anders aufteilen. In einer Privatwohnung in London zum Beispiel gefiel uns die architektonische Unterteilung der Glasfassade nicht besonders. Also haben wir versucht, mithilfe eines Vorhangs deren vertikale Struktur zu neutralisieren. Wir haben dazu einen breiten Saum, der sich über den gesamten kreisförmigen Raum erstreckte, als horizontales Strukturelement eingesetzt. Das hat dem Raum architektonisch eine ganz andere Qualität gegeben.
Außerdem benutzen wir die Vorhangschiene als eine Art Pfad: Sie choreografiert und bestimmt die Bewegung des Objektes. Indem man die Schiene unabhängig von der Form des Raums gestaltet, kann man einen Raum im Raum erschaffen und damit der vorgegebenen architektonischen Logik entkommen. Mithilfe von abgerundeten Ecken, Kurven oder einfach durch die Veränderung der Raumgröße lassen sich die architektonischen Regeln außer Kraft setzen. Auf diese

Weise haben wir die symmetrische Gestaltungslogik im Haus der Kunst in München aufgebrochen und zum Asymmetrischen hin geändert. Und schließlich kann man auch die Raumakustik vollkommen verändern, was man im Haus der Kunst ebenso erleben kann wie bei vielen weiteren unserer Projekte, bei denen die akustischen Eigenschaften und die Flexibilität des Raums eine wichtige Rolle spielen – so zum Beispiel in den Konzertsälen und Proberäumen der Casa da Música in Porto.

Welche Vorteile hat die textile Konstruktion und wo liegen ihre Grenzen?

Für Textilien kann man keine Lebensdauer von 25 oder 50 Jahren garantieren; da gibt es natürlich Grenzen. Sie verschleißen mit der Zeit, und genau das ist das Schöne. Sobald man mit Textilien zu arbeiten beginnt, setzt auch schon ihr langsamer Verfallsprozess ein. Sicherlich halten die vielen neuen Gewebe – aus Materialien wie Metall,

PVC, Kohle oder Glasfaser – wesentlich länger, wenn nicht gar für immer. Dagegen hat das klassische Gewebe natürlich nur eine begrenzte Haltbarkeit. Mit gewebten und ungewebten Stoffen ist konstruktionstechnisch vieles möglich; in Bezug auf Dehnbarkeit und Gewicht sind ihnen aber Grenzen gesetzt. Und immer noch kann man mit ihnen kein Gebäude bauen, ohne auf irgendwelche festen Strukturen zurückzugreifen. Wenn man aber ein Gewebe in ein flüssiges, sich verfestigendes Material integriert, wie es in der Raumfahrttechnologie oder bei Produktverpackungen der Fall ist, kann die Lebensdauer beider Materialien zusammen durchaus unbegrenzt sein.

Gerade die Verschmelzung von Funktion und Ästhetik macht den besonderen Reiz Ihrer Arbeit aus. Funktionale Anforderungen wie Veränderung des Lichts, des Klimas, der Akustik und der Raumsituation werden durch die bewusste Verwendung *der spezifischen Textileigen-schaften gelöst. Mit dieser Vorgehensweise heben Sie die verschiedenen textilen Materialeigenschaften und Verarbeitungstechniken hervor und machen sie un-mittelbar erlebbar. Aus der Anforderung ergibt sich die Materialität und die Form der textilen Konstruktion. Verwenden Sie lieber Ihre eigenen Lösungen oder nutzen Sie auch vorgefertigte technische Textilien? Gibt es neue textile Entwicklungen und Techniken, mit denen Sie arbeiten?*

Normalerweise verwenden wir vorgefertigte gewebte oder ungewebte Stoffe. Wir arbeiten ein wenig nach dem Prinzip Louis Kahns, der fragte: „Was hätten Sie denn gerne, Ziegelstein?" Jedes Material ist hinsichtlich seiner spezifischen Verwendungs-möglichkeiten und Grenzen einzigartig. Und es macht Spaß, die „Botschaft" des jeweiligen Materials „entzif-fern" zu lernen, indem man immer wieder damit herum-experimentiert und spielerisch

mit ihm umgeht. Wir arbeiten kaum mit vorgefertigten technischen Lösungen – im Sinne von fertigen Materi-alien, die so, wie sie sind, eingesetzt werden. Aber wir benutzen gewöhnlich vorge-fertigte Textilien als Grund-lage. Wir sind ständig auf der Suche nach Materialien, die feuerbeständig sind, nicht schmelzen, geruchlos sind, keine Giftstoffe freisetzen, wenn sie erhitzt werden usw. Im Fall von öffentlichen Gebäuden müssen unend-lich viele Vorschriften und Verbote beachtet werden. Das ist deshalb interessant, weil es bedeutet, dass man nur mit einer begrenzten Anzahl von Materialien arbeiten kann und gezwungen ist, sie zu ver-ändern und zu etwas umzuge-stalten, das faszinierender ist als ihr Originalzustand. Die Materialien müssen gründlich geprüft und getestet werden, um herauszufinden, wo ihre Möglichkeiten und Grenzen liegen und was man aus ihnen machen könnte. Solche Einschränkungen können also sehr inspirierend sein.

*Das Textil ist ein äußerst formbares und flexibles Ma-terial und kann sich daher den wechselnden mensch-lichen Bedürfnissen sehr gut anpassen. Im Kontrast dazu steht der eher statische Cha-rakter von Gebäuden. Wie gehen Sie bei Ihrer Arbeit mit diesen beiden ge-gensätzlichen Eigenschaften um?*

Gerade wegen dieser gegen-sätzlichen Eigenschaften ist es sehr einfach, sie zu kombi-nieren. Die Kombination von hartem und weichem Material kann sehr reizvoll sein. Es ist jedoch sehr wichtig, sich bereits in der Entwurfspha-se eines Gebäudes darüber im Klaren zu sein, wie man die Textilien einsetzen will. Denn die Implikationen und Möglichkeiten der Verwen-dung von Textilien lassen sich viel leichter erfassen, wenn man auch mit dem gesamten architektonischen Entwurf vertraut ist. Oder sogar mit der Statik des Baus, da Textilien sehr schwer sein können. Oft müssen sie allein schon aus akustischen

Gründen ein bestimmtes Gewicht und eine gewisse Fülle haben. Manchmal muss die gesamte Gebäudestruktur an diese Stoffmasse angepasst werden. Zudem muss man die Vorhänge auch irgendwo verstauen, wenn sie nicht be-nutzt werden. Da ist es dann schön, mit den Architekten zusammenzuarbeiten, um zu entdecken, wie die unter-schiedlichen Materialien, aus denen ein Innenraum besteht, zusammenpassen, und eine Komposition zu finden, die verborgenen Stauraum und Platz für die Motoren bietet – sodass das Verschwinden und Erscheinen des Vorhangs seine ganz eigene Choreogra-fie entwickelt.

*Durch den Einsatz von Textilien besteht die Mög-lichkeit, Raumsituationen zu schaffen, die die Archi-tektur nicht dauerhaft und grundlegend verändern. Das Temporäre und Veränderbare ist dem Textil eigen. Erweist sich diese Nicht-Architektur des Textils als Vorteil und wie nutzen Sie dies?*

Ich frage mich gerade, warum wir keine dauerhafte Architektur schaffen. Das Wesen unserer Arbeit bis zum heutigen Zeitpunkt besteht ja gerade darin, dass sie nicht dauerhaft ist. Mir kommt es oft so vor, als würde ich unter einer bestimmten Form von Klaustrophobie leiden, als würde mir alles, was permanent, nicht transparent oder nicht auf irgendeine Weise durchlässig ist, fast den Atem abschnüren.

*Sie arbeiten mit beweglichen, sich anpassenden Materialien wie Textilien und Pflanzen. Ist dies zufällig oder steht eine bewusste Haltung dahinter?*

Mir ist Folgendes aufgefallen: Wenn man zum Beispiel Gärten entwirft, stellt sich die Frage nach der Zeit auf genau umgekehrte Weise, als wenn man mit Textilien arbeitet. Bei Textilien setzt der Verfallsprozess ein, sobald man sie benutzt. Gärten hingegen brauchen Zeit – erst nach 20, 50 oder gar 100 Jahren nehmen sie die Form an, die man beim Entwerfen vor Augen hatte. Während seiner Entwicklung durchläuft ein Garten immer wieder jahreszeitlich bedingte Zyklen: von der Phase des Schlafes und des scheinbaren Todes zum Stadium der Verjüngung, wenn sich Knospen bilden und alles wieder zu wachsen beginnt. Durch diese

wiederkehrende Abfolge von Tod und Geburt findet ein Garten allmählich zu seiner Gestalt. Ein Textilobjekt entsteht dagegen innerhalb eines einzigen durchgehenden Schaffensprozesses und erreicht seine endgültige Form in relativ kurzer Zeit; dann ist es fertig, kann installiert und wie geplant sofort genutzt werden. Und dann beginnt auch schon der Zerfall: An verschiedenen Stellen bleicht der Stoff aus und wird dünner; man sieht Flickstellen, lose Fäden und all die Spuren der Vergänglichkeit, die gerade die Schönheit eines Stoffes ausmachen … bis er sich ganz auflöst – wenn er nicht durch kuratorische Sorgfalt gerettet wird und in einer dunklen Schublade in einem Museum verschwindet.

*Oftmals ist zeitgenössische Architektur eher reduziert und kühl. Sehen Sie es als Eigenschaft und Aufgabe des Textils, Architektur in eine menschliche Dimension zu bringen?*

So dachte man früher. Moderne Gebäude wurden damals oft als streng und minimalistisch beschrieben. Der Einsatz üppiger und weicher Stoffe wie Seide und Velours war da ein willkommener Kontrast. Diese Sichtweise ist aber zu einfach. Das Textil hat inzwischen auch viele andere Rollen übernommen; es erfüllt zahlreiche

Funktionen und wird vielen Bedürfnissen gerecht, die die Architektur allein nicht immer befriedigen kann. Wir haben das die „Emanzipation des Vorhangs" genannt. Der Vorhang, so wie wir ihn verwenden, ist schon fast konkurrenzfähig geworden.

*Oft kommt das Textil nachträglich zum Einsatz – also wenn das Gebäude fertig geplant oder sogar schon gebaut ist –, um „Probleme" zu lösen bzw. „Schwächen" des Gebäudes zu beheben wie beispielsweise mangelnder Sichtschutz oder Wärmeentwicklung. Sie werden verstärkt bereits in der Konzeptphase hinzugezogen. Wie wirkt sich Ihre Mitarbeit in diesem frühen Projektstadium auf das Endresultat bzw. die Qualität des Gebäudes aus?*

Im letzten Jahr traf ich beim Fahrradfahren zufälligerweise Herman Herzberger, der gerade an einem neuen Universitätsgebäude in Utrecht arbeitete. Er wollte in der zweiten Etage an einer Ecke des Gebäudes einen Außenhörsaal mit überhängendem Betondach bauen und fragte mich, ob er dort einen Vorhang im Freien installieren könne und was er dabei beachten müsse. Wir haben ihm dann in einem ausführlichen Gespräch die wichtigsten Punkte erläutert: dass er die Vorhangschiene in das

Betondach integrieren könne und dass die Befestigungsweise, Form und Schienentyp von Qualität, Größe und Gewicht des Vorhangs abhingen; dass die Witterungsverhältnisse, der Bewegungsspielraum und Fragen der Aufbewahrung des Vorhangs beachtet werden sollten … etc. Seitdem haben wir nie wieder etwas von ihm gehört, aber höchstwahrscheinlich wird er mit unseren Vorschlägen irgendetwas angefangen haben.
Ich wage nicht zu beurteilen, ob solche Konsultationen und Interventionen die Qualität eines Gebäudes immer positiv beeinflussen, aber sie fügen in jedem Fall eine andere Sichtweise hinzu; hin und wieder können sie ungeahnte Möglichkeiten eröffnen oder Lernprozesse auslösen. Architekten können sich auf uns und unsere Arbeit verlassen, wenn es darum geht, Probleme zu lösen, sie gibt ihnen größere Freiheit im Gebrauch dünner und transparenter Hüllen. Denken Sie an das dünne Dach des Glaspavillons von Sejima & Nishizawa in Toledo; oder an die Glasfassaden in den Konzertsälen der Casa da Música von OMA.

*In Ihrer Arbeit reagieren Sie auf bestehende bzw. geplante Raumsituationen und entwickeln dafür Lösungen als eine Art Ergänzung. Würde es Sie reizen, darüber*

*hinaus ein gesamtes Gebäude bestehend nur aus Textilien zu entwickeln?*

Auf Raumsituationen zu reagieren war bisher immer die größte Herausforderung. Es ist auch interessant, mit verschiedenen Architekten eng zusammenzuarbeiten, die völlig verschiedene Ansichten haben.

Tatsächlich ein gesamtes Gebäude selbst zu entwickeln ist nicht mein persönliches Ziel, weil ich der Meinung bin, dass unsere Arbeit bereits eine Form von Architektur ist. Es ist ja nicht so, dass Vorhänge vorhandene Räume nur ausgestalten oder verändern, sondern sie sind selbst Räume. Außerdem werden Größe, Form, Struktur, Falten, Knicke und die technischen Implikationen eines Vorhangs zu Teilen der Architektur, der er dient. Aber es stimmt, dass wir ständig auf der Suche sind nach selbsttragenden Textilien – um die Architektur von Wänden, Decken oder anderen festen Strukturen zu befreien. Bis jetzt ist diese Suche aber ergebnislos geblieben.

*Textilien wurden jahrhundertelang aufgrund ihrer besonderen funktionalen, aber auch ästhetischen Eigenschaften im architektonischen Kontext eingesetzt. Mit dem Fortschritt technischer Entwicklungen im Bereich der Wärmeregulierung von Gebäuden sowie einem Wandel der Architekturauffassung zu Beginn des 20. Jahrhunderts verlor das Textil – bis auf einige wenige Ausnahmen – mehr und mehr an Bedeutung im architektonischen Gebrauch. Erst in letzter Zeit hat man den Eindruck, dass Textilien, einhergehend mit einer gewissen „Emotionalisierung" der Architektur, wieder vermehrt zum Einsatz kommen. Wie sehen Sie diese Entwicklung und damit den Stellenwert des Textils in der Architektur heute?*

Das Textil selbst ist nie aus der Architektur verschwunden, aber Vorhänge waren eine Zeitlang tabu. Dennoch gab es sie in gewisser Weise auch in der modernen Architektur. Architekten wie Le Corbusier und Mies van der Rohe setzten sie ein – obwohl sie dies sicherlich abgestritten hätten. Im Grunde wurde aber die weiße Wand als eine Art Vorhang behandelt; deshalb glaube ich, dass auch der Vorhang als Phänomen nie wirklich verschwunden ist. Teppiche, Läufer oder Wandschirme haben vielleicht vorübergehend seine Rolle übernommen. Aber nun kehrt er in seiner klassischen Form zurück: als Vorhang, Wandbedeckung und Raumteiler. Besonders in Japan haben Architekten gerade wieder begonnen, Textilien in Innen- und Außenräumen als Sichtschutz oder zur Definition von Raum einzusetzen. Im Westen werden Textilien in opulenter, großbürgerlicher, barocker Weise vor allem in Privaträumen wieder zur Dekoration verwendet – und natürlich in Theatern. Sogar Modedesigner wie Issey Miyake werden in letzter Zeit eingeladen, Theatervorhänge zu gestalten … das ist eine positive Entwicklung!

Wie wir in den letzten Jahren mit Textilien arbeiten, ist meiner Ansicht nach jedoch hauptsächlich von der sogenannten „Blob-Architektur" beeinflusst worden – eine Bewegung, die in den 1980er Jahren entstanden ist. Seit dieser Zeit werden Gebäude digital entworfen; so lassen sich weiche und fließende Formen entwickeln, die tatsächlich nicht flexibel sind, aber so wirken. Auch wenn diese Formen faszinierend und komplex sein mögen, so sind sie doch – wenn ich das sagen darf – nur selten funktional. Aber wie dem auch sei: Diese sehr „organisch" wirkenden und dadurch sehr dekorativen Strukturen erwecken jedenfalls nicht gerade den Wunsch nach Textilien als einem weiteren weichen, üppigen Material in den Innenräumen. Interessanterweise verlangen diese gefalteten, plissierten und gewundenen Formen mit ihren oft dünnen, leichten oder transparenten Fassaden und Dachbelägen aber geradezu nach robusten und funktionalen Ergänzungen, um neue Lösungen für jene Probleme zu finden, die Sie bereits erwähnt haben – wie etwa Klima, Akustik, Lichtverhältnisse und Raumaufteilung. Wir haben festgestellt, dass sich diese funktionalen Anforderungen mithilfe von Textilien erfüllen lassen; und wir sind umso begeisterter, weil unsere Arbeit nun viel subtiler, relativ unsichtbar und dabei noch stärker in den Entwurfsprozess integriert ist als zuvor.

Unsere Interventionen, so präsent sie auch manchmal sein mögen, lösen auch unterbewusste Erfahrungen aus und können unerwartete Wirkungen erzielen; so nähert sich unsere Innenraumgestaltung immer mehr der natürlichen, biologischen Umwelt an, in der wir genauso gerne arbeiten. In der Architektur gewinnen Textilien gegenwärtig also ganz klar an Bedeutung – und nicht unbedingt nur im dekorativen Sinne.

---

*Die niederländische Designerin **Petra Blaisse** ist in vielen Bereichen kreativ tätig: Sie beschäftigt sich unter anderem mit Textildesign, Landschaftsgestaltung und Ausstellungsarchitektur. 1991 gründete sie das Büro **Inside Outside** in Amsterdam.*

---

LIGHT
*leicht*

# HEAVY
*schwer*

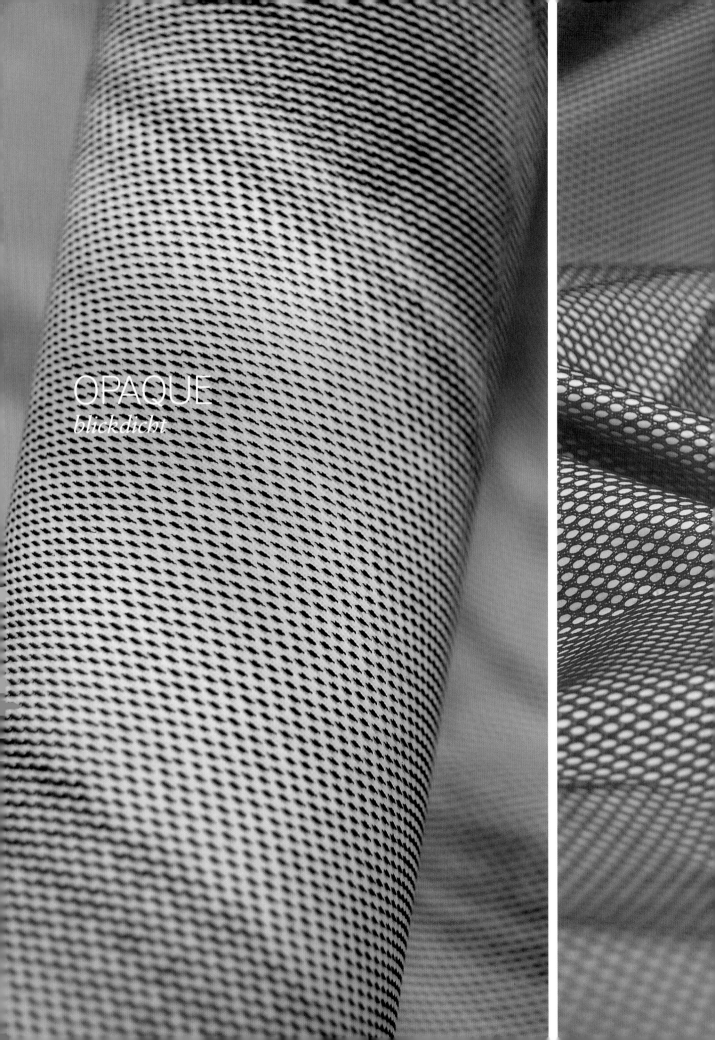

OPAQUE
*blickdicht*

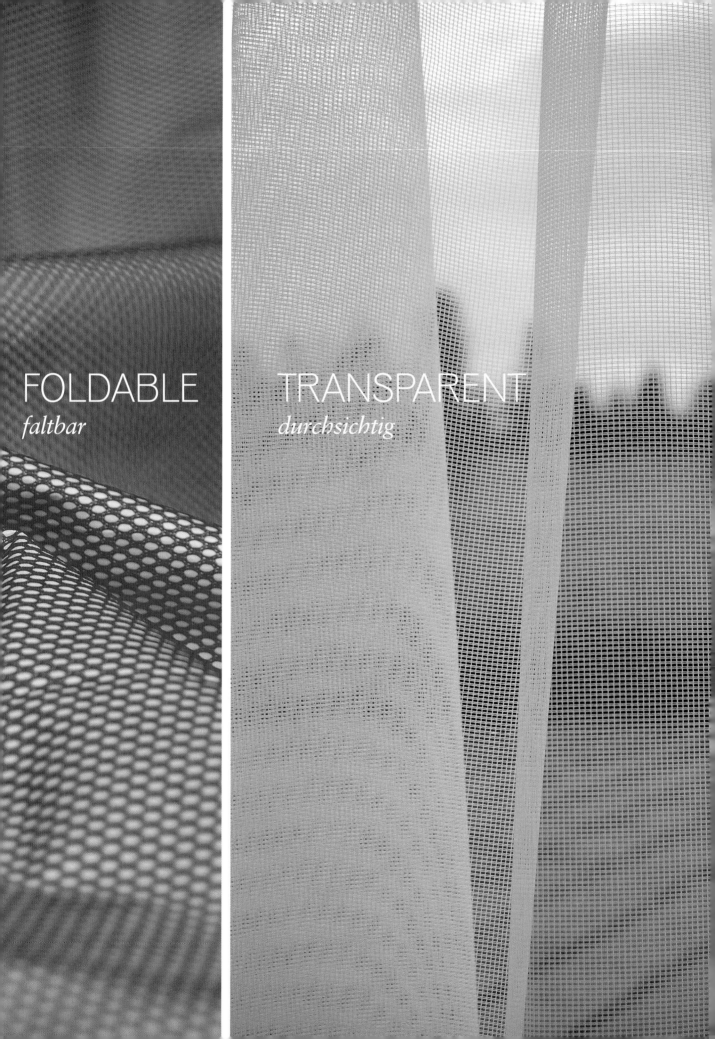

FOLDABLE

*faltbar*

TRANSPARENT

*durchsichtig*

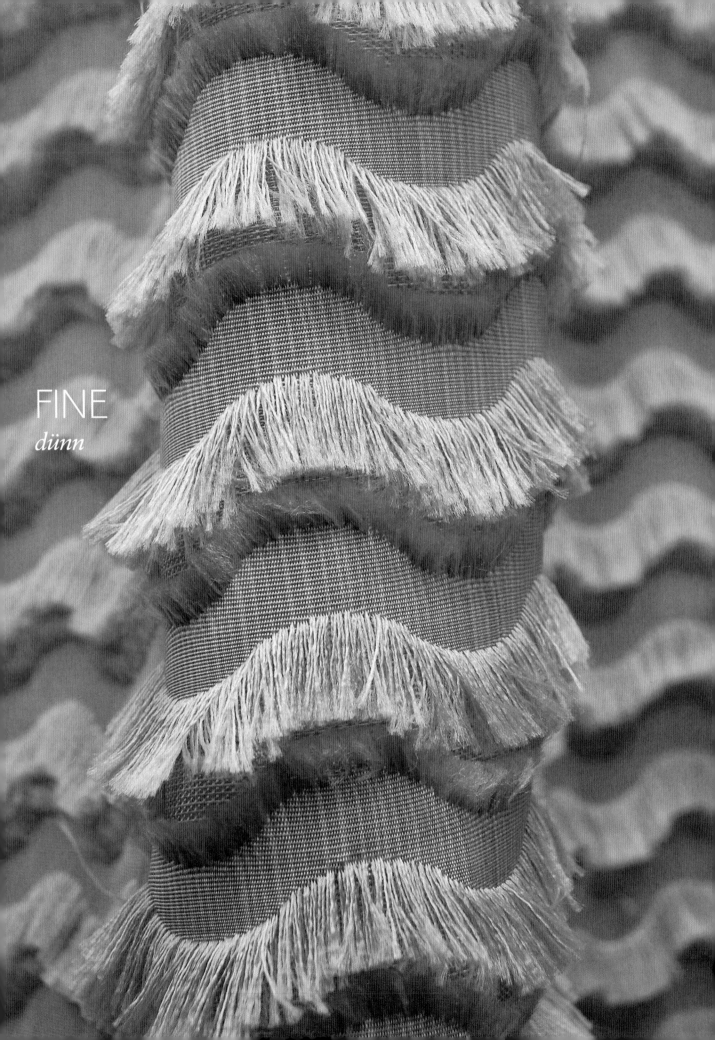

FINE
*dünn*

THICK
*dick*

DELICATE
*zart*

# BULKY
*voluminös*

# SOFT
*weich*

# VERTICAL SPACE DEFINER
## *VERTIKALER RAUMABSCHLUSS*

# HISTORICAL OVERVIEW
## *HISTORISCHER ÜBERBLICK*

The transience of textile materials means that hardly any finds have been made that date back to the beginning of human construction to provide proof of the application of textiles in architecture. When reconstructing historical developments, one is forced to depend on written and graphic depictions apart from a few grave and archaeological finds; such evidence shows that textile construction coincides with the very beginnings of building.

According to Gottfried Semper's "Theory of Dressing," fences for animal pens, woven with branches, were the earliest manmade partition walls and thus the first vertical space definers. As time passed by, the branches were gradually replaced by plant fibres and by threads spun from animal wool to produce textile mats.[1]

The ancient civilisations of Egypt, the Orient, Greece, and Asia used textiles for both representational purposes and as weather and visual protection. It is known that the ancient civilisations of Central and South America were also already commonly using textiles as mats, blankets and wall hangings in their living environments from the fourth century BC. Apart from their everyday use, holy cloths were of great significance for all ancient civilisations within a sacral context. Such cloths were used as protective or lucky objects during rites of passage such as births, weddings, and deaths.

To this day, primitive races in South America, Africa, and Asia still use mats, blankets and curtains as wall coverings or partitions in interior spaces. Apart from separation, they also protect against cold, sun, and insects.[2]

Aufgrund der Vergänglichkeit des textilen Materials sind kaum Fundstücke vom Beginn des menschlichen Bauens erhalten, die den Gebrauch von Textilien in architektonischer Anwendung belegen. Bei der Rekonstruktion der geschichtlichen Entwicklung ist man neben den wenigen Grab- und Bodenfunden auf schriftliche und bildliche Darstellungen angewiesen, die jedoch darauf hinweisen, dass die ersten textilen Konstruktionen mit den Anfängen des Bauens zusammenfallen.

Laut Gottfried Sempers Bekleidungstheorie ist der aus Zweigen geflochtene Zaun des Pferches die früheste von Menschen hergestellte Trennwand und somit der erste vertikale Raumabschluss. Die Zweige wurden mit der Zeit durch Bast ersetzt und später wurden Pflanzenfasern bzw. gesponnene Fäden aus tierischer Wolle verwebt, um textile Matten herzustellen.[1]

Bereits die Hochkulturen Ägyptens, des Vorderen Orients, Griechenlands und Asiens verwendeten Textilien sowohl zu Repräsentationszwecken als auch als Witterungs- und Sichtschutz. Auch bei den Hochkulturen Mittel- und Südamerikas waren Wohntextilien wie Matten, Decken und Wandbehänge schon seit dem 4. Jahrtausend vor Christus bekannt. Neben dem profanen Gebrauch hatte in allen Hochkulturen der sakrale Einsatz von heiligen Tüchern eine hohe Bedeutung. Bei Übergangsriten wie Geburt, Hochzeit oder Tod wurden Tücher als Schutz oder glücksbringendes Objekt verwendet.

Bis heute nutzen Naturvölker in Südamerika, Afrika und Asien Matten, Decken und Vorhänge als Wandverkleidung oder Raumtrennung im Innenraum. Sie dienen neben der Abgrenzung auch dem Kälte-, Sonnen- und Insektenschutz.[2]

---

### Exterior Curtain

The term "exterior curtain" refers to textiles that are used in outside areas to partially or entirely enshroud scaffolding or building façades in a vertical direction.

As a symbol of lordly power during the antiquity, it was a widely practiced custom to cover multilevel, grandly adorned timber scaffolding in rich draperies that were then burned at masters' burial ceremonies. In line with Asian custom, Alexander had a multilevel funeral pyre clad in elaborately draperied precious fabrics in honour of Hephaestion (fourth century BC). Gottfried Semper also describes the funeral ceremony of the Roman Emperor Septimius Severus in 211 AD, which ended in the incineration of a multilevel funeral pyre clad in gold-embroidered covers.

Draperied funeral pyre, Roman consecration medal / Bekleideter Scheiterhaufen, Römische Konsekrationsmedaille

During the antiquity, monuments, public squares, and streets were temporarily decorated using magnificent draperies. On the occasion of the festive procession of Manius Valerius Maximus Corvinus Messalla (263 BC), Rome's monuments were hung with canvases on which battle scenes of the victory over the Carthaginians were depicted.[3] The tradition of temporary festive façade decoration continued in the Byzantine Empire, as depictions of the imperial box in the hippodrome of Byzantium – from whose balustrades a richly decorated fabric hung – show.[4]

Temporary festive hangings, Samarkand, around 1425 / Temporärer Festbehang, Samarkand, um 1425

Marco Polo (1254–1324) also reported of the huts and wooden halls of the Tanguts that were covered in silk fabrics along the cremation paths of East Turkestan.[5]

Basilica di San Lorenzo enshrouded for the funeral of Enrico IV, Florence, 1610 / Verhüllung der Basilica di San Lorenzo anlässlich des Begräbnisses von Enrico IV., Florenz, 1610

Gottfried Semper (1803–1879) reported of a papal coronation in Rome where he had the opportunity to marvel at the hangings and carpets that lined the path of the coronation procession as well as the magnificent hangings that were suspended from all palace façades and balconies.[6]

Festive façade hanging has since become rare. In 1995, Christo und Jeanne-Claude artistically broached the topic of the enshrouding of monuments in their temporary wrapping of the Reichstag in Berlin. Cables were used to wrap over 100,000 square-metres of aluminium-coated polypropylene fabric around the building.

Textile building site protection to protect passers-by from dust represents a more functional application of textile façade cladding. Such temporary coverings are often used for advertising. It is becoming increasingly common to print such textile canvases with an image of the future building to give an impression of how the façade behind it will look when finished.

## Außenvorhang

Unter dem Begriff „Außenvorhang" werden Textilien verstanden, welche im Außenbereich vertikal ein Gerüst oder eine Gebäudefassade komplett oder teilweise verhüllen.

Als Zeichen herrschaftlicher Macht war es in der Antike ein weitverbreiteter Brauch, prachtvoll geschmückte, mehrstöckige Holzgerüste mit reichen Stoffdrapierungen zu überziehen und sie bei den Totenfeiern der Herrscher zu verbrennen. Alexander ließ nach asiatischem Brauch zu Ehren des Hephaistion (4. Jh. v. Chr.) einen mehrstöckigen Scheiterhaufen mit aufwendig drapierten, kostbaren Stoffen bekleiden. Ferner beschreibt Gottfried Semper die Totenfeier des römischen Kaisers Septimius Severus im Jahr 211, die mit der Verbrennung des mehrstöckigen, mit goldbestickten Decken verkleideten Scheiterhaufens endete.

Zu festlichen Anlässen wurden in der Antike Monumente, öffentliche Plätze und Straßen temporär mittels prächtiger Stoffdrapierungen ausgeschmückt. Anlässlich des Festzugs des Manius Valerius Maximus Corvinus Messalla (263 v. Chr.) wurden die Monumente Roms mit Leinwänden behängt, auf denen Kampfszenen des Sieges über die Karthager zu sehen waren.[3] Seine Fortsetzung fand die Tradition der temporären festlichen Fassadenverkleidung im Byzantinischen Reich, wie Darstellungen der kaiserlichen Loge im Hippodrom von Byzanz zeigen, von deren Brüstung ein reich dekorierter Stoff herabhing.[4]

Auch Marco Polo (1254–1324) berichtete von den mit Seidenstoffen verhüllten Hütten und Holzhallen der Tanguten entlang des Krematkonsweges in Ost-Turkestan.[5] Gottfried Semper (1803–1879) berichtete von einer Papstkrönung in Rom, bei der er selbst die Gelegenheit hatte, den von Tapeten und Teppichen gesäumten Weg der Krönungsprozession und die Prachtdecken zu bestaunen, die von allen Palastfassaden und Balkonen herabhingen.[6]

Die festliche Fassadenverhüllung ist heute selten geworden. Die künstlerische Auseinandersetzung des Themas der Bekleidung von Monumenten setzten Christo und Jeanne-Claude 1995 mit ihrer temporären Reichstagsverhüllung in Berlin um. Mit Seilen wurden über 100.000 Quadratmeter feuerfestes, aluminiumbedampftes Polypropylengewebe um das Gebäude gewickelt.

Eine eher zweckbezogene Fassadenbekleidung ist der textile Baustellenschutz, um den Passanten vor Staub zu schützen. Diese temporären Verhüllungen werden oftmals als Werbeflächen genutzt. Um schon während der Bauzeit den Anschein der dahinter liegenden Fassade zu erwecken, werden die textilen Planen zunehmend auch mit dem Abbild der zukünftigen Fassade bedruckt.

---

## Curtain Wall

The curtain wall is positioned behind large-area glass façades, providing light and visual protection. Its predecessor is the wall hanging, which decorated interior spaces and protected against cold stonewalls.

Just like exterior façades, the interior spaces of ancient temples and secular buildings were temporarily clad in wall hangings for festive occasions.[7] Ornate draperies decorated the walls to emphasise the festive spirit and to make such halls more habitable – as the following

two examples show: "At a banquet held by Cleopatra for Antonius, the walls of the grand chamber were enveloped in gold-embroidered purple hangings"[8] and "At the wedding banquet of the Macedonian Caranus, an oikos was draped in white batiste draperies, which opened to allow torch-bearers to step forward."[9]

In ancient Peru, the most important Inca temples were decorated inside with fine woollen fabrics.[10]

Temporarily erected tents were also festively draped: in Ion by Euripides (approximately 480–406 BC) a huge tent in Delphi is described whose interior was entirely clad in precious tapestries from the temple treasury.[11]

So-called podea were mounted under the icons of the churches of Byzantium – these hangings were not only ornamentally decorated, they also featured religious depictions or an image of their sponsor. Secular buildings were equally grandly furnished with wall hangings. Western visitors reported with fascination of the incredible luxuriousness of precious textiles at the imperial court of Byzantium.[12]

The wall has been draped with curtains in antiquity style, fifth century AD / Die Wand ist auf antike Weise mit Vorhängen drapiert, 5. Jahrhundert

In medieval times, apart from serving as decoration and representation, wall hangings provided protection from cold stonewalls. Decorated with religious and symbolic motifs, they were also used in churches. In the secular realm, they decorated aristocratic private households. As friezes they were mounted behind benches and chairs as back protection.[13]

The dining area is surrounded by lengths of fabric as was above all common in the north, late fifteenth century / Der Essplatz ist von Stoffbahnen umkleidet, wie es vor allem im Norden üblich war, Ende des 15. Jahrhunderts

Tapestries were used as temporary decoration "to furnish provisional accommodation or tents for rulers while journeying and on military expeditions."[14] Delegations took them along as representative gifts and they were used as articles of exchange and trade at masses, imperial diets and councils.[15] In the late fifteenth century, people began to cover white walls in fabrics. In France, it became the custom to change the wall hanging according to the season as a result of the alternating holding of the Burgundy court. A silk wall covering was used to provide cooling in summer while woollen tapestries were hung up in winter to protect against the cold.[16]

In the early nineteenth century, the edges of rooms were veiled in extravagant temporary and permanent fabric draperies in front of the walls and windows.[17]

Bedroom of Queen Louise of Prussia, design, 1809, Karl Friedrich Schinkel / Schlafzimmer der Königin Luise von Preußen, Entwurf, 1809, Karl Friedrich Schinkel

In expression of the fashion of the time, a tent room was arranged in Charlottenhof Palace in Potsdam around 1829; its walls were covered in a fabric-like blue and white striped wallpaper. Sloping canvas was spanned over green-painted metal rods to form the roof of the tent. Fabric drapes of the same pattern were mounted at the windows and over the beds.[18]

Tent room, Charlottenhof Palace, Potsdam, 1830, Karl Friedrich Schinkel / Zeltzimmer, Schloss Charlottenhof, Potsdam, 1830, Karl Friedrich Schinkel

These "excrescences of draped fashion"[19] came to an end in the late nineteenth century. Interior spaces were freed of their "dust catchers" for both aesthetical and hygienic reasons. Changes in living comfort brought about by the introduction of heating also meant that warming lining was no longer desired in interior spaces.

Textile interior decoration was further reduced with the beginning of "New Objectivity" after the First World War. People limited themselves to purely functional forms, banishing the decorative, which was reflected in frugal textile interior design.[20] At the Bauhaus in Dessau, textile wall coverings were produced under the direction of Gunta Stölzl as long-lasting substitutes for wallpaper or wall hangings and as sound-absorbing covering fabrics.[21]

However, textile wall coverings were gradually replaced by the large-area application of curtains for increasingly larger glass façades. At the Bauhaus Dessau, light curtain fabrics were developed as space-defining elements that could also be changed quickly if required; this was compatible to a desire for a flexible way of life.

Curtains were often used behind the large glass fronts of the buildings by Mies van der Rohe to provide temporary protection from the outside space. For example, curtains of black velvet as well as black and silver-grey silk could be pulled closed at night before the large glass front of the Tugendhat House in Brno (1929–1930). They prevented a feeling of being lost that could easily arise at night as a result of the reflection of the interior space in the black glass walls.[22]

Tugendhat House, Brno, Czech Republic, 1929–1930, Ludwig Mies van der Rohe / Haus Tugendhat, Brünn, Tschechien, 1929–1930, Ludwig Mies van der Rohe

Curtains were also generously applied to the Farnsworth House – built in Plano, Illinois (USA) in 1950–1951 – to temporarily isolate the interior space from the outside world. When the curtains were open, the borders of the house flowed into the outside space as a result of the glass façade.

Farnsworth House, Plano, Illinois, USA, 1950–1951, Ludwig Mies van der Rohe / Farnsworth House, Plano, Illinois, USA, 1950–1951, Ludwig Mies van der Rohe

The windows of the glass façade of the apartment building erected at 860 Lake Shore Drive in Chicago in 1949–1951 were uniformly equipped with vertically sliding blinds and with curtains that could be horizontally opened and closed. A second movable skin was thus established behind the glass façade. The residents could change it as required, always altering the appearance of the façade.[23]

**Vorhangwand**

Die Vorhangwand befindet sich hinter großflächigen Glasfassaden und bietet Schutz vor Licht und Einblick. Ihr Vorläufer ist der Wandbehang, der Innenräume ausschmückte sowie vor kalten Steinmauern schützte.

Ebenso wie die Außenfassaden wurden auch die Innenräume von antiken Tempeln und von profanen Gebäuden zu festlichen Veranstaltungen temporär mit Wandbehängen bekleidet.[7] Kunstvolle Drapierungen schmückten die Wände, um den festlichen Aspekt zu betonen und zugleich den Saal wohnlicher zu gestalten – wie die beiden folgenden Beispiele zeigen: „Bei einem Gastmahle, das Kleopatra dem Antonius gab, waren die Wände des Prachtgemaches besonders zu diesem Feste mit goldgestickten Purpurtapeten umspannt."[8] Und: „Beim Hochzeitsmale des Makedoniers Karanos war ein Oikos ringsrum mit weissen Battistdraperien behangen, die sich aufthaten und hinter welchen Fackelträger hervortraten."[9]

In Alt-Peru waren die wichtigsten Inka-Tempel im Inneren mit feinen Wolltüchern geschmückt.[10]

Auch temporär aufgestellte Zelte wurden festlich ausgekleidet: Im Ion des Euripides (ca. 480–406 v. Chr.) wird ein riesiges Zelt in Delphi beschrieben, dessen Inneres vollständig mit kostbaren Bildteppichen aus dem Tempelschatz verkleidet war.[11]

In den Kirchen von Byzanz wurden unterhalb der Ikonen sogenannte „Podea" angebracht – nicht nur ornamental, sondern auch mit religiösen Darstel-

lungen oder auch dem Bild des Stifters geschmückte Behänge. Gleichermaßen wurden profane Bauten im Inneren mit Wandbekleidungen prachtvoll ausgestattet. So berichteten westliche Besucher fasziniert von dem immensen Aufwand an kostbaren Textilien am kaiserlichen Hof von Byzanz.[12]

Im Mittelalter dienten Wandbehänge neben der Dekoration und der Repräsentation auch dem Schutz vor kalten Steinmauern. Mit religiösen und symbolischen Motiven versehen, kamen sie in Kirchen zum Einsatz. Im profanen Bereich wurden sie als Dekoration des vornehmen Privathaushalts genutzt. Als friesartige Variante wurden sie hinter Bänken und Stühlen als Rückenschutz angebracht.[13] Als temporäre Dekoration wurden die Tapisserien „von den Fürsten auf Reisen und Kriegszügen zur Ausstattung provisorischer Unterkünfte oder Zelte verwendet".[14] Gesandtschaften führten sie als repräsentative Gastgeschenke mit sich und bei Messen, Reichstagen und Konzilien wurden sie als Tausch- und Handelsware verwendet.[15] Ende des 15. Jahrhunderts begann man, ganze Wände mit Stoff zu bespannen. In Frankreich war es aufgrund der wechselhaften Hofhaltung der Burgunder Brauch geworden, je nach Jahreszeit den Wandbehang zu wechseln: Im Sommer verwendete man eine Tapete aus Seidenstoff als Kühlespender; im Winter wurden wollene Wirkteppiche als Schutz vor der Kälte aufgehängt.[16]

Zu Beginn des 19. Jahrhunderts wurden die Grenzen des Raums durch prunkvolle temporäre wie auch permanente Stoffdrapierungen vor den Wänden und Fenstern verschleiert.[17]

Als Ausdruck des Zeitgeschmacks wurde um 1829 im Schloss Charlottenhof in Potsdam ein Zeltzimmer eingerichtet, dessen Wände mit einer stoffartigen, blau-weiß gestreiften Tapete bezogen wurden. Als Zeltdach wurde Leinwandstoff schräg über grün gestrichene Metallstangen gespannt. An den Fenstern und über den Betten wurden Stoffdrapierungen in der gleichen Musterung angebracht.[18]

Diese „Auswüchse des drapierten Zeitgeschmacks"[19] nahmen gegen Ende des 19. Jahrhunderts ein Ende und sowohl aus hygienischen als auch aus ästhetischen Gründen wurde der Innenraum von den „Staubfängern" befreit. Weiter trug die Veränderung des Wohnkomforts mit dem Aufkommen der Heizung dazu bei, dass das Bedürfnis nach wärmender Auskleidung des Innenraums schwand. Mit dem Beginn einer „Neuen Sachlich-

keit" nach dem Ersten Weltkrieg wurde die textile Innenausstattung weiter reduziert. Man beschränkte sich auf die reine Zweckform und verbannte das Dekorative, was sich in einer sparsamen textilen Raumgestaltung widerspiegelte.[20] Im Bauhaus Dessau wurden unter der Leitung von Gunta Stölzl textile Wandbespannungen als haltbarer Ersatz für Tapeten oder Wandbehänge sowie schalldämpfende Spannstoffe hergestellt.[21]

Die textile Wandbespannung wurde jedoch zusehends durch den großflächigen Einsatz des Vorhangs vor den immer größer werdenden Glasfassaden abgelöst. Im Bauhaus Dessau wurden leichte Vorhangstoffe entwickelt, die raumbestimmendes Element sein konnten, sich aber bei Bedarf schnell verändern ließen, was dem Bedürfnis nach flexibler Lebensform entgegenkam.

Hinter den großen Glasfronten der Gebäude Mies van der Rohes wurden oftmals Vorhänge eingesetzt, um sich bei Bedarf temporär vom Außenraum abzugrenzen. Zum Beispiel ließen sich bei Dunkelheit vor der großen Glasfront des Hauses Tugendhat in Brünn (1929–1930) Vorhänge aus schwarzem Samt sowie schwarzer und silbergrauer Seide zuziehen. Sie verhinderten ein Verlorenheitsgefühl, welches sich bei Nacht durch die schwarzen, das Innere reflektierenden Glaswände leicht einstellte.[22]

Auch bei dem 1950–1951 in Plano, Illinois (USA) erbauten Farnsworth House wurden Vorhänge großzügig eingesetzt, um das Innere temporär von der Außenwelt abzuschotten. Bei geöffnetem Zustand der Vorhänge sind aufgrund der transparenten Glasfassade die Grenzen des Hauses zur Außenwelt fließend.

Die Fenster der Glasfassade des von 1949–1951 in Chicago erbauten Apartmenthauses 860 Lake Shore Drive wurden einheitlich mit vertikal verschiebbaren Rollos und horizontal auf- und zuziehbaren Vorhängen ausgestattet. Hinter der transparenten Glasfassade entstand so eine zweite bewegliche textile Haut. Die Bewohner können sie je nach Bedarf verändern und somit das Erscheinungsbild der Fassade ständig variieren.[23]

**Partition**

The term "partition" refers to a curtain that divides a space; by opening and closing a partition different spatial situations can be created.

The classical civilisations of the antiquity already used the curtain to create interplay between concealing and revealing – as a way of separating the holy from the unsanctified. Sacred places in temples or divine images were concealed by a curtain of carpets, which were only opened at certain times. They were otherwise left closed to protect the sanctuary or holy statues. The Incas also kept godly figures behind finely woven curtains.[24]

The Old Testament describes how the sanctuary was enclosed by a boundary made of linen that was attached to wooden columns. However, the absolute sanctum was again separated from the other sanctuary by a linen curtain with blue, red and crimson woollen threads running through it that hung on four gold-covered columns.[25]

Gottfried Semper describes festive events at holy places that were temporarily enclosed by carpets. These were held by servants, some of whom stood on multilevel scaffolds to reach the desired height.[26]

Carpet holders as decoration on back rests, Kujundshik, Mesopotamia / Teppichträger als Dekoration an Stuhllehnen, Kujundshik, Mesopotamien

Apart from concealing the sanctum in temple buildings, similar mantling customs were handed down from the ancient ruling cults.[27] Eastern rulers completely segregated themselves from their subjects using curtains. This custom was carried forward at the Sassanid court: "When the court gathered, the king was hidden by a curtain. He showed himself at public audiences by having the curtain opened theatrically."[28] Such orchestrations of the ruler were initially rejected in the West, however they gradually established themselves and became a fixed part of court rituals. Curtains were used to alternate between withdrawal and appearance. On opening the curtain, the ruler could appear subject-friendly.[29] The description of a scene in 1856 at Southampton station on the occasion of a visit by Queen Oude to England demonstrates just how long this oriental mantling custom remained alive: "So that she and her female court would not be contaminated by the curious gazes of the faithless English, eunuchs formed a double cordon with outspread magnificent shawls and

carpets along the path that led from the closed carriages to the compartment of the railway wagon and stood there as still as statues until the train left."[30]

One example of the mantling of the spaces between columns as temporary festive decoration is the description of a celebration held by King Xerxes I (519–465 BC) in the palace at Susa: "White and blue curtains made of precious fabrics were hung between the alabaster columns, fastened using white and crimson cords and silver rings."[31]

The Romans also used large curtains as decoration or as space definers, as hooks found in houses in Pompeii and Herculaneum prove. According to Semper, the atriums of residential buildings were divided using draperies that were rich in pleats or carpets that were hung on movable scaffolds in order to open or close a space as required. Similarly, doors inside private Roman houses were often closed using curtains, known as portières.[32] "As Vergil reports (Georgica III/25), curtains decorated with figures were also commonly used as stage curtains in the Roman theatre."[33]

The mantling of the spaces between columns was widespread in Europe until medieval times. "The Liber Pontificalis gives an impression of the amount of curtains that were used in churches, particularly in the eighth and ninth century. Pope Leo IV donated to St. Peter's alone: three for the main entrance, forty-six for the central nave, ten for the confessional, twenty-five for the high altar, thirty-four for the presbytery and eighteen for various other places. And more than 1,000 curtains are listed under Hadrian I (722–795), which the pope gave to various churches in Rome."[34]

Lengths of fabric draped between columns, around 1000 AD / Drapierte Stoffbahnen zwischen Säulen, um 1000

Textile also had a significant role in medieval living space. Carolingian miniatures constituted heavy portières, which were fixed to round arches using grommets, thus completely filling out the doorways. The spaces between columns and pillars were similarly closed using curtains; these were knotted together as required since pulling devices had not yet been

developed. Such partitioning curtains—heavy wool or velvet portières—were used as flexible door closings well into the nineteenth century. Draperies, ruffled fabric curtains, were used to partition spaces.[35]

Partitioning curtain, Annette von Droste-Hülshoff's room in the "Fürstenhäusle," Meersburg, around 1841 / Raumteilender Vorhang, Zimmer der Annette von Droste-Hülshoff im „Fürstenhäusle", Meersburg, um 1841

However, textile partitions were increasingly replaced in Europe by solid materials. Traditional Japanese sliding walls spanned with translucent paper are a non-European example of flexible partitions for variable interior design; they are still in use today.

One example of an early twentieth century flexible living situation is the large living and working area on the main floor of the Tugendhat House. There, individual areas could be separated by curtains as required without disturbing the unity of the whole space.[36] Grete Tugendhat spoke of a basic spatial and living feeling of "isolation, being alone but always feeling a sense of belonging to a larger whole."[37]

**Raumteiler**

Unter „Raumteiler" wird ein den Raum trennender Vorhang verstanden, durch dessen Öffnung und Verschluss verschiedene Raumsituationen geschaffen werden können.

Bereits bei den klassischen Hochkulturen der Antike wurde der Vorhang für das Wechselspiel zwischen Verbergen und Enthüllen verwendet – als Mittel zur Trennung des Heiligen vom Nichtgeweihten. Ehrwürdige Orte in Tempeln oder Götterbilder wurden durch Teppichvorhänge verborgen, die nur zu bestimmten Zeiten geöffnet wurden. Sonst blieben sie zum Schutz des Heiligtums bzw. der Götterstatue geschlossen. Auch bei den Inka wurden Götterfiguren hinter Vorhängen aus feinen Geweben verwahrt.[24]

Im Alten Testament wird beschrieben, wie das Heiligtum von einer Abgrenzung aus leinenen Planen umschlossen wurde, die an Holzsäulen angebracht waren. Das Allerheiligste wiederum wurde vom übrigen Heiligtum durch einen mit blauen, roten und karmesinroten Wollfäden

durchzogenen Leinenvorhang getrennt, der an vier golden überzogenen Säulen aufgehängt war.[25]

Gottfried Semper beschreibt feierliche Handlungen an geweihten Orten, die temporär mit Teppichen umschlossen wurden. Diese wurden von Dienern gehalten, welche teilweise auf mehrstöckigen Gerüsten standen, um die gewünschte Höhe zu erreichen.[26]

Neben der Verhüllung des Allerheiligsten in Tempelbauten sind ähnliche Verhüllungsbräuche für den antiken Herrscherkult überliefert.[27] Östliche Herrscher sonderten sich durch den Gebrauch von Vorhängen vollständig von ihren Untertanen ab. Am Sassanidenhof wurde dieser Brauch fortgesetzt: „Bei Zusammenkünften des Hofes war der König durch den Vorhang verborgen, bei öffentlichen Audienzen zeigte er sich, indem der Vorhang theaterhaft geöffnet wurde."[28] Derartige Inszenierungen des Herrschers stießen im Westen zunächst auf Ablehnung, setzten sich aber nach und nach durch und wurden fester Bestandteil des Hofzeremoniells. Man nutzte den Vorhang für den Wechsel von Entrückung und Erscheinung. Mit der Öffnung des Vorhangs konnte sich der Herrscher als untertanenfreundlich darstellen.[29] Wie lange sich diese orientalischen Verhüllungsbräuche am Leben erhielten, zeigt die Beschreibung einer Szene im Bahnhof von Southampton anlässlich des Besuchs der Königin von Oude in England 1856: „Damit sie und ihr weiblicher Hofstaat von den neugierigen Blicken der englischen Ungläubigen nicht verunreinigt werde, bildeten Eunuchen mit ausgebreiteten prachtvollen Shawls und Teppichen auf dem Wege, der von den geschlossenen Kutschen in das Coupé des Eisenbahnwagens führte, doppeltes Spalier und standen Statuen gleich unbeweglich bis zur Abfahrt des Zuges."[30]

Ein Beispiel für das Verhängen von Säulenzwischenräumen als temporäre textile Festausstattung ist die Beschreibung des Festes von König Xerxes I. (519–465 v. Chr.) im Palast zu Susa: „Zwischen Alabastersäulen waren weiße und blaue Vorhänge aus kostbaren Stoffen aufgehängt, befestigt mit weißen und purpurroten Schnüren und silbernen Ringen."[31]

Die Römer verwendeten große Vorhänge ebenfalls als Schmuck oder als Raumabschluss, was Funde von Haken in Häusern in Pompeji und Herculaneum belegen. Die Atrien der Wohnhäuser wurden Semper zufolge mittels faltenreicher Drapierungen oder auf beweglichen Gerüsten aufgespannter

Teppiche unterteilt, um den Raum je nach Bedarf schließen oder öffnen zu können. Ebenso wurden die Türen im Inneren der römischen Privathäuser oftmals mit Vorhängen, den Portieren, verschlossen.[32] „Wie Vergil berichtet (Georgica III/25), waren mit Figuren geschmückte Vorhänge auch im römischen Theater als Bühnenvorhang gebräuchlich."[33]

Das Verhängen von Säulenzwischenräumen war in Europa bis ins Mittelalter weitverbreitet. „Der Liber Pontificalis gibt insbesondere für das 8. und 9. Jahrhundert eine Vorstellung von der Menge von Vorhängen, die in den Kirchen verwendet wurden. Für St. Peter allein stiftete Papst Leo IV. drei für den Haupteingang, 46 für das Mittelschiff, zehn für die Confessio, 25 für den Hochaltar, 34 für das Presbyterium und 18 für verschiedene andere Stellen, und unter Hadrian I. (722–795) sind mehr als 1000 Vorhänge genannt, die der Papst an die verschiedenen Kirchen Roms schenkte."[34]

Auch im mittelalterlichen Wohnraum spielten Textilien eine bedeutende Rolle. Karolingische Miniaturen stellen schwere Portieren dar, welche durch Ösen an Rundbögen befestigt wurden und somit die Türen komplett ausfüllten. Ebenso wurden Säulen- und Pfeilerzwischenräume durch Vorhänge geschlossen, welche bei Bedarf zusammengeknotet wurden, da man noch keine Zugvorrichtungen kannte. Diese raumtrennenden Vorhänge hielten sich als flexibler Türverschluss in Form von schweren Woll- und Samtportieren bis ins 19. Jahrhundert. Draperien, geraffte Stoffvorhänge, wurden zur Raumtrennung verwendet.[35]

Jedoch wurde die textile Raumtrennung im europäischen Raum zunehmend durch feste Materialien ersetzt. Als außereuropäisches Beispiel flexibler Raumtrennung sind die traditionellen, mit durchscheinendem Papier bespannten Schiebewände in Japan, die eine variable Raumgestaltung ermöglichen, weiterhin im Gebrauch.

Ein Beispiel der Bildung flexibler Raumsituationen vom Anfang des 20. Jahrhunderts ist die Gestaltung des großen Wohn- und Arbeitsbereiches des Hauptgeschosses des Hauses Tugendhat. Dort ließen sich bei Bedarf durch Vorhänge einzelne Bereiche abtrennen, ohne dass dadurch die Einheit des Ganzen gestört worden wäre.[36] Grete Tugendhat sprach von einem grundlegenden Raum- und Lebensgefühl von „Abgrenzung, Für-Sich-Sein, aber immer in dem Gefühl der Zugehörigkeit zu einem größeren Ganzen."[37]

**Room in Room**

The term "room in room" refers to a space that can be opened and closed using vertical expanses of textile that are mounted inside solid built spaces. The bed curtain, which surrounded a bed on all sides, was a "room in room" structure that was already popular during the antiquity.[38]

Depiction of a woman on a day bed, mosaic from Centocelle, first century / Darstellung einer Frau auf dem Ruhebett, Mosaik aus Centocelle, 1. Jahrhundert

The mantling custom had been a part of wedding rituals since time immemorial. In that sense, the groom used to enter the tent of the bride. During the Roman antiquity, the bridal bed, enshrouded in draperies was erected in the atrium as a provisional enclosed space. This tradition continued with the Christian canopy bed.[39] In medieval times, the use of bed curtains became common practice. The bed was overhung by a canopy of wood or fabric, which was carried by four pillars and enclosed by bed curtains on the sides in order to keep dust and insects out and above all to protect from cold and drafts. Since there was no separate bedroom and the bed usually stood in the heated living room in which several people often slept, the closed bed curtain created a certain private sphere.[40]

Open bed curtain, manuscript from 1448 / Offener Bettvorhang, Manuskript von 1448

During the baroque period, the textile design of four-poster beds using curtains, canopies and opulently arranged drapes of silk, damask or brocade, became increasingly more elaborate. The state bed as a type of throne spread from France to other European ruling houses.

Four-poster bed commonly found in France, seventeen-sixties / In Frankreich übliches Himmelbett, sechziger Jahre des 18. Jahrhunderts

Notes / *Anmerkungen*

[1] Cf. Semper, Gottfried: *Der Stil.* Volume 1. Reprint of the 1860 Frankfurt on Main edition. Mittenwald 1977, pp. 227–228

[2] Cf. Seiler-Baldinger, Annemarie: "Le confort sauvage. Die Vielfalt des Wohnens." In: *Stoffe und Räume. Eine textile Wohngeschichte der Schweiz.* Langenthal 1986, pp. 9–25

[3] Cf. Semper, Gottfried: *Der Stil.* Volume 1, pp. 290–292 and pp. 314–317

[4] Cf. Heinz, Dora: *Europäische Wandteppiche I.* Brunswick 1963, p. 26

[5] Cf. Polo 1963, p. 69, according to Seiler-Baldinger: "Le confort sauvage. Die Vielfalt des Wohnens", p. 23

[6] Cf. Semper, Gottfried: *Der Stil.* Volume 1, pp. 319–320

[7] Cf. Eberlein, Johann Konrad: *Apparatio regis – revelatio veritatis. Studien zur Darstellung des Vorhanges in der bildenden Kunst von der Spätantike bis zum Ende des Mittelalters.* Wiesbaden 1982, p. 22

[8] Socrates Rhod. in Athens. IV. 29, according to Semper, Gottfried: *Der Stil.* Volume 1, p. 289

[9] Hippolochos in Athens. IV. 5, according to Semper, Gottfried: *Der Stil.* Volume 1, pp. 288–289

[10] Cf. Blas Valera in Baudin 1959, p. 115, according to Seiler-Baldinger: "Le confort sauvage. Die Vielfalt des Wohnens", p. 23

[11] Cf. Ion des Euripides, Vers 141 et seq., Heinz, Dora: *Europäische Wandteppiche I,* p. 20

[12] Cf. Heinz, Dora: *Europäische Wandteppiche I,* p. 26

[13] Cf. Vuilleumier-Kirschbaum, Ruth: "Textile Wandverkleidungen in der Schweiz. Gestaltungsmöglichkeiten und Ausdruck der Zeit." In: *Stoffe und Räume. Eine textile Wohngeschichte der Schweiz.* Langenthal 1986, p. 26, and Lang, Hans: *Gotische Bildteppiche.* Stuttgart circa 1975, p. 8

[14] Heinz, Dora: *Europäische Wandteppiche I,* p. 20

[15] Cf. Lang, Hans: *Gotische Bildteppiche,* p. 9

[16] Cf. Vuilleumier-Kirschbaum, Ruth: "Textile Wandverkleidungen in der Schweiz", p. 26

[17] Cf. Giedion, Siegfried: *Die Herrschaft der Mechanisierung.* Frankfurt on Main 1982, p. 381

[18] Cf. Bauakademie der DDR, Institut für Städtebau und Architektur (Ed.): *Karl Friedrich Schinkel.* Exhibition catalogue. Berlin 1982, p. 238

[19] Weinberg Staber, Margit: "Der drapierte Zeitgeschmack." In: *Stoffe und Räume. Eine textile Wohngeschichte der Schweiz.* Langenthal 1986, p. 128

[20] Cf. Weinberg Staber, Margit: "Der drapierte Zeitgeschmack", p. 128, and Meier-Oberist, Edmund: *Kulturgeschichte des Wohnens im abendländischen Raum.* Hamburg 1956, pp. 317–318

[21] Cf. Stiftung Bauhaus Dessau (Ed.): *Gunta Stölzl. Meisterin am Bauhaus Dessau. Textilien, Textilentwürfe und freie Arbeiten 1915–1983.* Ostfildern-Ruit 1997, p. 228

After the social upheaval of the French Revolution, simple forms of living were desired and people bedded themselves more modestly. Heavy pleated textile mantles were replaced by brighter, lighter curtains of voile and mousseline. The bed was situated in a bedroom and no longer in the lounge. Increasingly high demands on hygiene and practicability meant that the canopy bed including curtains disappeared from bedrooms as time passed by.[41]

Another type of "room in room" structure shaped much exhibition design; for example, the "Exposition de la Mode" in Berlin in 1927. The interior space was divided using lengths of fabric.[42] The fact that the curtains were slidable meant that temporary spaces could be formed and changed as required.

16

"Exposition de la Mode," Berlin, 1927, Ludwig Mies van der Rohe with Lilly Reich / „Exposition de la Mode", Berlin, 1927, Ludwig Mies van der Rohe mit Lilly Reich

## Raum im Raum

Mit dem Begriff „Raum im Raum" wird hier ein variabel verschließbarer und zu öffnender Raum aus vertikalen textilen Flächen verstanden, der sich inner-

halb eines Raums massiver Bauweise befindet.

Als „Raum-im-Raum"-Konstruktion war der das Bett allseitig umgebende Bettvorhang bereits in der Antike bekannt.[38] Der Verhüllungsbrauch war von jeher Bestandteil des Hochzeitsritus. In diesem Sinne betrat der Bräutigam das Zelt der Braut. In der römischen Antike wurde das mit Tüchern verhängte Brautbett als provisorisch abgeschlossene Räumlichkeit im Atrium aufgestellt. Diese Tradition setzte sich im christlichen Brauthimmel fort.[39]

Im Mittelalter wurde die Verwendung von Bettvorhängen zum Allgemeingut. Das Bett wurde von einem Betthimmel aus Holz oder Stoff überragt, der von vier Säulen getragen und seitlich von Bettvorhängen umschlossen wurde, um Staub und Ungeziefer fernzuhalten, vor allem aber auch um vor Kälte und Zugluft zu schützen. Da ein separates Schlafzimmer nicht vorhanden war und das Bett somit im beheizten Wohnraum stand, wo oftmals mehrere Personen schliefen, schaffte der geschlossene Bettvorhang eine gewisse Privatsphäre.[40]

Mit dem Barock wurde die textile Gestaltung des Himmelbetts durch Vorhänge, Baldachine und üppig arrangierte Drapierungen aus Samt, Damast oder Brokat zusehends aufwendiger. Das Paradebett als eine Art Thronsitz nahm von Frankreich aus Einzug in die europäischen Herrscherhäuser.

Nach dem sozialen Umsturz der Französischen Revolution suchte man nach einfacheren Wohnformen und bettete sich schlichter. Schwere faltenreiche textile Verhüllungen wurden durch helle, leichte Voile- und Mousseline-Vorhänge ersetzt. Das Bett wurde nicht mehr im Gesellschaftsraum, sondern im Schlafzimmer aufgestellt. Mit zunehmend höheren Anforderungen an Hygiene und Praktikabilität verschwand der Betthimmel samt Vorhängen im Laufe der Zeit aus dem Schlafzimmer.[41]

Eine andere Form der „Raum-im-Raum"-Konstruktion prägte so manche Ausstellungsgestaltung; wie etwa jene der „Exposition de la Mode" von 1927 in Berlin. Der Innenraum war durch Stoffbahnen unterteilt.[42] Durch die Möglichkeit des Verschiebens der Vorhänge ließen sich temporäre Räume ausbilden, die je nach Bedarf verändert werden konnten.

## Contemporary Application

The past importance of vertical space definers as a means of representation is no longer relevant today. Similarly, technical developments in window insulation and heating have made fabric curtains less relevant these days for protection against cold and drafts.

As a result of their flexibility, they are now more often used for visual protection and for variable spatial separation or organisation of both public and private space.

Textiles continue to be used before and within façades to flexibly protect interior spaces–particularly behind large glass façades–from sunlight and therefore glare and from too much heat input. Textiles are also used to improve the acoustics of interior spaces. They serve temporary decoration, building site protection and as information and advertising surfaces on exterior façades.

## Heutige Verwendung

Die Bedeutung, die der vertikale Raumabschluss in der Vergangenheit als Mittel der Repräsentation innehatte, kommt ihm heute nicht mehr zu. Ebenso wird der Stoffvorhang heutzutage aufgrund der technischen Entwicklung im Bereich der Fensterisolierung und der Heizung seltener als Schutz vor Kälte oder Zugluft eingesetzt.

Aufgrund seiner Flexibilität übernimmt er vielmehr die Funktionen des Sichtschutzes und der variablen Raumtrennung oder Raumgliederung im öffentlichen wie im privaten Bereich. Weiterhin werden Textilien vor wie innerhalb der Fassade genutzt, um das Rauminnere besonders hinter großen Glasfassaden variabel vor dem Sonnenlicht und damit vor Blendung und zu großem Wärmeeintrag zu schützen. Im Innenraum werden Textilien auch zur Verbesserung der Raumakustik verwendet. An der Außenfassade dienen sie temporär als Dekoration, als Baustellenschutz und als Informations- bzw. Werbeträger.

[32] Cf. Tegethoff, Wolf: Mies van der Rohe. Die Villen und Landhausprojekte. Essen 1981, p. 95

[33] Cf. Harather, Karin: Haus-Kleider. Zum Phänomen der Bekleidung in der Architektur, pp. 103–108

[34] Cf. Eberlein, Johann Konrad: Apparatio regis – revelatio veritatis, p. 22, and Semper, Gottfried: Der Stil. Volume 1, p. 281, and Murra 1962, p. 719, according to Seiler-Baldinger: "Le confort sauvage. Die Vielfalt des Wohnens", p. 19

[35] Cf. Old Testament, 2. Moses, 27

[36] Cf. Semper, Gottfried: Der Stil. Volume 1, pp. 272–273

[37] Cf. Eberlein, Johann Konrad: Apparatio regis – revelatio veritatis, p. 22

[38] Eberlein, Johann Konrad: Apparatio regis – revelatio veritatis, p. 23

[39] Cf. Eberlein, Johann Konrad: Apparatio regis – revelatio veritatis, pp. 23–24

[40] Semper, Gottfried: Der Stil. Volume 1, p. 272

[41] Old Testament, Esther I, 6–7

[42] Cf. Heinz, Dora: Europäische Wandteppiche I, p. 22, and Semper, Gottfried: Der Stil. Volume 1, pp. 278–279, and Durm, Josef: Die Baukunst der Etrusker. Die Baukunst der Römer. Darmstadt 1885, p. 224

[43] Heinz, Dora: Europäische Wandteppiche I, p. 22; Cf. Durm, Josef: Die Baukunst der Etrusker. Die Baukunst der Römer, p. 340

[34] Heinz, Dora: Europäische Wandteppiche I, p. 24, and Cf. Schmidt, Heinrich Jakob: Alte Seidenstoffe. Brunswick 1958, pp. 32–33

[35] Cf. Meier-Oberist, Edmund: Kulturgeschichte des Wohnens im abendländischen Raum, p. 70, and Mundt, Barbara: Historismus, Kunstgewerbe zwischen Biedermeier und Jugendstil. 1981, pp. 142–143, according to Weinberg Staber, Margit: "Der drapierte Zeitgeschmack", pp. 120–121 and p. 123; Cf. Meier-Oberist, Edmund: Kulturgeschichte des Wohnens im abendländischen Raum, p. 246

[36] Cf. Tegethoff, Wolf: Mies van der Rohe. Die Villen und Landhausprojekte, p. 95

[37] Hammer-Tugendhat, Daniela/Tegethoff, Wolf: Ludwig Mies van der Rohe. Das Haus Tugendhat. Vienna 1998, pp. 18–19

[38] Cf. Meier-Oberist, according to Harather, Karin: Haus-Kleider. Zum Phänomen der Bekleidung in der Architektur, p. 67

[39] Cf. Eberlein, Johann Konrad: Apparatio regis – revelatio veritatis, p. 39

[40] Cf. Brunner-Littmann, Birgit: "Textile Bettgeschichten". In: Stoffe und Räume. Eine textile Wohngeschichte der Schweiz, pp. 59–60 and Cf. Meier-Oberist, Edmund: Kulturgeschichte des Wohnens im abendländischen Raum, pp. 85–86

[41] Cf. Brunner-Littmann, Birgit: "Textile Bettgeschichten", p. 63 and pp.68–70

[42] Cf. Cohen, Jean-Louis: Ludwig Mies van der Rohe. Paris 2007, Second and extended edition, p. 64

Vertical Space Definer
*Vertikaler Raumabschluss*

# CONSTRUCTION & FUNCTION
*KONSTRUKTION & FUNKTION*

| Exterior Curtain | Curtain Wall | Partition | Room in Room |
| *Außenvorhang* | *Vorhangwand* | *Raumteiler* | *Raum im Raum* |

Vertical Space Definer
*Vertikaler Raumabschluss*

# EXTERIOR CURTAIN
## *AUSSENVORHANG*

Exterior Curtain *Like a second skin in front of actual building volumes, textiles provide visual and sun protection. Their application extends from exterior curtains in front of single window and door openings through to curtains that enshroud whole façades. While they can be tautly fixed or adjustable, the degree of transparency and the amount of light entering can be altered by sliding the curtains. Textiles are temporarily installed on outside façades as dust-absorbing building-site curtains, for decorative purposes and as bearers of information and advertising.*

Außenvorhang *Wie eine zweite Haut vor dem eigentlichen Baukörper angebracht, schützen Textilien vor Einblick und Sonnenlicht. Die Bandbreite reicht von Außenvorhängen vor einzelnen Fenster- und Türöffnungen bis zu ganze Fassaden verhüllenden Vorhängen; sie können straff fixiert oder wandelbar sein, sodass sich durch Verschieben der Grad der Transparenz und der Lichteinstrahlung variabel ändern lässt. Temporär werden Textilien an Außenfassaden als staubabsorbierende Baustellenvorhänge, als Dekoration und als Informations- bzw. Werbeträger verwendet.*

House 47°40'48"n/13°8'12"e, Adnet, Austria, 2005–2007,
**Maria Flöckner and Hermann Schnöll**
*Haus 47°40'48"n/13°8'12"e, Adnet, Österreich, 2005–2007,*
***Maria Flöckner und Hermann Schnöll***

# EXTERIOR CURTAIN / temporary
## AUSSENVORHANG / temporär

Rosemarie Trockel

Alfonso Hüppi

"Frontside," Basel, Switzerland, 2001, **Littmann Kulturprojekte**
As a temporary intervention in public space, net vinyl tarpaulins designed by artists mantled twenty-one façades in Basel. The aesthetics of large-surface advertising messages were picked up and the surrounding area changed, thus provoking a new perception of the urban space.

„Frontside", Basel, Schweiz, 2001, **Littmann Kulturprojekte**
Als temporäre Intervention im öffentlichen Raum verhüllten von Künstlern gestaltete Netzvinylplanen 21 Fassaden Basels. Spielerisch wurde die Ästhetik großflächiger Werbebotschaften aufgegriffen, die gewohnte Umgebung verändert und eine neue Wahrnehmung des Stadtraums provoziert.

"Movements Exhibition," Storefront for Art & Architecture, New York, USA, 2000, **Inside Outside**
A 15 x 20 meter large curtain covered the whole façade of the gallery on the occasion of a retrospective of the work so far carried out by Inside Outside.

„Movements Exhibition", Storefront for Art & Architecture, New York, USA, 2000, **Inside Outside**
Anlässlich einer Retrospektive der bisherigen Arbeit von Inside Outside bedeckte ein 15 x 20 Meter großer Vorhang die gesamte Fassade der Galerie.

Paris, France, 2004
Paris, Frankreich, 2004

Venice, Italy, 2008
Venedig, Italien, 2008

"Baugerüste" photo series
by **Deidi von Schaewen**
Bildreihe „Baugerüste"
von **Deidi von Schaewen**

Dresden, Germany, 1990
Dresden, Deutschland, 1990

Temporary veiling of the Basilica di
San Lorenzo for the funeral of Enrico
IV, Florence, Italy, 1610
Temporäre Verhüllung der Basilica di
San Lorenzo anlässlich des Begräb-
nisses von Enrico IV., Florenz, Italien,
1610

"Liquid Façade," Los Angeles, USA,
2002, **Infranatural – Jenna Didier**
Stretchable Lycra was spanned over
semicircular bars anchored in the
façade for "Materials & Applications,"
the temporary sculptural covering
of the Architecture and Landscape
Centre.
„Liquid Façade", Los Angeles, USA,
2002, **Infranatural – Jenna Didier**
Für die temporäre skulpturale
Verhüllung des Architektur- und
Landschaftszentrums „Materials
& Applications" wurde dehnbares
Lycra über halbrunde, in der Fassade
verankerte Stangen gespannt.

# EXTERIOR CURTAIN / adjustable
## *AUSSENVORHANG / wandelbar*

Theodoric Palace, Ravenna, Italy, around 540 AD
Theoderichpalast, Ravenna, Italien, um 540

Piazza San Marco, Venice, Italy, 1973
Markusplatz, Venedig, Italien, 1973

Saragossa, Spain, 2007
Saragossa, Spanien, 2007

Madrid, Spain, 2008
Madrid, Spanien, 2008

Curtain Wall House, Tokyo, Japan, 1994–1995, **Shigeru Ban Architects**
Following in the footsteps of traditional Japanese houses, this modern residential home embodies the creation of an "open living style" with contemporary materials. Huge white curtains surround the building to make the façade as changeable as possible. Visual and lighting conditions inside are influenced by opening and closing the "curtain wall". The façade is further closed in winter by glass doors.

Curtain Wall House, Tokio, Japan, 1994–1995, **Shigeru Ban Architects**
Nach dem Vorbild traditioneller japanischer Häuser verkörpert dieses moderne Wohnhaus die Umsetzung des „offenen Lebensstils" mit aktuellen Materialien. Um die Fassade so wandelbar wie möglich zu halten, umschließen riesige weiße Vorhänge das Gebäude. Die Sicht- und Lichtverhältnisse im Inneren werden durch Öffnen und Schließen der „Curtain Wall" beeinflusst. Im Winter wird die Fassade zusätzlich durch Glastüren geschlossen.

Adjustable bast mats veil the upper floors of traditional houses in the district of Gion, Kyoto, Japan, 2003
Wandelbare Bastmatten verhüllen die oberen Etagen traditioneller Häuser im Stadtteil Gion, Kyoto, Japan, 2003

# EXTERIOR CURTAIN / adjustable
## *AUSSENVORHANG / wandelbar*

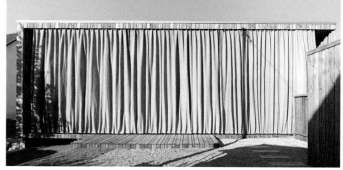

Berkhan House, Grosselfingen, Germany, 2006,
**Fischer Berkhan Architects**
Over-dimensioned curtains that are fixed to the roof overhang above the entrance area and the terrace of this residential house provide visual and sun protection. The semitransparent curtain fabric made of a PE-ribbon weave guarantees a hazy view towards the outside but none towards the inside. Varying degrees of openness and closure can be had by sliding the curtains. The curtains can be closed to create a protected outside space in the terrace area.

Haus Berkhan, Grosselfingen, Deutschland, 2006,
**Fischer Berkhan Architekten**
Am Dachüberstand über dem Eingangsbereich und der Terrasse des Wohnhauses befestigte überdimensionale Vorhänge dienen als Sicht- und Sonnenschutz. Der halbtransparente Vorhangstoff aus PE-Bändchen-Gewebe gewährt einen schemenhaften Ausblick, aber keinen Einblick. Durch das Verschieben der Vorhangbahnen lassen sich verschiedene Situationen von Offenheit oder Geschlossenheit erzeugen. Bei geschlossenem Vorhang entsteht zudem ein geschützter Außenraum im Bereich der Terrasse.

"Radial View," Exhibition, deSingel, Antwerp, Belgium, 2008, **Inside Outside**
The lawn area was vertically "reflected" by hanging up a curtain printed with a "grass structure" along the interior courtyard of the art centre. This and other much more subtle interventions in the existing situation changed the perception of the building and garden, suggesting to visitors new paths through them.

Ausstellung „Radial View", deSingel, Antwerpen, Belgien, 2008, **Inside Outside**
Durch die Aufhängung eines mit einer „Grasstruktur" bedruckten Vorhangs entlang des Innenhofs des internationalen Kunstzentrums wurde die Rasenfläche vertikal „reflektiert". Mit diesem und weiteren subtilen Eingriffen in die vorhandene Situation wurde die Wahrnehmung des Gebäudes und des Gartens verändert und dem Besucher eine neue Wegführung vorgeschlagen.

Golestan Palace, Tehran, Iran
Golestan-Palast, Teheran, Iran

## EXTERIOR CURTAIN / fixed
*AUSSENVORHANG / nicht wandelbar*

"Canvas" Restaurant, Tokyo, Japan, 2003, **Nendo**
The building is completely clad in a textile envelope,
both inside and outside.
Restaurant „Canvas", Tokio, Japan, 2003, **Nendo**
Das Gebäude ist außen und innen komplett mit einer
textilen Hülle bekleidet.

Design for the Pinault Foundation for Contemporary Art, Boulogne-
Billancourt, France, 2001, **Dominique Perrault Architecture**
The textile envelope covers the building like a veil, allowing new
spatial volumes to develop in the exterior area.
Entwurf für die Pinault Stiftung für zeitgenössische Kunst, Boulogne-
Billancourt, Frankreich, 2001, **Dominique Perrault Architecture**
Wie ein Schleier bedeckt die textile Hülle das Gebäude und lässt im
Außenbereich neue Raumvolumen entstehen.

Serpentine Gallery Pavilion 2007, London, Great Britain,
**Olafur Eliasson and Kjetil Thorsen**
A complex geometrical structure was designed for the
temporary pavilion at the Serpentine Gallery; it appears to
transform with each step forward. The façade of the 140-
metre-long spiral ramp was partially enclosed by twisted
screens made of polyester cables.
Serpentine Gallery Pavillon 2007, London, Großbritannien,
**Olafur Eliasson und Kjetil Thorsen**
Für den temporären Pavillon der Serpentine Gallery wurde
eine komplexe geometrische Struktur entworfen, die sich
mit jedem Schritt zu wandeln schien. Die Fassade der 140
Meter langen Spiralrampe war abschnittsweise von in sich
gedrehten Lichtblenden aus Polyesterseilen eingefasst.

Music Theatre, Graz, Austria, 1998–2008, **UNStudio**
A net façade of stainless steel mesh conceals the printed
glass façade of this building. The transparency of the building
envelope and thus its pellucidity change with alternating lighting conditions during the day and at night.
Musiktheater, Graz, Österreich, 1998–2008, **UNStudio**
Eine Netzfassade aus Edelstahlgewebe verhüllt die bedruckte
Glasfassade des Gebäudes. Aufgrund der wechselnden Lichtverhältnisse bei Tag und Nacht ändert sich die Transparenz
der Gebäudehülle und somit die Durchsicht.

# CURTAIN WALL
## *VORHANGWAND*

Curtain Wall *There is a long history behind decorating and/or insulating textile wall coverings. Portable wall hangings and later tapestries provided protection from cold stone walls. Adjustable curtains in front of windows kept the sun and gazes from outside at bay. Contemporary large-area glass façades and their inherent transparency are making adjustable curtains an ever-more popular means of controlling heat build-up in interior spaces. The spectrum extends from transparent textiles, which provide visual protection but allow daylight to enter, to opaque materials such as blackening textiles, which can completely darken a room during the day. Particularly voluminous materials or special acoustic textiles can improve the sound quality of spaces.*

Vorhangwand *Textile Wandbespannungen mit schmückender und/oder isolierender Funktion haben eine lange Geschichte. Der transportable Wandbehang und später die Tapisserie schützten vor kalten Steinmauern. Variable Vorhänge vor dem Fenster hielten die Sonne ebenso ab wie fremde Blicke. Aufgrund großflächiger Glasfassaden und der damit verbundenen Transparenz werden wandelbare Vorhangwände heute verstärkt eingesetzt, um die Wärmeentwicklung im Innenraum steuern zu können. Die Bandbreite des Materials reicht dabei von transparenten Stoffen, die vor Einblick schützen, aber noch Tageslicht eindringen lassen, bis zu blickdichten Materialien wie beispielsweise Verdunklungstextilien, die den Raum auch tagsüber völlig abdunkeln. Besonders voluminöse Stoffe oder spezielle Akustiktextilien tragen zur Verbesserung der Raumakustik bei.*

Stage curtain "Liquid Gold," The Netherlands Dance Theater, The Hague,
The Netherlands, 1987 (replica 1999), **Inside Outside**
*Bühnenvorhang "Liquid Gold", Niederländisches Tanztheater, Den Haag,*
*Niederlande, 1987 (erneuert 1999),* **Inside Outside**

# CURTAIN WALL / adjustable
## *VORHANGWAND / wandelbar*

"The Modern Curtain," Birkerød Sports and Leisure Centre, Denmark, 2007,
**Astrid Krogh Design; Architecture: SHL Architects**
This variable sun protection made of fibreglass lamellas controls the amount of light entering the building, guaranteeing it a pleasant atmosphere. When the blinds are closed, black circles on the individual lamellas combine to form a large-area pattern.
„The Modern Curtain", Sport- und Freizeitzentrum, Birkerød, Dänemark, 2007,
**Astrid Krogh Design; Architektur: SHL Architects**
Der variable Sonnenschutz aus Glasfaserlamellen steuert den Lichteinfall ins Gebäudeinnere und sorgt dort für eine angenehme Atmosphäre. Bei geschlossenen Jalousien verbinden sich die schwarzen Kreise auf den einzelnen Lamellen zu einem großflächigen Muster.

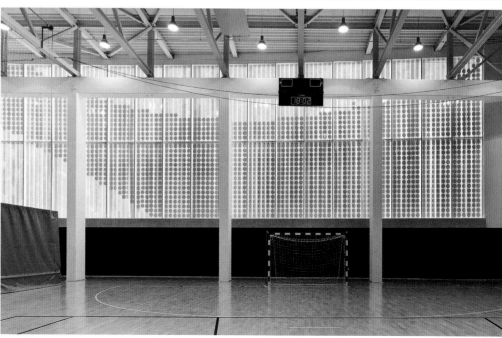

Villa Leefdaal, Leefdaal, Belgium, 2003–2004, **Inside Outside**
**Architecture: Macken en Macken**
The changeability of the curtains facilitates continual interac-
tion between the house and its inhabitants: they shape or
separate spaces, darken them, or reflect the sunlight. The
double-sidedness and various layers of the curtains guarantee multifaceted appearances. During daytime, transparent,
colourless layers open the interior spaces to the outside world
and when night falls, they are replaced by colourful textiles,
which create a warm, more enclosed, atmosphere.
Villa Leefdaal, Leefdaal, Belgien, 2003–2004, **Inside Outside**
**Architektur: Macken en Macken**
Die Veränderbarkeit der Vorhänge ermöglicht eine kontinuier-
liche Interaktion zwischen dem Haus und seinen Bewohnern:
Sie bilden oder trennen variabel Räume, verdunkeln sie oder
reflektieren das Sonnenlicht. Die Doppelseitigkeit und die
verschiedenen Lagen der Vorhänge gewährleisten facetten-
reiche Erscheinungsformen: Tagsüber öffnen transparente und
farblose Lagen die Innenräume zur Außenwelt, bei Anbruch
der Nacht werden sie durch farbenfrohe Textilien ersetzt, die
eine warme, eher abgeschlossene Atmosphäre erzeugen.

"House for a Couple," German Build-
ing Exhibition, Berlin, Germany, 1931,
**Ludwig Mies van der Rohe**
„Wohnhaus für ein Paar", Deutsche Bau-
ausstellung, Berlin, Deutschland, 1931,
**Ludwig Mies van der Rohe**

CURTAIN WALL / adjustable
*VORHANGWAND / wandelbar*

Darkening curtain in McCormick Tribune Campus
Centre, Chicago, USA, 1998–2004,
**Inside Outside; Architecture: OMA**
Verdunkelungsvorhang im McCormick Tribune
Campus Centre, Chicago, USA, 1998–2004,
**Inside Outside; Architektur: OMA**

Farnsworth House, Plano, Illinois, USA, 1950–1951,
**Ludwig Mies van der Rohe**
Farnsworth House, Plano, Illinois, USA, 1950–1951,
**Ludwig Mies van der Rohe**

Information Centre Court of Rotterdam, Netherlands, 2007–2008, **Atelier Kempe Thill**
The information centre fits as an independent
building volume into the glazed public interim
space within the Rotterdam court complex. The
inviting building volume is totally transparent. If
necessary, the conference rooms can be closed
using curtains to temporarily shield them from the
public sphere. These light-reflecting silver curtains also serve sun protection and improve the
acoustics of the space. In counterbalance to the
hermetics of the building, they provide a softer,
more tangible component.

Gerichts-Informationszentrum Rotterdam, Niederlande, 2007–2008, **Atelier Kempe Thill**
Das Informationszentrum passt sich als eigen-
ständiger Baukörper in den öffentlichen, mit
einem Glasdach überdeckten Zwischenraum
innerhalb des Rotterdamer Gerichtskomplexes
ein. Der einladende Baukörper ist vollständig
durchsichtig. Bei Bedarf werden die Bespre-
chungsräume mittels Vorhängen geschlossen, um
sie temporär von der Öffentlichkeit abzuschirmen.
Die lichtreflektierenden, silbernen Vorhänge wirken
auch als Sonnenschutz und tragen zur Verbesserung der Raumakustik bei. Als Gegengewicht
zur Hermetik des Gebäudes geben sie ihm etwas
Weiches und Fassbares.

## CURTAIN WALL / fixed
*VORHANGWAND / nicht wandelbar*

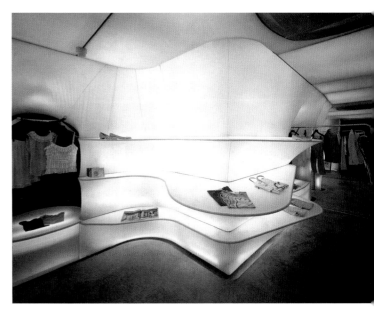

Tent room in Charlottenhof Palace, Potsdam, Germany,
Retrofit 1826–1829, **Karl Friedrich Schinkel**
Zeltzimmer im Schloss Charlottenhof, Potsdam, Deutsch-
land, Umbau 1826–1829, **Karl Friedrich Schinkel**

"A-POC Making" exhibition, Vitra Design Museum Berlin,
Germany, 2001, **Issey Miyake and Dai Fujiwara**
Ausstellung „A-POC Making", Vitra Design Museum Berlin,
Deutschland, 2001, **Issey Miyake und Dai Fujiwara**

United Bamboo Store, Tokyo, Japan, 2003, **Acconci Studio**
A covering of lengths of PVC stretches like a second skin from
the ceiling to the walls of this showroom in the basement floor of
a fashion store. The material curves around bent horizontal-run-
ning poles to create an amorphous structure that forms both the
shelves and sales desk. It conceals the structure behind and the
lamps, whose light penetrates the translucent skin to spread out
into the space.
United Bamboo Store, Tokio, Japan, 2003, **Acconci Studio**
Wie eine zweite Haut legt sich ein Bezug aus PVC-Bahnen von der
Decke über die Wände des Verkaufsraums im Untergeschoss des
Modeladens. Das Material wölbt sich über gebogene, horizontal
verlaufende Stangen und formt eine amorphe Struktur, die sowohl
die Regale als auch den Verkaufstresen bildet. Der Bezug verbirgt
die dahinter liegende Struktur und die Leuchten, deren Licht durch
die transluzente Haut dringt und sich im Raum ausbreitet.

Gala Event, Whitney Museum, New York, USA, 1999,
**Gisela Stromeyer Design**
The entrance area of the museum was completely
transformed for one evening – the walls and ceiling of
a tunnel that leads into the building and the lobby were
entirely clad in white spandex and soaked in magenta-
coloured light.
Gala Event, Whitney Museum, New York, USA, 1999,
**Gisela Stromeyer Design**
Für einen Abend wurde der Eingansbereich des Mu-
seums komplett verwandelt, indem die Wände und die
Decke des ins Gebäude führenden Tunnels sowie die
Lobby vollständig mit weißem Elastan bekleidet und in
magentafarbenes Licht getaucht wurden.

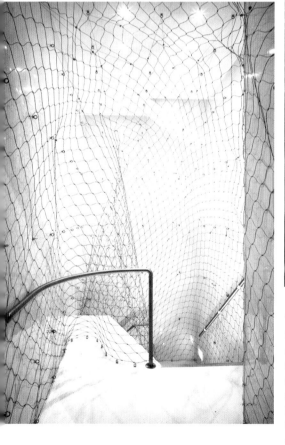

Bordello Bar, London, Great Britain, 2008, **Sam Buxton**
The flowing movement of a net structure clads the different spaces with
numerous arches and niches to visually connect them to one another. The
ceiling and walls of a cool and sober looking entrance area have been
spanned by stainless steel wire netting. Guests are received by a warm
soft atmosphere in the actual bar area – its walls and pillars are wrapped in
a knotted net of fire-proof-treated polypropylene rope.

Bordello Bar, London, Großbritannien, 2008, **Sam Buxton**
Um die verschiedenen Räume mit ihren zahlreichen Torbögen und Nischen
optisch miteinander zu verbinden, sind sie in einer fließenden Bewegung
von einer Netzstruktur überzogen. Die Decke und die Wände des kühl
und nüchtern wirkenden Eingangsbereiches sind von einem Drahtnetz
aus rostfreiem Stahldraht überspannt. Im eigentlichen Barbereich wird der
Gast von einer warmen und weichen Atmosphäre empfangen: Dort sind
die Wände und Säulen von einem geknoteten Netz aus rotem, feuerfest
behandeltem Polypropylenseil umwickelt.

# PARTITION
## *RAUMTEILER*

Partition *From the "classical" curtain to sliding padded lamella structures to spanned canvas elements: textile partitions allow different spatial situations to be created as required, so that individual areas can be used simultaneously for different functions or – when the partitions are retracted – the space can be experienced as a whole. Partitions can usually be guided vertically along ceiling* tracks *or can be horizontally raised and lowered; their design incorporates storage room for the folded textile when not in use. Various degrees of separation can be had depending on the transparency and volume of the material – from light, solely optical separation to acoustically effective spatial partition.*

Raumteiler *Vom „klassischen" Vorhang über verschiebbare gepolsterte Lamellenstrukturen bis hin zu verspannten Segelelementen: Mit textilen Raumteilern lassen sich je nach Bedarf unterschiedliche Raumsituationen erzeugen, bei denen wahlweise einzelne Bereiche parallel unterschiedlich genutzt werden können oder – bei geöffneten Raumteilern – der Raum als Ganzes erlebbar ist. Zumeist* lassen sich Raumteiler vertikal an Deckenschienen verfahren oder horizontal senken und heben und sind so konzipiert, dass sich die nicht benötigten Textilien zusammengefaltet verstauen lassen. Je nach Transparenz und Volumen des Materials sind verschiedene Grade der Trennung möglich – von leichten, lediglich optischen Abgrenzungen bis zu auch akustisch wirksamen Raumteilern.*

Spatial partition, Germany, 1999.
**Sylvie Krüger**
*Raumteiler, Deutschland, 1999.*
**Sylvie Krüger**

## PARTITION / adjustable
### *RAUMTEILER / wandelbar*

Eventquest Advertising Agency, New York, USA, 1994,
**Gisela Stromeyer Design**
Translucent sails made of spandex divide the 220 square-metre space into working areas in which the sculptural-seeming separation still offers enough openness for dialogue between employees.
Werbeagentur Eventquest, New York, USA, 1994,
**Gisela Stromeyer Design**
Transluzente Segel aus Elastan unterteilen den 220 Quadratmeter großen Raum in Arbeitsbereiche, wobei die skulptural anmutende Trennung genug Offenheit für den Dialog der Mitarbeiter bietet.

Clouds, 2009, **Ronan & Erwan Bouroullec** in collaboration with **Kvadrat**
Spatial partitions made of connectable textile components.
Clouds, 2009, **Ronan & Erwan Bouroullec** in Zusammenarbeit mit **Kvadrat**
Raumteiler aus zusammensteckbaren textilen Elementen.

Three-part spatial partition made of spinnaker nylon with flock print, Germany, 1998, **Claudia Strobel**
Dreiteiliger Raumteiler aus Spinnackernylon mit Flockdruck, Deutschland, 1998, **Claudia Strobel**

Elie Tahari Showroom, New York, USA, 2002, **Gisela Stromeyer Design**
Vertically spanned fabric sails made of translucent inflammable spandex divide the space into four areas that can be combined for large events. The ceiling, walls, and the central pillar are also covered in sails.
Elie Tahari Showroom, New York, USA, 2002, **Gisela Stromeyer Design**
Vertikal verspannte Stoffsegel aus transluzentem, nicht brennbarem Elastan trennen den Raum in vier Bereiche, die bei Veranstaltungen zusammengelegt werden können. Zusätzlich sind die Decke, die Wände und die zentrale Stütze mit Segeln bespannt.

## PARTITION / adjustable
*RAUMTEILER / wandelbar*

Temporary Hall Divider, Neue Messe Karlsruhe, Germany, 2003, **Gerriets GmbH**
Temporäre Hallenunterteilung, Neue Messe Karlsruhe, Deutschland, 2003, **Gerriets GmbH**

"Liquid Gold" stage curtain, The Netherlands Dance Theatre, The Hague, The Netherlands, 1987 (replica 1999), **Inside Outside**
This sound and light absorbing black curtain of heavy wool velvet separates the stage from the auditorium. Gold dots that have been printed on it are reflected in a "flowing" manner depending on light intensity, exposure to light, and the movement of the curtain.
Bühnenvorhang „Liquid Gold", Niederländisches Tanztheater, Den Haag, Niederlande, 1987 (erneuert 1999), **Inside Outside**
Der geräusch- und lichtabsorbierende schwarze Vorhang aus schwerem Wollsamt trennt die Bühne vom Zuschauerraum. Bedruckt ist er mit goldenen Punkten, die je nach Lichtintensität, Lichteinfall und Bewegung des Vorhangs in einem „fließenden" Effekt reflektiert werden.

Paul Horn-Arena, Tübingen, Germany, 2003–2004,
**Allmann Sattler Wappner Architects**
The playing field of the sports hall can be divided into three
separate parts by lowering separating curtains – a netting
combination made of flame-resistant nylon netting and artificial
leather – that are stored in the ceiling. There are ball protection
nets at each end of the playing field which can equally be stored
in packages on the ceiling.
Paul Horn-Arena, Tübingen, Deutschland, 2003–2004,
**Allmann Sattler Wappner Architekten**
Das Spielfeld der Sporthalle wird bei Bedarf in drei Bereiche
geteilt, indem zwei im Deckenbereich verstaute Trennvorhänge
– eine Netzkombination aus schwer entflammbaren Nylonnetz
und Kunstleder – herabgelassen werden. An den Stirnseiten des
Spielfelds befinden sich Ballschutznetze, die ebenfalls an der
Decke in Paketen verstaut werden können.

Stage Curtain, Grand Palais,
Lille, France, 1994–1995,
**Inside Outside**
Bühnenvorhang, Grand Palais,
Lille, Frankreich, 1994–1995,
**Inside Outside**

## PARTITION / adjustable
### *RAUMTEILER / wandelbar*

Spatial Partition, 1999, Germany, **Sylvie Krüger**
This double-sided spatial partition consists of six foam panels that are each covered with white felt on one side and with a grey, PVC-coated fabric on the other.
Raumteiler, 1999, Deutschland, **Sylvie Krüger**
Der zweiseitige Raumteiler besteht aus sechs Schaumstoffpaneelen, die jeweils auf der einen Seite mit einem weißen Filz und auf der anderen Seite mit einem grauen, PVC-beschichteten Gewebe bespannt sind.

Near Koya-San, Wakayama prefecture, Japan, 2008
Nahe Koya-San, Wakayama Präfektur, Japan, 2008

Curtains inside the Frieze Art Fair Tent, London, Great Britain, 2008,
**Caruso St. John**
1,800 metres of wool fabric were used to form temporary spaces
inside the Frieze Art Fair Tent. The "walls" of different rooms such as
the entrance area, the VIP lounge, and the restaurant, were formed by
coloured, generously pleated curtains.
Vorhänge innerhalb des Zeltes der Kunstmesse „Frieze", London,
Großbritannien, 2008, **Caruso St. John**
1800 Meter Wollstoff wurden verwendet, um temporär Räume
innerhalb des Zeltes der Kunstmesse „Frieze" zu bilden. Farbige, in
großzügige Falten gelegte Vorhänge formten die „Wände" verschiedener Räume wie den Eingangsbereich, die VIP-Lounge und das
Restaurant.

Exhibition space at the 1912 World Fair in Brussels,
Belgium, Section of the German Empire, commis-
sioned by the automobile industry, **Peter Behrens**
Ausstellungsraum auf der Weltausstellung 1912 in
Brüssel, Belgien, Sektion des Deutschen Reichs, im
Auftrag der Linoleumindustrie, **Peter Behrens**

## ROOM IN ROOM
## *RAUM IM RAUM*

Room in Room *Vertical expanses of textile allow convertible rooms – that can be opened up or closed at will – to be created within solid walled spaces. As an early "room in room" structure, the four-poster bed provided a certain degree of privacy in cramped living spaces, and also protected against the cold. These days, closed textile structures can become self-contained, temporary havens or individual areas for diverse uses. Depending on the transparency and volume of the material, which slides along ceiling tracks, such structures can also provide visual and additional acoustic separation. As long as the surrounding noise can be absorbed effectively, a quiet, concentrated atmosphere can be established within a temporary room in room.*

Raum im Raum *Mithilfe vertikaler textiler Flächen lässt sich innerhalb eines Raums massiver Bauweise ein variabel verschließbarer und zu öffnender zusätzlicher Raum schaffen – als frühe „Raum im Raum"-Konstruktion gewährleistete das Himmelbett in beengten Wohnverhältnissen eine gewisse Privatsphäre und schützte zudem vor Kälte. Heutzutage bilden geschlossene textile Konstruktionen bei Bedarf eigenständige, temporäre Rückzugsorte bzw. einzelne Bereiche für unterschiedliche Nutzungen. Je nach Transparenz und Volumen des an Deckenschienen bewegten textilen Materials dient die Konstruktion einer optischen oder zusätzlich auch einer akustischen Trennung. Werden die Umgebungsgeräusche wirksam gedämpft, entsteht innerhalb des temporären Raums im Raum eine ruhige, konzentrierte Atmosphäre.*

Extension to School Complex, Hirzenbach. Zurich,
Switzerland, 2005–2007, **Boltshauser Architects
with Alex Herter**
*Erweiterung Schulanlage Hirzenbach. Zürich,
Schweiz, 2005–2007, **Boltshauser Architekten
mit Alex Herter***

ROOM IN ROOM / convertible
*RAUM IM RAUM / wandelbar*

"The Wedding Night," 1767
„Die Brautnacht", 1767

Nyamasari, Kenya, 2006
Nyamasari, Kenia, 2006

Travelling showroom, Portugal, 2008,
**ex.studio. Patricia Menses + Iván Juárez**
Developed for the presentation of Portuguese
fashion designers, this showroom toured various
cities throughout Portugal in 2008. The relationship
between space, transparency, and light was a defin-
ing factor within the design process. It was inspired
by the incredible intensity of light in the streets of
Portugal and the special shape of an elliptical type of
door in the Barrio Alto district of Lisbon. The shape
of the door was interpreted through a sequence of
several vertical layers of white lengths of material with
elliptical openings that were attached to the ceiling.
The space, formed by that sequence of identical
elements and open to the sides, invited the visitor to
a visual game between interior and exterior. Direct
white light radiated from the ceiling and roof through
the translucent textiles, making the showroom appear
ethereal and flowing.

Travelling showroom, Portugal, 2008,
**ex.studio. Patricia Menses + Iván Juárez**
Entwickelt für die Präsentation portugiesischer
Modedesigner, tourte der Showroom 2008 durch
verschiedene Städte Portugals. Beim Entwurf stand
die Beziehung zwischen Raum, Transparenz und Licht
im Vordergrund. Inspiration hierfür war die enorme
Intensität des Lichtes in den Straßen Portugals und
die besondere Typologie einer elliptischen Türform aus
dem Barrio Alto in Lissabon. Die Form der Tür wurde
durch eine Staffelung mehrerer vertikaler Ebenen
aus weißen, an der Decke befestigten Textilbahnen
mit elliptischen Öffnungen interpretiert. Der von einer
Sequenz gleicher Elemente gebildete, seitlich offene
Raum lud den Besucher zu einem visuellen Spiel
zwischen innen und außen ein. Von Decke und Boden
strahlte direktes weißes Licht durch die transluzenten
textilen Ebenen, was den Showroom als ätherischen,
fließenden Raum erscheinen ließ.

## ROOM IN ROOM / convertible
*RAUM IM RAUM / wandelbar*

Danish Cultural Ministry, Copenhagen, Denmark, 2005,
**Louise Campbell and Marianne Britt Jørgensen**
Five free-standing steel frames in the shape of cubes, which could be closed on two sides by hand-dyed curtains, were erected to separate the desks of seven members of staff from the official entrance to the minister's office without architecturally altering the space inside the monument-protected building. They act as variable sun protection towards the window front and separate the working area from the passageway to create a concentrated working atmosphere.

Dänisches Kulturministerium, Kopenhagen, Dänemark, 2005,
**Louise Campbell und Marianne Britt Jørgensen**
Um die Arbeitsplätze von sieben Mitarbeitern vom offiziellen Durchgang zum Büro des Ministers abzugrenzen, ohne den Raum innerhalb des denkmalgeschützten Gebäudes architektonisch zu verändern, wurden fünf frei stehende Stahlrahmen in Form von Kuben aufgestellt, die jeweils an zwei Seiten mit handgefärbten Vorhängen verschließbar sind. Sie fungieren als variabler Sonnenschutz zur Fensterfront hin und trennen bei Bedarf den Arbeitsbereich vom Durchgang, um eine konzentrierte Arbeitsatmosphäre zu ermöglichen.

"Samt und Seide" Café inside the "Die Mode der Dame" exhibition, Berlin, Germany, 1927,
**Ludwig Mies van der Rohe with Lilly Reich**
These room curtains in black, red, and orange coloured velvet as well as gold, silver, black, and lemon-yellow silk divide the exhibition cafe variably into individual areas, creating protected spatial situations.
Café „Samt und Seide" innerhalb der Ausstellung „Die Mode der Dame", Berlin, Deutschland, 1927,
**Ludwig Mies van der Rohe mit Lilly Reich**
Die Raumvorhänge aus schwarzem, rotem und orange-farbenem Samt sowie goldener, silberner, schwarzer und zitronengelber Seide unterteilten das Ausstellungscafé variabel in einzelne Bereiche und bildeten geschützte Raumsituationen.

Kunsthaus Bregenz, Austria, 2004, **Thomas Demand** in collaboration with **Caruso St. John Architects**
On the occasion of his solo exhibition at the Kunsthaus Bregenz, the artist Thomas Demand created a temporary room for screening a film in the foyer in conjunction with architects Adam Caruso and Peter St. John. Two motor-driven, floor-to-ceiling dark blue curtains moved on tracks into the space in a spiral shape, forming an enclosed dark room for a few minutes, which disappeared again when the curtains were opened.
Kunsthaus Bregenz, Österreich, 2004, **Thomas Demand** in Zusammenarbeit mit **Caruso St. John Architects**
Anlässlich seiner Einzelausstellung im Kunsthaus Bregenz gestaltete der Künstler Thomas Demand zusammen mit den Architekten Adam Caruso und Peter St. John für die Aufführung eines Kurzfilms einen temporären Raum im Fo-yer des Gebäudes. Zwei raumhohe dunkelblaue Vorhänge bewegten sich, von Motoren angetrieben, an Schienen spiralförmig in den Raum hinein und bildeten für einige Minuten einen geschlossenen, dunklen Raum, der mit dem Öffnen der Vorhänge wieder verschwand.

Vertical Space Definer
*Vertikaler Raumabschluss*

CURRENT PROJECTS
*AKTUELLE PROJEKTE*

MARIA FLÖCKNER
AND HERMANN SCHNÖLL,
MASSIMILIANO AND DORIANA FUKSAS,
RENZO PIANO BUILDING WORKSHOP,
INSIDE OUTSIDE,
RONAN & ERWAN BOUROULLEC,
DIENER & DIENER ARCHITECTS,
BOLTSHAUSER ARCHITECTS,
HERZOG & DE MEURON,
STUDIO MAKKINK & BEY.

## MARIA FLÖCKNER AND HERMANN SCHNÖLL

House 47°40'48"n/13°8'12"e, Adnet, Austria, 2005–2007
*Haus 47°40'48"n/13°8'12"e, Adnet, Österreich, 2005–2007*

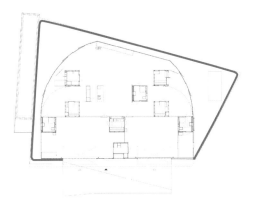

Its architects describe this house, located on green pastures and surrounded by mountains, as a "shelter with a glass curtain." Two horizontal reinforced concrete slabs define the living area. The gaze wanders sideways, uninterrupted, through a circumferential glass wall to the surrounding landscape. The transparency of this house can be regulated on three sides by a mobile, black exterior curtain made of UV-proof PE raschel fabric, which, if need be, can be fixed to floor anchors using expander ropes. From complete closure to the outside space through snippets of scenery to total openness; there is a wide spectrum of possible options. The transparency of the textile and varying light situations, depending on time of day and year, create diverse lighting conditions inside the building. The roof protrudes on two corners to create outside spaces; spaces of transition to the landscape. These can be opened or closed using the curtain, which also serves adjustable weather protection against sun, rain or wind.

Als „Unterstand mit Glasvorhang" beschreiben die Architekten das in Wiesen gelegene und von Bergen umgebene Wohnhaus. Zwei horizontale Stahlbetonplatten begrenzen den bewohnten Raum. Seitlich gleitet der Blick ungehindert durch die umlaufende Glaswand in die umge-bende Landschaft. Die Transparenz des Hauses ist an drei Seiten durch einen mobilen schwarzen Außenvorhang aus UV-beständigem PE-Raschelgewirk regulierbar, der bei Bedarf mit Expanderseilen an Bodenösen fixiert werden kann. Von einer völligen Verschließbarkeit gegenüber dem Außenraum über szenische Ausschnitte bis hin zur völligen Öffnung sind verschiedene Szenarien möglich. Die Durch-lässigkeit des textilen Materials sowie unterschiedliche Lichtsituationen je nach Tages- und Jahreszeit bewirken variable Lichtverhältnisse im Gebäudeinneren. Aufgrund des an zwei Ecken weit ausladenden Daches entstehen Außenräume bzw. Übergangsräume zur Landschaft, die sich mittels des Vorhangs öffnen oder schließen lassen. Er fungiert hier als einstellbarer Witterungsschutz vor Sonne, Regen oder Wind.

## MASSIMILIANO AND DORIANA FUKSAS

Zénith Concert Hall, Strasbourg, France, 2003–2007
*Zénith Musikhalle, Straßburg, Frankreich, 2003–2007*

A light textile membrane, reminiscent of the transportable tents used by travelling shows, enshrouds the massive building volume of this concert hall. The reinforced concrete shell of the concert hall, which seats 10,000, has good acoustics, preventing sound from penetrating to the outside. Five ellipsoidal rings, which lean slightly towards one another and are supported by steel columns, form the structure of the 12,000 square-meter silicon-reinforced envelope of fibreglass fabric that makes the building appear compact and opaque from the outside during the day. At night it transforms into a giant, glowing Chinese lantern as a result of its translucent skin, onto which announcements of future events can be projected.

Eine leichte textile Membran, die an die transportablen Zelte fahrender Shows erinnert, umhüllt den festen Baukörper der Musikhalle. Der mit 10.000 Sitzplätzen bestückte Konzertraum gewährleistet aufgrund einer verstärkten Betonschale eine gute Akustik und verhindert, dass Geräusche nach außen dringen. Fünf ellipsenförmige, leicht zueinander verschobene und von Stahlstützen gehaltene Ringe bilden die Konstruktion für die 12.000 Quadratmeter große silikonverstärkte Hülle aus Glasfasergewebe, die den Bau von außen bei Tageslicht wie eine kompakte, opake Skulptur erscheinen lässt. Nachts verwandelt sie sich aufgrund ihrer durchscheinenden Haut in einen riesigen leuchtenden Lampion, auf den Ankündigungen für bevorstehende Veranstaltungen projiziert werden können.

## RENZO PIANO BUILDING WORKSHOP

Luna Rossa team base, Valencia, Spain, 2005–2006
*Luna Rossa Operationsbasis, Valencia, Spanien,*
*2005–2006*

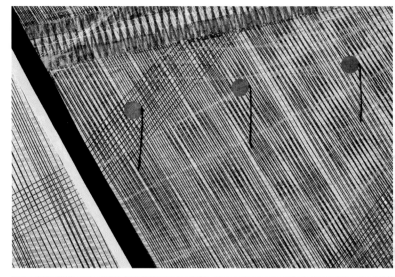

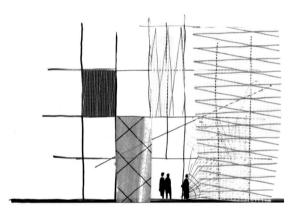

The exterior appearance of the Luna Rosa team base, built for the "America's Cup 2007," makes reference to the sailing regatta that takes place in Valencia annually; fifty used sails were cut up, reassembled and fixed to 485 frames with which the façade of the building was made. In order to make the sails more resistant they were laminated to polycarbonate honey-comb panels using acrylic glue and made air and water tight. The membrane was prestressed to make it a stiff structural element that changed the light entering, depending on the levels of translucency of the various sails. While the façade envelope appears opaque during the day, it becomes translucent when lit up from behind at night, providing insights into the structure of the façade system and the interior spaces.

Die äußere Erscheinung der für den „America's Cup 2007" erbauten Luna Rossa Operationsbasis ist eine Referenz an die alljährlich in Valencia stattfindende Segelregatta: 50 gebrauchte Segel wurden zerschnitten, neu zusammengesetzt und auf 485 Rahmen befestigt, mit denen die Fassade des Gebäudes gebildet wurde. Um die Segel widerstandsfähiger zu machen, wurden sie mithilfe von Acrylkleber auf Polykarbonat-Wabenpaneele aufkaschiert und luft- sowie wasserdicht versiegelt. Durch die Vorspannung wurde die Membran zu einem steifen Strukturelement, das den Lichteinfall je nach Grad der Lichtdurchlässigkeit der verschiedenen Segel steuert. Während die Fassadenhülle tagsüber opak erscheint, ist sie nachts bei Beleuchtung von innen durchscheinend und gewährt Einblicke in die Struktur des Fassadensystems sowie in die Innenräume.

## INSIDE OUTSIDE
### Architecture: OMA

Casa da Música, Porto, Portugal, 1999–2004
*Casa da Música, Porto, Portugal, 1999–2004*

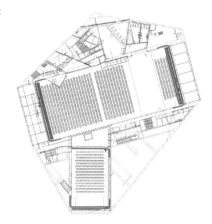

The Casa da Música, built by OMA, rises like a mighty polygonal crystal of white cement above the old town of Porto. Inside, two concert halls and other rooms are piled like boxes on top of and beside each other. The large concert hall opens up to its surroundings via a giant glass front, allowing daylight to stream in. Three curtains are layered one behind the other along that opening; these can be moved separately or in combination with one another to vary the amount of light, the view, and the acoustics. The wide variety within those curtains, from very delicate layers through to spatially defined structures – such as a view-blocking "veil" made of knotted strips of voile – create various degrees of transparency, overlapping, and volume. Three further curtains have been installed to similar effect in the small concert hall. Electrically powered, the fire-proof curtains can be stored in cavities in walls and ceilings. For acoustic reasons, two wool curtains, into which windows of transparent plastic sheeting have been integrated, drape the walls of the rehearsal rooms, creating a visual connection between them and the conducting cabin and public spaces, even when the curtains are closed. The colourlessness of the curtains attracts attention to the structure of the textiles.

Small concert hall
Kleiner Konzertsaal

Large concert hall
Großer Konzertsaal

Wie ein gewaltiger polygonaler Kristall aus
weißem Beton erhebt sich die von OMA erbaute
Casa da Música über der Altstadt Portos, in deren Inneren zwei Konzertsäle und weitere Räume
wie Boxen auf- und nebeneinander gestapelt
sind. Der große Konzertsaal öffnet sich an den
Stirnseiten über riesige Glasfronten zur Umgebung und lässt Tageslicht einströmen. Daran
entlang lassen sich separat oder in Kombination
jeweils drei hintereinander geschichtete Vorhänge
bewegen, um den Lichteinfall, die Sicht und die
Akustik zu variieren. Die große Variationsbreite
der Vorhänge, von sehr zarten Schichten bis hin
zu plastischen, räumlich wirksamen Strukturen
– wie der aus Voilestreifen geknotete, die Sicht
verwehrende „Schleier" – erzeugen verschiedene
Stufen von Transparenz, Überlagerung und Volumen. Im kleinen Konzertsaal werden drei weitere
Vorhänge in ähnlicher Funktion eingesetzt. Von
Motoren gesteuert, lassen sich die feuerbestän-
digen Vorhänge in Hohlräumen der Wände sowie
der Decken verstauen. Die Wände der Pro-
beräume werden aus akustischen Gründen von
zwei Wollvorhängen bedeckt, in die Fenster aus
transparenter Kunststofffolie integriert sind, um
auch bei geschlossenem Vorhang eine Einsicht
von den Regiekabinen und den öffentlichen
Bereichen zu gewährleisten. Aufgrund der Farb-
losigkeit der Vorhänge wird die Aufmerksamkeit
auf die Struktur der Textilien verlagert.

**RONAN & ERWAN BOUROULLEC**

North Tiles, Showroom Kvadrat, Stockholm, Sweden, 2006
*North Tiles, Showroom Kvadrat, Stockholm, Schweden, 2006*

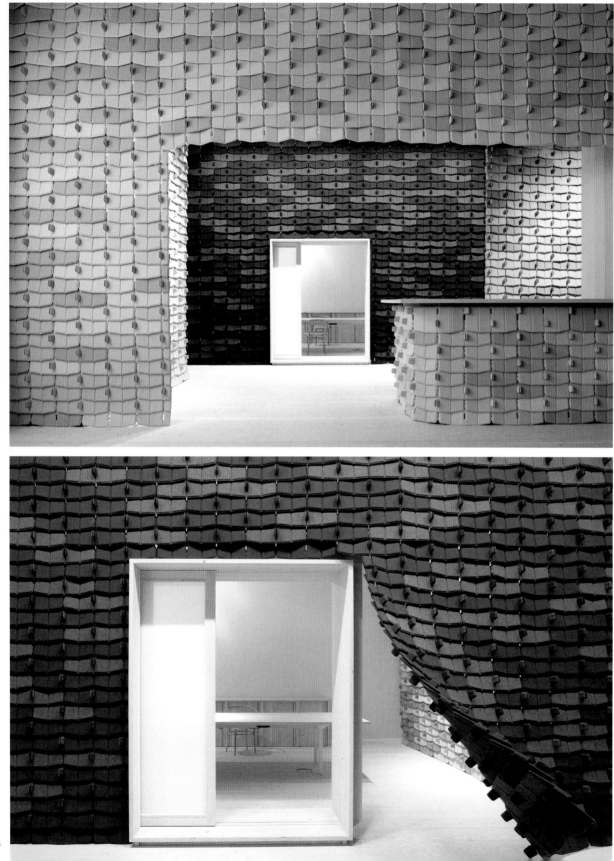

Originally developed for the showroom of Kvadrat textile manufacturers, "North Tiles" can be used to form spaces, as spatial separators and as wall cladding. The approximately 28 x 65 centimetre large textile tiles consist of a rigid foam core covered in two layers of material; their noise-absorbing properties enable them to improve the acoustics of spaces. The simple push-fit system allows them to be combined to form alterable walls without extra mechanical support. Spatial structures can be continually developed as the system allows changes to be made to entrances, corridors, and transitions. Its modularity means that it can be used for a wide variety of applications and adapted to spatial situations using linear or organic shapes. Diverse spatial atmospheres can be created by combining different colours.

Ursprünglich für den Showroom des Textilherstellers Kvadrat in Stockholm entwickelt, lassen sich mit den „North Tiles" ohne großen Aufwand Räume bilden und voneinander abgrenzen, aber auch Wände bekleiden. Die etwa 28 x 65 Zentimeter großen textilen Ziegel bestehen aus einem von zwei Stoffschichten ummantelten Hartschaumkern und verbessern aufgrund ihrer geräuschdämpfenden Eigenschaft die Raumakustik. Mithilfe eines einfachen Stecksystems lassen sie sich ohne weitere mechanische Unterstützung zu wandelbaren Wänden zusammenfügen. Durch die Veränderung von Zugängen, Gängen und Übergängen bietet das System die Möglichkeit, die räumliche Struktur fortlaufend weiterzuentwickeln. Das Bausteinprinzip erlaubt die Berücksichtigung multipler Anwendungen und die Anpassung an räumliche Gegebenheiten mittels linearer oder organischer Formen. Durch die Kombination unterschiedlicher Farben können differenzierte Raumatmosphären geschaffen werden.

## DIENER & DIENER ARCHITECTS
### with Peter Suter

Presentation of Switzerland at the Frankfurt Book Fair, Frankfurt on Main, Germany, 1998
*Präsentation der Schweiz auf der Frankfurter Buchmesse, Frankfurt am Main, Deutschland, 1998*

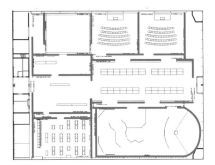

Rather than erecting its own pavilion, Switzerland, the guest of honour country, adapted an existing warehouse on the trade fair grounds for its presentation at the Frankfurt Book Fair. Floor-to-ceiling curtains divided the warehouse into different areas, which still remained acoustically connected, so that the provisional character of the interior remained preserved. This spatial and material dimension stood in pleasant contrast to the density, constriction, and hectic of the surrounding trade fair bustle.

Each area accommodated a different function. The central and largest space formed a library, around which two lecture rooms, a television studio, a restaurant, a cloakroom, and the foyer were arranged. A narrow channel was installed as a double layer between the restaurant and the neighbouring spaces to prevent them from disturbing each other. Three different materials were used for the strong-coloured curtains: cotton fabric and felt, both made flame-resistant through impregnation, and chintz made of highly flame-resistant polyester fibres.

Das Gastland Schweiz nutzte anstatt eines eigens errichteten Pavillons eine bereits bestehende Lagerhalle auf dem Messegelände für seine Landespräsentation auf der Frankfurter Buchmesse. Die Lagerhalle wurde durch raumhohe Vorhänge in verschiedene Bereiche aufgeteilt, die jedoch akustisch verbunden blieben, womit der provisorische Charakter auch im Inneren gewahrt wurde. Die räumliche und stoffliche Dimension hob sich angenehm von der Dichte, Enge und Hektik des umliegenden Messebetriebs ab.

In den einzelnen Bereichen wurden unterschiedliche Nutzungen untergebracht. Den zentralen und größten Raum bildete eine Bibliothek, um die sich zwei Vortragsräume, ein Fernsehstudio, ein Restaurant, eine Garderobe und das Foyer gruppierten. Eine schmale Schleuse, die als doppelte Schicht zwischen dem Restaurant und den angrenzenden Räumen eingezogen wurde, verhinderte ihre gegenseitige Störung. Für die in kräftigen Farben gehaltenen Vorhänge wurden drei verschiedene Materialien verwendet: ein Baumwollstoff und ein Filz, beide schwer entflammbar imprägniert, sowie ein Chintz aus schwer entflammbaren Polyesterfasern.

## INSIDE OUTSIDE
### Architecture: UNStudio

Mercedes-Benz Museum, Stuttgart, Germany, 2001–2006
*Mercedes-Benz Museum, Stuttgart, Deutschland, 2001–2006*

The floor plan of this museum, designed by UNStudio, is similar to a three-leafed clover. Like a helix, the building components wind about each other, forming a spiral-like circuit along a connecting ramp from the ground floor to the topmost exhibition level.

Curtains have been given different functions within the building. Various spatial and lighting situations can be created in the multifunctional room on the ground floor by opening or closing an adjustable curtain. The curtain, which runs along a semicircular rail, is made of heavy, grey, long mohair velvet, onto which a wide seam made of a black "sauerkraut" structure is sewn. The exterior of the curtain is lined with a transparent plastic foil. A second layer, consisting of a further curtain made of a silver, light-reflecting film can be moved along parallel rails. In the espresso bar, a concave "brush wall" with a long fringe-like surface absorbs the background noise, surrounding the space like a three-dimensional veil.

On the top floor, a lemon-green curtain lined by a black "sauerkraut" structure borders the atrium and encloses the restaurant and the lounge. Its opacity creates a soft lighting situation, while the partially open surface allows visitors to look through it.

Curtain of the restaurant
Vorhang des Restaurants

Espresso bar
Espressobar

Multifunctional room
Multifunktionsraum

Der Grundriss des von UNStudio erbauten Museums erinnert
an ein dreiblättriges Kleeblatt. Gleich einer Helix winden sich die
Gebäudestränge umeinander und bilden über Verbindungsrampen
einen spiralartigen Rundgang vom Erdgeschoss bis in die oberste
Ausstellungsebene.

Innerhalb des Gebäudes werden Vorhänge in verschiedenen
Funktionen eingesetzt. Im Erdgeschoss lassen sich im Multifunktionsraum durch Öffnen oder Schließen eines flexiblen Vorhangs
verschiedene Raum- und Lichtsituationen schaffen. Der in einem
Halbrund verlaufende Vorhang besteht aus einem schweren, grau-
en, langhaarigen Mohair-Samt, an den ein breiter Saum aus einer
schwarzen „Sauerkraut"-Struktur genäht ist. Die Außenseite des
Vorhangs ist mit einer transparenten Kunststofffolie überzogen. An
parallel verlaufenden Schienen wird in einer zweiten Schicht ein
weiterer Vorhang aus einer silbernen, Licht reflektierenden Folie
bewegt. In der Espressobar dämpft eine konkave „Bürstenwand"
mit einer langen fransenartigen Oberfläche die Geräuschkulisse
und umgibt den Raum wie einen dreidimensionalen Schleier.
In der obersten Etage säumt ein limonengrüner Vorhang mit einer
Rückseite aus schwarzer „Sauerkraut"-Struktur das Atrium und
umschließt das Restaurant sowie die Lounge. Seine Lichtun-
durchlässigkeit hat eine gedämpfte Lichtsituation zur Folge,
während die halb offene Oberfläche es den Besuchern erlaubt,
hindurchzublicken.

# BOLTSHAUSER ARCHITECTS
## with Alex Herter

Extension to School Complex, Hirzenbach, Zurich, Switzerland, 2005–2007
*Erweiterung Schulanlage Hirzenbach, Zürich, Schweiz, 2005–2007*

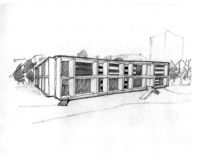

A single-storey kindergarten was added to the north of the existing school building, while a sports hall was half-sunken into the ground on the southern side. Artist Alex Herter designed curtains with wide coloured horizontal stripes in green and white, red and white, and yellow and black for the interior spaces. By reacting to the spatial structures, they blend into the existing building while also standing on their own as independent elements, which, in conjunction with the fixed spatial boundaries–concrete walls, sliding windows, glass brick walls–allow the spaces to be shaped at will. These curtains serve both the need for protection and for the greatest possible openness. They are used in the sports hall and the kindergarten as sun protection along the façade and also as space-shaping and separating elements in the interiors of both. The soft haptics of their noise-absorbing material, made of flame-resistant polyester, temper the hard smooth surfaces of the surrounding materials that include concrete and glass.

Das bestehende Schulhaus wurde im Norden mit einem eingeschossigen Kindergarten und im Süden mit einer halb in den Boden versenkten Sporthalle erweitert. Für die Innenräume entwickelte der Künstler Alex Herter Vorhänge mit breiten farbigen Querstreifen in Grün/Weiß, Rot/Weiß und Gelb/Schwarz. Indem sie die räumlichen Strukturen aufnehmen, fügen sie sich einerseits in die bestehende Gebäudesituation ein,

Sports hall
Sporthalle

Adaptable dormitories in kindergarten
Wandelbare Schlafräume im Kindergarten

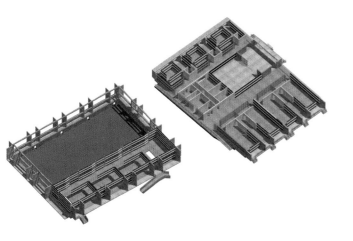

bilden aber andererseits ein eigenständiges Element, welches im Zusammenspiel mit den fest installierten Raumbegrenzungen – Betonwände, Schiebefenster und Glasbausteinwände – der variablen Raumbildung dient. Die Vorhänge bedienen sowohl das Bedürfnis nach Schutz als auch nach größtmöglicher Offenheit. Sie werden in der Sporthalle und im Kindergarten jeweils sowohl als Sonnenschutz entlang der Fassade als auch, im Inneren, in raumbildender bzw. -trennender Funktion verwendet. Die harten und glatten Oberflächen der umgebenden Materialien wie Beton und Glas werden durch die weiche Haptik des geräuschdämpfenden Stoffes aus schwer entflammbarem Polyester gemildert.

## HERZOG & DE MEURON

Concert Hall, European Month of Music, Basel, Switzerland, 2001
*Konzerthalle, Europäischer Musikmonat, Basel, Schweiz, 2001*

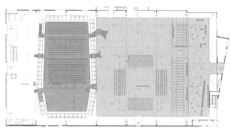

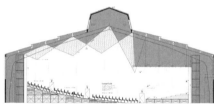

Concert hall interior view
Konzerthalle Innenansicht

Concert hall exterior view
Konzerthalle Außenansicht

Foyer and
"Salle modulable"
Foyer und
„Salle modulable"

Herzog & de Meuron designed a temporary concert hall on the occasion of the "European Month of Music 2001," which took place in Basel, in hall five of Basel trade fair grounds; diverse pieces of music by contemporary composers were performed there.

Several layers of coloured, semi-transparent curtains separated the "Salle modulable" from the foyer and bar. Electronic music performances could just about be made out though the protective visual layers from there. The actual concert hall was located behind the "Salle modulable." A wooden structure was festively decorated with black molleton. The audience entered the concert hall via three round openings. A white rear-lit transparent fabric was used to clad the interior walls; there was a gap of approximately half a metre between the walls and the material. The concert hall covering was made of transparent tulle. "Built of light," this temporary concert hall emanated a magical atmosphere, transporting its audience to another world and focusing its attention on the concerts.

Anlässlich des in Basel stattfindenden „Europäischen Musikmonats 2001" entwarfen Herzog & de Meuron in der Halle 5 der Basler Messe eine temporäre Konzerthalle, in der verschiedene Musikstücke zeitgenössischer Komponisten dargeboten wurden.

Durch mehrere Schichten farbiger, halb-transparenter Vorhänge wurde der „Salle modulable" von dem Foyer und der Bar abgetrennt. Von dort waren durch den visuellen Sichtschutz die Darbietungen elektronischer Musik schemenhaft zu erkennen. Die eigentliche Konzerthalle befand sich hinter dem „Salle modulable". Hierzu wurde ein Holzbau von außen mit schwarzem Molton festlich behängt. Über drei runde Öffnungen gelangte das Publikum in die Konzerthalle. Mit einem weißen, transluzenten Gewebe wurden die Wände im Innenraum in einem Abstand von etwa einem halben Meter verkleidet und hinterleuchtet. Nach oben wurde der Konzertsaal durch einen transparenten Tüll horizontal begrenzt. „Aus Licht gebaut", rief die temporäre Konzerthalle eine magische Atmosphäre hervor, um das Publikum in eine andere Welt zu transportieren und die Konzentration auf das Konzert zu fokussieren.

## STUDIO MAKKINK & BEY
**with the assistance of Eric Klarenbeek**

ROC Aventus Apeldoorn, The Netherlands, 2007
*ROC Aventus Apeldoorn, Niederlande, 2007*

Recreation room of the Tourism course
Empfangsbereich des Tourismusstudiengangs

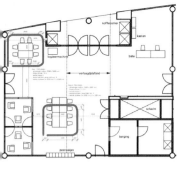

Recreation room of the Technology course
Empfangsbereich des Technologiestudiengangs

The recreation rooms of the Tourism and Technology course at the ROC vocational education centre in Apeldoorn have been deliberately left free of rigid walls. Adjustable separation using sliding curtains creates an intimate atmosphere while also preserving a feeling of openness. Since the curtains do not quite reach the ground, the surrounding noise is merely reduced rather than being entirely absorbed. Its users remain visually and acoustically aware of the presence of the others, causing them to respectfully lower their voices.

The curtains, floor and furniture of the recreation areas, in an unobtrusive blue, are printed with motifs of plants and people as well as text. Transparent flag fabric of varying length separates the four seating areas. Two seating areas in the recreational area are separated from their surroundings by opaque curtains made of tarpaulin and printed with technical motifs.

Die Aufentaltsräume des Tourismus- und Technologiestudiengangs der Technischen Berufsschule ROC Apeldoorn sind bewusst von starren Wänden frei gehalten. Durch die variable Trennung mittels verschiebbarer Vorhänge wird eine intime Atmosphäre geschaffen, die gleichzeitig ein Gefühl der Offenheit bewahrt. Da die Vorhänge nicht ganz bis auf den Boden reichen, wird der Umgebungslärm nicht völlig absorbiert, sondern lediglich reduziert. Die Nutzer sind sich visuell und auch akustisch der Präsenz der anderen bewusst, was sie veranlasst, respektvoll die Stimme zu senken.

Die Vorhänge, der Boden und die Möbel des in einem dezenten Blau gehaltenen Aufenthaltsbereiches des Tourismusstudiengangs sind mit Pflanzen- und Menschenmotiven sowie mit Texten bedruckt. Die vier Sitzbereiche werden hier durch einen transparenten Flaggenstoff in verschiedenen Längen abgeteilt. Im Aufenthaltsbereich des Technologiestudiengangs trennen mit technischen Motiven bedruckte Vorhänge aus blickdichter Lastwagenplane zwei Sitzbereiche von ihrer Umgebung.

# HORIZONTAL SPACE DEFINER
*HORIZONTALER RAUMABSCHLUSS*

# HISTORICAL OVERVIEW
## *HISTORISCHER ÜBERBLICK*

In addition to functioning as protection from the sun and rain, the horizontal textile space definer has been used since the antiquity as an instrument with which to honour dignitaries.

Neben der Funktion als Schutz vor Sonne oder Regen wurde der horizontale textile Raumabschluss bereits seit der Antike als Instrument zur Auszeichnung von Würdenträgern eingesetzt.

---

### Canopy

The term baldachin, now used in Europe to describe a horizontal textile membrane construction, can be traced back to an early form of the Italian name for the city of Bagdad, "Baldacco," and described a brocade-like silk fabric embroidered with gold thread that came from that city. As it was used mainly for throne canopies and to roof over altars, this term came in time to also be used for architectural structures.[1]

Tutankhamen under a baldachin, 1333–1323 BC / Tutanchamun unter einem Baldachin, um 1333–1323 v. Chr.

The "portable canopy," a transportable baldachin attached to four supports, was used for state and sacral ceremonies, processions and entrances. In England, it was specified in 1189 which barons were entitled to carry the baldachin of the king on his way to coronation. Also "the Norwegian King's daughter, who in 1257 travelled to Barcelona with Brother Alfonsos X to be married, was conducted away from Burgos under a baldachin."[2]

In its fixed variant, the baldachin was attached to a back wall, hung from a ceiling, or rested on supports to distinguish the seat or throne of a ruler, judge or ecclesiastical dignitary. Due to its easy detachability and transportability it was used in the various medieval residences of travelling monarchs.[3]

King Francis I under the throne baldachin, fourteenth century / König Franz I. unter dem Thronbaldachin, 14. Jahrhundert

Similarly, at table the host and/or the guest of honour, sometimes entire companies of diners, might be crowned with a baldachin. It was well known that this custom came from a concept of honouring the ruler that was derived from ancient Eastern thought.[4]

Like other honorific symbols, the baldachin was also transferred from state rites into sacred ceremony. "The first mention of the papal canopy, here called the 'mappula,' was around 1140 in the *Ordines Romani*."[5] The introduction of the portable canopy into the procession of the Feast of Corpus Christi in the fourteenth century distinguished the ecclesiastical dignitaries in the procession. As an endless band, it could extend over an entire square and so mark the path of the procession.[6]

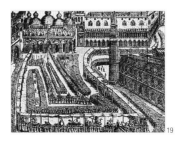

Procession for the Feast of Corpus Christi on St Mark's Square in Venice, seventeenth century / Fronleichnamsprozession auf dem Markusplatz in Venedig, 17. Jahrhundert

The baldachin was still used in an honorific function in the nineteenth century at the ceremonial departure of the bride of the heir to the throne, Rudolf II, outside Brussels stock exchange (1881).[7] Its use in distinguishing kings or prominent personalities disappeared with the advent of democratic forms of government. Baldachins, however, are still used today in ecclesiastical rites.

Procession, Steyr, Austria, 2007 / Prozession, Steyr, Österreich, 2007

In the profane world, canopies have been reduced to the function of providing protection from weather. In 1972, Frei Otto investigated the possibility of providing shade on the largest possible scale to enable agriculture in the desert in the project study "Shadow in the Desert." To achieve this, a mobile system of vertical masts and horizontally-stretched nets was developed, which could adapt to the expansion of plantings over time. Shading of seventy per cent could be achieved by mounting up to three layers of plastic netting one on top of the other, ensuring at the same time that the netting was permeable to precipitation. The addition of several canopies made it possible to shade large areas, resulting in a reduction in water evaporation and thus a decrease in water consumption.[8]

"Schatten in der Wüste," project study, Frei Otto, 1972 / „Schatten in der Wüste", Projektstudie, Frei Otto, 1972

Another twentieth century canopy construction is the roof structure of the Hajj Terminal of the King Abdul Aziz International Airport in Jeddah, Saudi-Arabia, built by Skidmore, Owings & Merrill in 1978–1981; its tent-like membrane structure, supported by masts, is reminiscent of a Bedouin tent. The goal was to protect passengers in the terminal from heat. The chosen construction, which is open at the sides, makes artificial air conditioning unnecessary. Its Teflon-coated fibreglass fabric, which deflects three quarters of the sun's heat radiation, allows diffuse light into the building, so there is no need for artificial lighting during the day. This and the ability to do without air conditioning saves both energy and costs.[9]

22

Hajj Terminal, King Abdul Aziz International Airport, Jeddah, Saudi Arabia, 1978–1981, Skidmore, Owings & Merrill / Haj-Terminal, King Abdul Aziz International Airport, Jeddah, Saudi-Arabien, 1978–1981, Skidmore, Owings & Merrill

## Baldachin

Der heute im europäischen Kulturraum verwendete Begriff Baldachin als Bezeichnung einer horizontalen textilen Membrankonstruktion geht auf eine frühe Form des italienischen Namens für die Stadt Bagdad, „Baldacco", zurück und bezeichnete den von dort stammenden, mit Goldfäden bestickten brokatähnlichen Seidenstoff. Da er hauptsächlich für den Thronhimmel und zur Überdachung des Altars verwendet wurde, ging diese Begrifflichkeit mit der Zeit auf das architektonische Gebilde über.[1] Beim herrschaftlichen wie auch beim sakralen Zeremoniell der Prozession und des Einzuges wurde der „Traghimmel", ein auf vier Stützen befestigter transportabler Baldachin, verwendet. In England wurde 1189 festgelegt, welche Barone den Baldachin des zur Krönung schreitenden Königs tragen durften. Auch „die norwegische Königstochter, welche 1257 zur Verehelichung mit einem Bruder Alfonsos X. nach Barcelona reist, wird von Burgos weg unter einem Baldachin geleitet."[2]

In seiner ortsfesten Variante wurde der Baldachin an einer Rückwand angebracht, von der Decke abgehängt oder er ruhte auf Stützen, um das Sitzen bzw. Thronen eines Herrschers, Richters oder kirchlichen Würdenträgers hervorzuheben. Aufgrund seiner leichten Abnehmbarkeit und Transportfähigkeit kam er in den verschiedenen mittelalterlichen Residenzen reisender Monarchen zum Einsatz.[3]
Ebenso wurden bei Tafelrunden der Gastgeber und/oder der Ehrengast, mitunter auch ganze Tischgesellschaften, mit einem Baldachin bekrönt. Man war sich durchaus bewusst, dass dieser Brauch aus der dem alten östlichen Denken entstammenden Vorstellung der Auszeichnung des Herrschers herrührte.[4]
Wie andere ehrende Zeichen ist auch der Baldachin aus dem herrschaftlichen Brauch ins sakrale Zeremoniell übernommen worden. „Erstmals ist um 1140 in den Ordines Romani vom päpstlichen Baldachin die Rede, der hier „mappula" genannt wird."[5] Seit Einführung der Fronleichnamsprozession im 14. Jahrhundert zeichnete der tragbare Baldachin kirchliche Würdenträger während des Prozessionsweges aus. Als endloses Band konnte er sich sogar über einen gesamten Platz erstrecken und gab somit den Prozessionsweg vor.[6]
Noch im 19. Jahrhundert wurde der Baldachin bei der Verabschiedung der Braut des Thronfolgers Rudolf II. vor der Brüsseler Börse (1881) in ehrender Funktion eingesetzt.[7] Mit dem Aufkommen demokratischer Staatsformen verschwand der Aspekt der Auszeichnung von Königen oder herausragenden Persönlichkeiten. Im kirchlichen Gebrauch werden jedoch noch heute Baldachine verwendet.
Im profanen Bereich hat sich die Funktion der Baldachinkonstruktion auf eine vor Witterung schützende reduziert. Frei Otto untersuchte 1972 in der Projektstudie „Schatten in der Wüste" die Möglichkeiten einer möglichst großflächigen Beschattung, um landwirtschaftliche Kulturen in der Wüste zu ermöglichen. Dafür wurde ein mobiles System aus vertikalen Masten und horizontal verspannten Netzen entwickelt, das sich der Ausdehnung der Anpflanzung im Laufe der Zeit anpassen konnte. Durch das Anbringen von bis zu drei übereinander liegenden Schichten eines Kunststoffnetzes konnte eine Beschattung von 70 Prozent erreicht werden. Gleichzeitig blieb die Durchlässigkeit des Gewebes für Niederschlag gewährleistet. Die Addition mehrerer Baldachine machte die Beschattung großer Flächen möglich – mit der Folge einer Reduzierung der Wasserverdunstung und somit einer Verringerung des Wasserverbrauchs.[8]
Eine weitere Baldachinkonstruktion des 20. Jahrhunderts ist die Dachstruktur des Haj-Terminals des von Skidmore, Owings & Merrill 1978–1981 erbauten King Abdul Aziz International Airport in Jeddah, Saudi-Arabien, dessen zeltartige Membranstruktur, unterstützt von Masten, an Beduinenzelte erinnert. Ziel war es, die Passagiere im Terminalbereich vor Hitze zu schützen. Aufgrund der gewählten, seitlich offenen Konstruktion konnte auf eine künstliche Klimatisierung verzichtet werden. Das teflonbeschichtete Glasfasergewebe, das drei Viertel der Wärmestrahlung der Sonne abhält, lässt diffuses Licht einfallen. Somit kann tagsüber auf eine künstliche Beleuchtung verzichtet werden, wodurch – ebenso wie durch den Verzicht auf eine Klimaanlage – Energie und Kosten eingespart werden.[9]

## Retractable Roof

From our earliest history, tents were probably already constructed so that large parts of the roof could be retracted or removed entirely. Retractable, moveable parts of tents were later also a fundamental and integral part of the construction of the Indian tipi and the tents of north Arabic nomads.[10]
Sun shades have been and are partly still used today across the entire Mediterranean area to roof over entire streets. In the antiquity, worn out ships' sails were hung free from buildings and masts on horizontal poles. A mosaic from the Sanctuary of Fortuna Prinigenia at Praeneste (80 BC) shows the use of such a sun shade.[11]

23

Sun shade in front of a temple. Mosaic from Praeneste, 80 BC / Sonnensegel vor einem Tempel. Mosaik von Praeneste, 80 v. Chr.

The Romans also covered the roof openings of their atrium houses with lengths of cloth to protect them from the sun.[12] "Around 65 BC Caesar, when giving gladiatorial games, had the Via Sacra leading from his house and the Clivius up to the Capitol covered with sun shades."[13]

In addition to roofing over streets and squares, the Romans also covered theatres, amphitheatres and stadiums with large, retractable roofs, the so-called *vela* (Latin for sail). In 69 BC, Quintus Lutatius Catulus had vela hung over a Roman theatre for the first time. However, these were not an urban Roman invention, but imitated Campanian roofing systems.[14] "The vela were regarded not as provisional fixtures, but as parts of the buildings."[15] "Their supporting structure consisted of upright masts towering over the exterior walls at regular intervals, and of horizontal poles or bars overhanging the interior that hung from the masts. Under these supporting poles hung a retractable tent roof of individual lengths of vela placed together in rows,[16] which were moved by a drawing mechanism. These were operated by seamen, suggesting that they were like those of sails (on ships). These retractable roofs must have had spans that were only to be achieved again in the mid-twentieth century. The roof over the Colosseum, the antiquity's biggest amphitheatre, must have covered 23,000 square metres – doubtless a technical tour de force for that time.

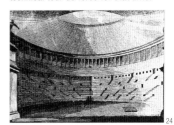

24

Vela roof of the Colosseum. Reconstruction by Canina, 1851 / Velumdach des Kolosseum. Rekonstruktion von Canina, 1851

The Roman vela roofs were not made retractable to comply with a wish to be protected from the sun yet sit in the open air in favourable weather as desired. It was, in fact, more due to the susceptibility of roofs of that size to wind and rain. They would be hastily retracted to protect them from damage if a wind blew up. The vela were made of linen dyed yellow, rust-red, and sky-blue. Stretched over the interiors of the amphitheatres and stadiums, they flooded these spaces with a light of the same colour as the fabric, which must have produced a very special atmosphere.[17] Particularly splendid specimens were elaborately embroidered. "The vela that Nero had erected in the amphitheatre imitated the night sky: they were sky-blue and emblazoned with stars."[18]

Amphitheatre with vela roof, painting, end of the nineteenth century / Amphitheater mit Velumdach, Gemälde, Ende des 19. Jahrhundert

Acquiring and deploying the vela must have been very expensive. Gladiatorial games in the amphitheatres were announced with the formula "Vela erunt" (Latin for "there will be vela")[19] to court the favour of the populace, which indicates that this was not common. The erection of vela was a special attraction in addition to the performances and games. They were used across almost the entire Roman sphere of control from the first century BC to the sixth century AD.[20]

The use of toldos as sun protection in Spain – a continuation of the Roman tradition of the vela – is documented from the sixteenth century. In addition to sun shades over market stalls and temporary stages, there were also the non-retractable so-called "procession toldos," which marked the path of a procession and protected those walking under it from the sun. The space-creating effect of the toldos came into its own on such festive occasions.

Procession for the Feast of Corpus Christi under a toldos in Seville, 1862 / Fronleichnamsprozession unter Toldos in Sevilla, 1862

In everyday life, "street toldos" were erected right across streets as permanent sun protection for public spaces. Lengths of cloth with grommets in them were extended on ropes in parallel, aligned according to the position of the sun, and retracted if it rained, because the canvas was delicate.

Toldos still serve today as protection against strong sun in the public spaces of southern Spanish cities, preventing the street beneath them from heating up. As well as the classic Spanish toldos, similar forms are used in countries throughout the Mediterranean area, such as Morocco, Egypt, Syria, and Turkey, and outside

Europe in South America and Japan.[21]
The origins of the smallest retractable roof, the awning, probably lie in the sun shades of sophisticated classical cultures. "Broad baldachins and awnings, whose stability could almost be doubted because of their size, were used from the sixteenth to eighteenth centuries in castles and palaces in Central Europe, in Persia, and India."[22] "In 1795 a large retractable sun shade was erected in Terracina on the occasion of a papal visit."[23]

Sun shade in Terracina, Italy, 1795 / Sonnensegel in Terracina, Italien, 1795

With the beginning of industrialisation in the nineteenth century, large panes of glass were used as shop windows and awnings were used to protect shops and residential buildings from the sun and weather.[24] The awning is attached on one side to a fixed wall. The other "open" side is extended from an overhanging bracket or easily removable supports. "In the space of the pavement, closed off from above, the gaze is drawn to the goods on display, the passer-by led through a protected climatic zone, which due to its lightness and adaptability, never creates a feeling of closeness or constriction."[25]
Technical developments in the areas of heat-insulating glazing and artificial air conditioning mean that awnings are now no longer used to the same extent as they once were. They can, however, still be seen in streets, more frequently in southern countries, providing protection from the sun.
In the middle of the twentieth century a new era began with the development of retractable roofs with large spans for covering open-air theatres and sports arenas. A pioneer in this area was Frei Otto. In 1955, he designed his first retractable roof for the Killesberg open-air theatre in Stuttgart. Made of impregnated cotton, the membrane was designed to cover 3,700 square metres as a temporary protection against rain, but the design was never implemented.
To shelter the open-air theatre performances held in summer at the abbey ruins in Bad Hersfeld from rain as required, the Institute for Lightweight Structures and Conceptual Design under the direction of Frei Otto developed a central retractable membrane roof in 1966, which

was built in 1968–1969. The roof construction was not permitted to touch the historical structure or detract from the spatial impression of the Romanesque stage setting. Open-air performances are still held there today in good weather. The membrane roof, originally made of double-sided, coated polyester fabric (the roof was renewed in 1993) hangs radially from a mast outside the ruins. The suspension ropes serve simultaneously as block lines, on which the retractable roof can be extended or retracted by rope traction motors within four minutes.[26]

Retractable roof above the abbey ruins, Bad Hersfeld, 1968–1969, Institute for Lightweight Structures and Conceptual Design / Wandelbares Dach über der Stiftsruine, Bad Hersfeld, 1968–1969, Institut für Leichte Flächentragwerke

In 1987, SL Rasch GmbH created a retractable inner courtyard roof for the Quba Mosque in Medina, whose construction is similar to that of the Spanish toldos. Every day, electrical motors extend and retract the folding roof that covers the courtyard without supports on steel cables from two sides in parallel over an area of around 1,000 square metres. In summer, the roof is closed during the day and opened at night. Because the translucent membrane, consisting of a two-ply, PVC-coated polyester net, offers protection from direct sun during the day and heat can escape through the open roof at night, there is no need for air conditioning in the courtyard. In winter the retractable roof is operated in precisely reverse order, so that the climate inside the building is naturally regulated.[27]

Retractable roof over the inner courtyard of the Quba Mosque, Medina, Saudi Arabia, 1987, SL Rasch GmbH / Wandelbares Dach über dem Innenhof der Quba-Moschee, Medina, Saudi-Arabien, 1987, SL-Rasch GmbH

One example from recent years of the use of retractable membrane constructions to roof over sports arenas is the roof

of the Rotherbaum Center Court in Hamburg, built in 1995–1997 by Schweger + Partners. It consists of permanent roofing for the rostrum and a radially-manoeuvrable inner membrane made of PVC-coated polyester fabric, allowing tennis matches to be played regardless of the weather.

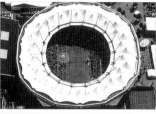

Retractable roof over the Rotherbaum Center Court, Hamburg, 1995–1997, Schweger + Partners / Wandelbares Dach über dem Center Court Rotherbaum, Hamburg, 1995–1997, Schweger + Partner

In recent years, events such as the Olympic Games or international football championships have been catalysts for new building and rebuilding at many stadiums. The new retractable roofs can be opened or closed depending on the weather and character of the event. Membranes however now cover not only stadiums, but also airport terminal buildings, railway stations, and port facilities.

### Wandelbares Dach

Mit großer Wahrscheinlichkeit wurden bereits in frühgeschichtlicher Zeit Zelte so konstruiert, dass größere Teile der Dachhaut gerafft oder ganz entfernt werden konnten. Wandelbare, bewegliche Zeltteile waren später ebenso bei den Tipi der Indianer oder den Zelten der nordarabischen Nomaden grundsätzlich Bestandteil der Zeltkonstruktion.[10]
Im gesamten Mittelmeerraum wurden und werden zum Teil bis heute Sonnensegel als Straßenüberdachungen verwendet. In der Antike wurden ausgediente Schiffssegel von Gebäuden und Masten mittels horizontaler Stangen frei abgespannt. Das Mosaik des Fortunaheiligtums von Praeneste (80 v. Chr.) zeigt die Benutzung solch eines Sonnensegels.[11]
Auch die Dachöffnungen ihrer Atrienhäuser überspannten die Römer zum Schutz vor der Sonne mit Tuchbahnen.[12] "Gegen 65 v. Chr. ließ Cäsar, als er Gla-

diatorenkämpfe gab, die Via sacra von seinem Hause ab und den Clivius bis zum Capitol mit Sonnensegeln überdeckten."[13]

Neben der Überdachung von Straßen und Plätzen wurden bei den Römern ebenso Theater, Amphitheater und Stadien mit wandelbaren Dächern sehr großer Spannweite, den sogenannten Vela (lat. für Segel), überspannt. Im Jahr 69 v. Chr. ließ Quintus Lutatius Catulus erstmals Vela über einem römischen Theater spannen. Jedoch waren sie keine stadtrömische Erfindung, sondern ahmten kampanische Überdachungen nach.[14] „Die Vela wurden nicht als provisorisches Zubehör, sondern als Teile der Gebäude angesehen."[15] „Ihr Tragwerk bestand aus senkrechten Masten, die in regelmäßigen Abständen die Außenmauern überragten, und aus horizontal über die Innenräume auskragenden Stangen oder Bäumen, die von den Masten abgehängt waren. Unter diesen Tragstangen hing ein raffbares Zeltdach aus einzelnen aneinander geneihten Velumbahnen"[16], die mithilfe von Zugvorrichtungen bewegt wurden. Die Bedienung erfolgte durch Seeleute, woraus zu schließen ist, dass sie ähnlich der von Segeln war. Diese wandelbaren Dächer müssen Spannweiten gehabt haben, wie sie erst wieder Mitte des 20. Jahrhunderts erreicht worden sind. Das Dach über dem Kolosseum, dem größten Amphitheater der Antike, müsste demzufolge 23.000 Quadratmeter überdeckt haben – zweifelsohne eine technische Meisterleistung zu dieser Zeit.

Die Wandelbarkeit der römischen Velumdächer entsprach nicht dem Wunsch, sich nur bei Bedarf vor Sonneneinstrahlung zu schützen und bei günstiger Witterung unter freiem Himmel zu sitzen. Sie war vielmehr in der Anfälligkeit dieser Dächer mit derartigen Spannweiten gegen Wind und Niederschlag begründet. Bei aufkommendem Wind wurden sie zum Schutz vor Beschädigung eilig gerafft. Die Vela bestanden aus gelb, rostrot und himmelblau gefärbtem Leinen. Über dem Innenraum der Amphitheater und Stadien aufgespannt, tauchten sie diesen in das jeweilige farbige Licht, was eine ganz besondere Stimmung erzeugt haben muss.[17] Besonders prachtvolle Exemplare wurden kunstvoll bestickt. Einen nächtlichen Himmel imitierten die Vela, die Nero im Amphitheater anbringen ließ: sie waren himmelblau und mit Sternen geschmückt."[18]

Die Anschaffung und Verwendung der Vela muss sehr kostspielig ge-

wesen sein. Bei Ankündigungen von Kampfspielen in Amphitheatern wurde mit der Formel „Vela erunt" (lat. für „es wird Vela geben")[19] um die Gunst des Volkes geworben, was darauf hinweist, dass dies durchaus nicht üblich war. Das Aufspannen der Vela war neben den Aufführungen und Spielen eine besondere Attraktion. Im nahezu gesamten römischen Machtbereich kamen sie zwischen dem 1. Jh. v. Chr. und dem 6. Jh. n. Chr. zum Einsatz.[20]

Seit dem 16. Jahrhundert ist der Gebrauch von Toldos – einer Weiterführung der römischen Tradition der Vela – als Sonnenschutz in Spanien belegt. Neben Sonnensegeln über Marktständen und temporären Bühnen gab es die sogenannten – nicht raffbaren – Prozessionstoldos, die den Weg einer Prozession markierten und die darunter Schreitenden vor der Sonne schützten. Die raumerzeugende Wirkung der Toldos kam bei solch feierlichen Anlässen besonders zur Geltung.

Im Alltag wurden Straßentoldos als permanenter Sonnenschutz im öffentlichen Raum quer über die Straße gespannt. Hierzu wurden Stoffbahnen mit Ösen an Seilen parallel verfahren, je nach Sonnenstand ausgerichtet und bei Regen eingezogen, da die Segeltücher sehr empfindlich waren.

Bis heute dienen Toldos im öffentlichen Raum der südspanischen Städte dem Schutz vor zu starker Sonneneinstrahlung und vermindern so das Aufheizen des darunter liegenden Straßenraums. Neben den klassischen spanischen Toldos treten verwandte Formen in Ländern des gesamten Mittelmeerraums wie Marokko, Ägypten, Syrien und der Türkei auf – außerhalb Europas in Südamerika sowie in Japan.[21]

Den Ursprung des kleinsten wandelbaren Daches, der Markise, bilden vermutlich die Sonnensegel der klassischen Hochkulturen. „Weitgespannte Baldachine und Markisen, deren Standsicherheit man aufgrund der Größe beinahe in Frage stellen möchte, finden sich im 16.–18. Jahrhundert in Schloß- und Palastanlagen Mitteleuropas, in Persien und Indien."[22] „1795 wurde in Terracina anlässlich des Papstbesuchs ein großes raffbares Sonnensegel aufgespannt."[23]

Als im 19. Jahrhundert mit der beginnenden Industrialisierung große Glasscheiben als Schaufenster eingesetzt wurden, kam die Markise als Sonnen- und Wetterschutz vor Ladengeschäften sowie Wohngebäuden auf.[24] Die Markise ist an einer Seite an einer fixen Wand

befestigt. Die andere „offene" Seite ist mittels einer auskragenden Abspannung oder leicht demontierbarer Stützen abgespannt. „Im nach oben geschlossenen Raum des Gehweges wird der Blick auf die Auslagen gelenkt, der Vorübergehende in eine geschützte Klimazone geleitet, die aufgrund ihrer Leichtigkeit und Wandelbarkeit nie das Gefühl der Enge oder Geschlossenheit bewirkt."[25]

Aufgrund technischer Entwicklungen im Bereich der Wärmeschutzverglasung und der künstlichen Klimatisierung wird die Markise heute nicht mehr in dem Ausmaß wie früher eingesetzt. Jedoch sieht man sie immer noch im Straßenraum, vermehrt in südlichen Ländern, als Schutz vor der Sonne.

Mitte des 20. Jahrhunderts begann eine neue Entwicklung wandelbarer Dächer mit großen Spannweiten über Freilichttheatern und Sportarenen. Pionier auf diesem Gebiet war Frei Otto. 1955 entwarf er sein erstes wandelbares Dach über dem Freilichttheater Killesberg in Stuttgart. Die Membran aus imprägnierter Baumwolle sollte als temporärer Regenschutz 3700 Quadratmeter überdachen, der Entwurf wurde jedoch nicht realisiert.

Um die Freilichtaufführungen der Sommerfestspiele der Stiftsruine in Bad Hersfeld bei Bedarf vor Regen zu schützen, entwickelte das Institut für Leichte Flächentragwerke unter der Leitung von Frei Otto 1966 ein zentral raffbares Membrandach, das 1968–1969 umgesetzt wurde. Die Dachkonstruktion durfte das historische Bauwerk nicht antasten und den Raumeindruck der romanischen Bühnenkulisse nicht beeinträchtigen. Bei guten Wetterverhältnissen finden die Vorstellungen noch heute unter freiem Himmel statt. Das Membrandach aus ursprünglich beidseitig beschichtetem Polyestergewebe (das Dach ist 1993 erneuert worden) ist an einem Mast außerhalb der Ruine aufgehängt, der strahlenförmig abgespannt ist. Die Abspannseile dienen gleichzeitig als Fahrseile, an denen das wandelbare Dach von Seiltraktoren innerhalb von vier Minuten aus- oder eingefahren wird.[26]

1987 konstruierte die SL-Rasch GmbH eine wandelbare Innenhofüberdachung für die Quba-Moschee in Medina, deren Konstruktionsweise mit den spanischen Toldos verwandt ist. Ein Faltdach, welches den Innenhof stützenlos überspannt, wird täglich mittels elektrischem Antrieb an Stahlseilen paral-

lel von zwei Seiten über einer Fläche von etwa 1000 Quadratmetern aus- und eingefahren. Im Sommer wird das Dach tagsüber geschlossen und nachts geöffnet. Da die transluzente Membran aus einem zweilagigen, PVC-beschichteten Polyesternetz tagsüber vor direkter Sonneneinstrahlung schützt und nachts die Wärme über das geöffnete Dach entweicht, kann auf eine Klimatisierung des Innenhofs verzichtet werden. Im Winter wird die wandelbare Überdachung genau gegenläufig bedient. Das Klima im Inneren des Gebäudes wird so auf natürliche Weise reguliert.[27]

Ein Beispiel für die Überdachung von Sportarenen mittels wandelbarer Membrankonstruktionen aus der näheren Vergangenheit ist die 1995–1997 von Schweger + Partner erbaute Überdachung des Center Court Rotherbaum in Hamburg. Sie besteht aus einer permanenten Tribünenüberdachung und einer radial verfahrbaren Innenmembran aus PVC-beschichtetem Polyestergewebe, aufgrund derer die Tennisspiele unabhängig von Witterungseinflüssen stattfinden können.

Veranstaltungen wie die Olympischen Spiele oder internationale Fußballmeisterschaften waren in den letzten Jahren Auslöser für Neu- und Umbauten zahlreicher Stadien. Die dort neu eingesetzten, wandelbaren Dächer können je nach Witterung und Charakter der Veranstaltung geöffnet oder geschlossen werden. Aber nicht nur über Stadien spannen sich Membrane, sondern auch über Abfertigungshallen von Flughäfen und Bahnhöfen ebenso wie über Hafenanlagen.

---

### Umbrella

The classic construction of the umbrella consists of a central mast, on which a substructure shaped like a spoked wheel moves by means of a ring and to open and close the umbrella. A membrane is attached above. Its portability makes the umbrella not only versatile, but also mobile. Originally used as a functional roof for protection from the sun and rain, it was carried in ancient Egypt, in the Orient and in China and Japan as a symbol of authority, being borne by a servant to shield his lord.[28]

Ashurnasirpal II (883–859 BC) in a ceremonial chariot under an honorific umbrella / Assurnasirpal II. (883–859 v. Chr.) in einem Prunkwagen unter einem Ehrenschirm

In Greece, use of the umbrella is documented from the fifth century BC. It was covered with fabric and was evidently foldable. It is often pictured carried in both hands, indicating its heavy weight. Originally borne at the head of religious festivals to distinguish the priests and priestesses, it was later also used by men as profane sun protection. For the Romans, an umbrella was not only a fashionable accessory for ladies but was also used to provide shelter from rain.

Like the baldachin, the umbrella, originally an instrument of distinction in state ceremony, came to be incorporated into sacral ceremonies. According to a fourteenth century document, the Doge was allowed to use an "umbrella of honour," whose oriental origins were well-known, at the conclusion of the papal-imperial Treaty of Venice in 1177.[29]

The umbrella continued to be used however, to distinguish secular dignitaries, as can be seen from a painting from 1660 showing the French chancellor Séguier with an honorific umbrella.

The French chancellor Séguier with an honorific umbrella, 1660 / Der französische Kanzler Séguier mit einem Ehrenschirm, 1660

The umbrella first reappears as an article of daily use in Italy in the sixteenth century and from here found its way into other European countries during the seventeenth century. Its whalebone frame and oilcloth cover meant that it was still very heavy. Originally constructed to protect against the sun, it has also been used since the eighteenth century to shield the bearer from rain.

In eighteenth century Japan, bamboo was used for the umbrella shaft and subconstruction and it was covered with oiled paper.[30]

"In 1806 an umbrella still weighed ten pounds. Only in 1852 did Englishman Samuel Fox replace the whalebone and wooden struts with relatively thin steel struts, distinctly reducing the umbrella's weight."[31] In 1928 the German Hans Haupt developed the "Knirps," the first telescopic umbrella.

Today's portable umbrella is like the first models in terms of the principles of its construction. Its dimensions are relatively small. Fixed umbrellas with a diameter of up to five metres that are temporarily erected to provide protection from the sun at markets, on the

beach, or cafés, are now just as widespread. Large areas can be covered by simply adding more umbrellas.

The technical development of large fixed umbrellas for roofing over venues began in the mid-twentieth century. Frei Otto developed three non-flexible umbrellas with a double white cotton fabric membrane that was stretched between two wooden rings each 6.5 metres in diameter, forming a hollow space, for the Bundesgartenschau (National Garden Show) 1955 in Kassel. These "Drei Pilze" (three mushrooms) marked a resting area and were illuminated at night. At the edge of the wooden rings there was a channel to divert rainwater through the hollow space into the hollow masts.[32]

"Drei Pilze," BUGA 1955, Kassel, Frei Otto / „Drei Pilze", BUGA 1955, Kassel, Frei Otto

The combination of umbrella and pneumatic constructions resulted in new roofing potentals. For the Expo 1970 in Osaka, Tanero Oki designed five pneumatically-opening textile umbrella roofs in various sizes, each covering an area of 180 to 700 square metres. Each pneu was divided into radial chambers and simply supported by the mast at its central point. The umbrellas, made of PVC-coated synthetic fibre fabric, were closed in case of high wind speeds.

Pneumatic umbrellas, Expo 1970, Osaka, Tanero Oki / Pneumatische Schirme, Expo 1970, Osaka, Tanero Oki

In contrast to previous traditional synclastic umbrellas, which had a textile membrane forming a dome-like covering over the struts, Frei Otto, working together with Ewald Bubner and Bodo Rasch developed the first large, adjustable, anticlastic umbrellas with diameters of fifteen to seventeen metres, for the Bundesgartenschau (National Garden Show) 1971 in Cologne. The membrane, made of PVC-coated polyester, was stretched in a funnel shape under the struts. Each umbrella covered an area of approximately 220 square metres and could be opened within about two and a half minutes.[33]

Large umbrellas at the BUGA 1971, Cologne, Frei Otto with Ewald Bubner and Bodo Rasch / Großschirme auf der BUGA 1971, Köln, Frei Otto mit Ewald Bubner und Bodo Rasch

Folding umbrellas using these types of construction have been frequently deployed in recent years in Arabic countries–such as in the large umbrellas in the two inner courtyards of the Mosque

Notes / Anmerkungen

[1] Cp. Brockhaus Enzyklopädie. Volume 2. Mannheim 1992, p. 506, and Schmidt. Heinrich J.: Alte Seidenstoffe. Brunswick 1958, p. 106 and p. 450

[2] Reinle, Adolf: Zeichensprache der Architektur, p. 337

[3] Cp. Reinle, Adolf: Zeichensprache der Architektur, p. 337 and p. 339

[4] Cp. Eberlein, Johann Konrad: Apparatio regis – revelatio veritatis. Wiesbaden 1982, p. 43

[5] Reinle, Adolf: Zeichensprache der Architektur, p. 337

[6] Cp. Reinle, Adolf: Zeichensprache der Architektur, p. 338

[7] Cp. Hoppe, Diether S.: Freigespannte textile Membrankonstruktionen. Vienna 2007, p. 212

[8] Cp. Institut für Leichte Flächentragwerke, University of Stuttgart ( Ed.): IL 7. Schatten in der Wüste. Stuttgart 1972, p. 32 et seq.

[9] Cp. Skidmore, Owings & Merrill (Ed.): SOM Skidmore, Owings & Merrill. Architektur und Städtebau 1973–1983. Stuttgart 1983, p. 383

[10] Cp. Institut für Leichte Flächentragwerke, University of Stuttgart (Ed.): IL 5. Wandelbare Dächer. Stuttgart 1972, p. 12

[11] Cp. Plinius XIX, 23–24, according to: Institut für Leichte Flächentragwerke (Ed.): IL 5. Wandelbare Dächer, p. 18, and Institut für Leichte Flächentragwerke, Universität Stuttgart (Ed.): IL 30. Schattenzelte – Sun and Shade. Toldos. Vela. University of Stuttgart 1984, p. 14

[12] Cp. Durm, Josef: Die Baukunst der Etrusker. Die Baukunst der Römer. Darmstadt 1885, p. 277

[13] Institut für Leichte Flächentragwerke (Ed.): IL 5. Wandelbare Dächer, p. 28

[14] Cp. Institut für Leichte Flächentragwerke (Ed.): IL 30. Schattenzelte – Sun and Shade. Toldos. Vela, p. 10, and Durm, Josef: Die Baukunst der Etrusker. Die Baukunst der Römer, p. 343, and Graefe, Rainer: Vela erunt. Mainz 1979, p. 4

[15] Graefe, Rainer: Vela erunt, p. 169

[16] Graefe, Rainer: Vela erunt, p. 147

[17] Cp. Institut für Leichte Flächentragwerke (Ed.): IL 5. Wandelbare Dächer, p. 24 and p. 30,

of the Prophet in Medina, Saudi Arabia, constructed by SL Rasch GmbH in 1993. Like the retractable roof in the Quba Mosque, the umbrellas improve the microclimate without destroying the character of the open courtyards.

37

Folding umbrellas in the inner courtyard of the Mosque of the Prophet in Medina, Saudi Arabia, 1993, SL Rasch GmbH / Wandelbare Schirme im Innenhof der Moschee des Heiligen Propheten in Medina, Saudi-Arabien, 1993, SL-Rasch GmbH

## Schirm

Die klassische Konstruktion des Schirms besteht aus einem Mittelmast, an dem die speichenförmige Unterkonstruktion mittels eines Rings bewegt und so mit der Schirm auf- und abgespannt wird. Darüber ist eine Membran befestigt. Aufgrund seiner Tragbarkeit ist der Schirm nicht nur variabel, sondern auch mobil. Ursprünglich als funktionelles Schutzdach vor Sonne und Regen eingesetzt, diente er im ägyptischen Altertum, im Orient, in China und Japan als Herrschaftssymbol, welches von einem Diener über seinem Herrn getragen wurde.[28]

In Griechenland ist der Gebrauch des Schirms seit dem 5. Jahrhundert v. Chr. belegt. Er wurde mit Stoff bespannt und war nachweislich zusammenklappbar. Auf Abbildungen wird er oft mit beiden Händen getragen, was auf ein hohes Gewicht hinweist. Ursprünglich bei religiösen Feiern in auszeichnender Funktion den Priestern und Priesterinnen voran getragen, wurde er später auch als profaner Sonnenschutz von Männern benutzt. Bei den Römern war der Schirm ein modisches Attribut der Damen und wurde auch als Regenschirm verwendet.

Ebenso wie der Baldachin ist der Schirm, ursprünglich ein Instrument der Auszeichnung aus dem herrschaftlichen Brauch, ins sakrale Zeremoniell übernommen worden. Nach einem Zeugnis des 14. Jahrhunderts wurde dem Dogen beim päpstlich-kaiserlichen Friedensschluss 1177 in Venedig erlaubt, einen Ehrenschirm zu verwenden, dessen orientalischer Herkunft man sich durchaus bewusst war.[29]

Jedoch auch als Auszeichnung weltlicher Ehrenpersonen wurde er weiterhin benutzt, was auf einem Gemälde von 1660 zu sehen ist, das den französischen Kanzler Séguier mit einem Ehrenschirm zeigt.

Als alltäglicher Gebrauchsgegenstand tauchte der Schirm erst wieder im Italien des 16. Jahrhunderts auf und fand von hier aus im Verlauf des 17. Jahrhunderts Eingang in die übrigen europäischen Länder. Aufgrund eines Fischbeingestells mit Wachstuchbezug war er noch sehr schwer. Ursprünglich als Schutz gegen die Sonne konstruiert, wurde er seit dem 18. Jahrhundert auch als Regenschirm genutzt.

In Japan verwendete man im 18. Jahrhundert als Material für den Stiel und die Unterkonstruktion Bambus und bespannte diese mit geöltem Papier.[30]

„1806 wog ein Regenschirm noch 10 Pfund. Erst 1852 ersetzte der Engländer Samuel Fox die Fischbein- und Holzstäbe durch relativ dünne Stahlreifen, wodurch das Gewicht des Schirms entschieden verringert wurde."[31] 1928 entwickelte der Deutsche Hans Haupt den „Knirps".

Der heutige tragbare Regenschirm ist konstruktiv im Prinzip mit den ersten Modellen vergleichbar. Seine Abmessungen sind relativ klein. Nicht mobile Schirme mit einem Durchmesser von bis zu fünf Metern, die temporär aufgestellt werden, um sich bei Märkten, am Strand oder im Café vor der Sonne zu schützen, sind ebenso weitverbreitet. Durch die Addition einzelner Schirme können größere Flächen überdacht werden.

Mitte des 20. Jahrhunderts begann eine technische Entwicklung hin zu ortsfesten Großschirmen für die Überdachung von Veranstaltungsorten. Frei Otto entwickelte für die Bundesgartenschau 1955 in Kassel drei nicht flexible Schirme mit einer hohlkörperbildenden Doppelmembran aus weißem Baumwollgewebe, die zwischen zwei Holzringen von je 6,5 Metern Durchmesser gespannt wurde. Die „Drei Pilze" markierten einen Rastplatz und leuchteten bei Nacht. Am Rand des Holzrings befand sich eine Rinne, die das Regenwasser durch den Hohlraum in die Rohrmasten ableitete.[32]

Durch die Kombination von Schirm- mit pneumatischen Konstruktionen ergaben sich neue Überdachungsmöglichkeiten. Für die Expo 1970 in Osaka entwarf Tanero Oki fünf pneumatisch zu öffnende textile Pilzschirmdächer in verschiedenen Größen, die jeweils eine Fläche von 180 bis 700 Quadratmetern überdachten. Jeder Pneu war radial in Kammern aufgeteilt und in seinem Mittelpunkt gelenkig am Mast gelagert. Bei hohen Windgeschwindigkeiten wurden die Schirme aus PVC-beschichtetem Kunstfasergewebe geschlossen.

Im Gegensatz zu den bisher traditionell synklastisch geformten Schirmen – die textile Membran spannt sich kuppelartig über ein Gestänge – entwickelte Frei Otto zusammen mit Ewald Bubner und Bodo Rasch für die Bundesgartenschau 1971 in Köln die ersten wandelbaren Großschirme mit Durchmessern von etwa 15 bis 17 Metern, die antiklastisch geformt waren: Die Membran aus PVC-beschichtetem Polyestergewebe wurde trichterförmig unter dem Gestänge gespannt. Jeder Schirm überdeckte eine Fläche von ca. 220 Quadratmetern und ließ sich innerhalb von etwa zweieinhalb Minuten ausfahren.[33]

Aufklappbare Schirme dieser Konstruktionsart wurden in den letzten Jahren häufig in arabischen Ländern eingesetzt – beispielsweise die 1993 von der SL-Rasch GmbH konstruierten Großschirme in den zwei Innenhöfen der Moschee des Heiligen Propheten in Medina, Saudi-Arabien. Ähnlich wie das wandelbare Dach in der Quba-Moschee sorgen die Schirme für ein verbessertes Klima, ohne den Charakter der offenen Höfe zu zerstören.

and Graefe, Rainer: Vela erunt, pp. 5–6 and p. 18

Plinius 19, 1, 24, according to Graefe, Rainer: Vela erunt, p. 7

Graefe, Rainer: Vela erunt, p. 8

Cp. Graefe, Rainer: Vela erunt, p. 169

Cp. Institut für Leichte Flächentragwerke (Ed.): IL 5. Wandelbare Dächer, p. 18, and Institut für Leichte Flächentragwerke (Ed.): IL 30. Schattenzelte – Sun and Shade. Toldos. Vela, p. 94 and p. 98

Burkhardt, Berthold: "Die Vielfalt der Zelte – oder Lernen vom Zelt", In: Der umgekehrte Weg. Cologne 1990, p. 30

Hoppe, Diether S.: Freigespannte textile Membrankonstruktionen, p. 212

Cp. Institut für Leichte Flächentragwerke (Ed.): IL 5. Wandelbare Dächer, p. 18

Burkhardt, Berthold: "Die Vielfalt der Zelte – oder Lernen vom Zelt" p. 31–32

[26] Cp. Institut für Leichte Flächentragwerke (Ed.): IL 5. Wandelbare Dächer, p. 252 et seq.

[27] Cp. SL-Rasch GmbH: Das Zitat im Internet. www.sl-rasch.de 20.05.09

[28] Cp. Hoppe, Diether S.: Freigespannte textile Membrankonstruktionen, p. 220, and Loschek, Ingrid: Reclams Mode- & Kostümlexikon. Stuttgart 1987, p. 409, and Reinle, Adolf: Zeichensprache der Architektur, p. 339

[29] Cp. Mart. XIV, 28; XI, 73 and Juv. IX, 50, according to: Institut für Leichte Flächentragwerke (Ed.): IL 5. Wandelbare Dächer, p. 18, and Reinle, Adolf: Zeichensprache der Architektur, pp. 337–338

[30] Cp. Loschek, Ingrid: Reclams Mode- & Kostümlexikon, p. 409, and Institut für Leichte Flächentragwerke (Ed.): IL 5. Wandelbare Dächer, p. 24

[31] Loschek, Ingrid: Reclams Mode- & Kostümlexikon, p. 409

[32] Cp. Otto, Frei/Stromeyer, Peter: "Zelte". In: db deutsche bauzeitung. Issue 7, 1960, p. 351 et seq.

[33] Cp. Institut für Leichte Flächentragwerke (Ed.): IL 5. Wandelbare Dächer, p. 305 and p. 312

Horizontal Space Definer
*Horizontal Raumabschluss*

CONSTRUCTION & FUNCTION
*KONSTRUKTION & FUNKTION*

Canopy
*Baldachin*

Retractable Roof
*Wandelbares Dach*

Umbrella
*Schirm*

CANOPY
*BALDACHIN*

Canopy A canopy is a horizontally-spanned, fixed expanse of textile that is attached to a supporting structure. In the past, canopies were used to honour lordly or Christian dignitaries. These days, they are no longer of such symbolic function outside sacral ceremonies. They can be fixed to a wall or can alternatively be attached to the ceiling in interior spaces. In the portable version, the horizontally spanned textile is attached at its corners to four carrying stakes; this is used during religious processions to honour Christian dignitaries. Contemporary, fixed canopy-like structures are mainly used for weather protection.

*Baldachin Ein Baldachin ist eine horizontal verspannte, nicht wandelbare textile Fläche, die an einer tragenden Konstruktion befestigt ist. In der Vergangenheit wurde er als Auszeichnung herrschaftlicher oder christlicher Würdenträger benutzt. In dieser symbolischen Funktion wird er heute nur noch im sakralen Bereich eingesetzt. Er wird an der Wand, im Innenraum alternativ auch an der Decke befestigt. In seiner transportablen Version ist das horizontal gespannte Textil an den äußeren Ecken an vier Tragstützen befestigt und dient bei religiösen Umzügen der Auszeichnung kirchlicher Würdenträger. Gegenwärtig werden feststehende, baldachinartige Konstruktionen vor allem als Witterungsschutz verwendet.*

Waste Control Department, Munich, Germany,
1997–1999, **Ackermann and Partners**
*Amt für Abfallwirtschaft, München, Deutschland,
1997–1999,* **Ackermann und Partner**

CANOPY / portable
*BALDACHIN / tragbar*

Entry of Cardinal Francis, Francis I
and Charles V into Paris, 1540
Einzug Kardinal Franceses, Franz I.
und Karls V. in Paris, 1540

Good Friday Procession, Cuenca,
Spain, 2006
Karfreitagsprozession, Cuenca,
Spanien, 2006

Steyr, Austria, 2007
Steyr, Österreich, 2007

El Viejo, Nicaragua, 2005
El Viejo, Nicaragua, 2005

Corpus Christi Procession, Marija
Bistrica, Croatia, 2008
Fronleichnamsprozession, Marija
Bistrica, Kroatien, 2008

# CANOPY / fixed
## BALDACHIN / ortsfest

Waste Control Department, Munich, Germany, 1997–
1999, **Ackermann and Partners**
The filigree tent roof construction–weather protection for
the fleet of vehicles belonging to the Central Waste Control Department–makes reference to the nearby Olympic
stadium. A translucent roof covers an area of 8400 square
metres; it consists of a punctually-supported membrane
construction made of a PTFE-coated fibreglass fabric
supported by a steel structure in a grid of 10 x 12 metres.
Amt für Abfallwirtschaft, München, Deutschland, 1997–
1999, **Ackermann und Partner**
Die filigrane Zeltdachkonstruktion – Wetterschutz für den
Fuhrpark des zentralen Amtes für Abfallwirtschaft – nimmt
Bezug zum nahe gelegenen Olympiastadion. Das transluzente Dach überdeckt eine Fläche von 8400 Quadratmetern und besteht aus einer punktgestützten Membrankonstruktion aus PTFE-beschichtetem Glasfasergewebe, das
von einer leichten Stahlkonstruktion im Achsraster von 10
x 12 Metern getragen wird.

Ericeira, Portugal, 2007
Ericeira, Portugal, 2007

Project study "Shadow in the Desert," 1972,
**Frei Otto**
Projektstudie „Schatten in der Wüste", 1972,
**Frei Otto**

Market stand, Munich, Germany, 2008
Marktstand, München, Deutschland, 2008

Announcement of the 1574 Amnesty in front of the
"Maison du Roi," Brussels, Belgium
Verkündigung der Amnestie von 1574 vor dem „Maison
du Roi", Grande-Place, Brüssel, Belgien

## RETRACTABLE ROOF
*WANDELBARES DACH*

Retractable Roof *A simple awning over an entrance or an electrically-powered, automatic rollout roof construction; both are retractable roofs – flexible, textile membranes that can be horizontally opened and closed. Their primary function is to provide rain and sun protection, like the parallel-movable textile sunroofs that give shade to squares and streets in southern countries. They slide along wires that span horizontally between the building façades. Translucent textiles are often used as they provide sun protection but do not completely block out the light.*

Wandelbares Dach *Eine simple Markise über einem Eingang oder die elektrisch gesteuerte, automatisch ausfahrbare Dachkonstruktion über einem Stadion: Beides sind wandelbare Dächer – flexible, textile Membrane, die sich horizontal verfahren – öffnen und schließen – lassen. Sie dienen in erster Linie dem Schutz vor Regen oder Sonne, wie die parallel beweglichen textilen Sonnendächer, die über Plätzen und Straßen südlicher Länder Schatten spenden. Dabei werden sie an Seilen bewegt, die zwischen Häuserfassaden horizontal verspannt sind. Häufig werden transluzente Textilien eingesetzt, die vor der Sonne schützen, jedoch den Lichteinfall nicht komplett unterbinden.*

Rothenbaum, Hamburg, Germany, 1995–1997,
**Schweger and Partners;**
**Roof construction: Werner Sobek**
*Rothenbaum, Hamburg, Deutschland, 1995–1997,*
***Schweger und Partner;***
***Dachkonstruktion: Werner Sobek***

# RETRACTABLE ROOF
*WANDELBARES DACH*

Sun shade, Terracina,
Italy, 1795
Sonnensegel, Terracina,
Italien, 1795

Hong Kong, China, 2007
Hongkong, China, 2007

Ghent, Belgium, 2007
Gent, Belgien, 2007

Hoyerswerda, Germany, 2008
Hoyerswerda, Deutschland, 2008

Rotterdam, The Netherlands, 2006
Rotterdam, Niederlande, 2006

# RETRACTABLE ROOF
## *WANDELBARES DACH*

Processional toldo, Feast of Corpus
Christi, Seville, Spain, circa 1900
Prozessionstoldo, Fronleichnam, Sevilla,
Spanien, ca. 1900

Vista Alegre, Córdoba, Spain, 2007
Vista Alegre, Córdoba, Spanien, 2007

Seville, Spain, 2008
Sevilla, Spanien, 2008

Historic city centre, Mexico City,
Mexico, 2007
Historisches Zentrum, Mexiko-Stadt,
Mexiko, 2007

Retractable street covering, Japan
Wandelbare Straßenüberdachung, Japan

# RETRACTABLE ROOF
## *WANDELBARES DACH*

Demonstration by teachers, Mexico City,
Mexico, 1998
Demonstration von Lehrern, Mexiko-Stadt,
Mexiko, 1998

Toldo over a court of the Inquisition, Madrid,
Spain, seventeenth century
Toldo über einem Inquisitionsgericht, Madrid,
Spanien, 17. Jahrhundert

Retractable roof over the inner
courtyard of the Quba Mosque,
Medina, Saudi Arabia, 1987,
**SL Rasch GmbH**
Wandelbares Dach über dem Innen-
hof der Quba-Moschee,
Medina, Saudi-Arabien, 1987,
**SL Rasch GmbH**

Arcade Courtyard Roofing, Vienna City Hall, Austria, 2000, **Tillner & Willinger** in cooperation with **Schlaich Bergermann and Partners**
Like an accordion, the retractable membrane roof over the Arcade Courtyard of Vienna's city hall can be extended and folded together. Steel rails are attached to the long sides of the roof on which the carriages of the track cables that run in a transverse direction are extended. A membrane made of translucent PVC-coated polyester fabric is attached to these. The roof spans an area of 34 x 32 metres and has provided shelter from the sun and rain for countless events.
Arkadenhofüberdachung, Rathaus Wien, Österreich, 2000, **Tillner & Willinger** in Zusammenarbeit mit **Schlaich Bergermann und Partner**
Wie eine Ziehharmonika lässt sich das wandelbare Membrandach über dem Arkadenhof des Wiener Rathauses ausfahren und zusammenfalten. An den Längsseiten des Daches sind Stahlschienen angeordnet, auf denen die Laufwagen der in Querrichtung gespannten Tragseile verfahren werden. Daran ist die Membran aus transluzentem PVC-beschichtetem Polyestergewebe befestigt. Als Regen- und Sonnenschutz für zahlreiche Veranstaltungen überdeckt das Dach eine Fläche von 34 x 32 Metern.

Valencia, Spain, 2008
Valencia, Spanien, 2008

# RETRACTABLE ROOF
## *WANDELBARES DACH*

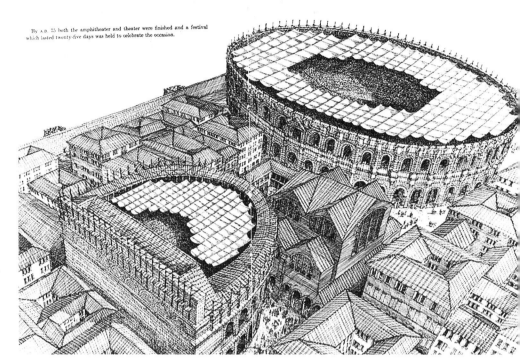

Retractable roof covering over an
amphitheatre and a theatre, 75 AD,
Reconstruction by Macauley, 1974
Wandelbare Überdachung eines
Amphitheaters und eines Theaters,
75 n. Chr., Rekonstruktion von
Macauley, 1974.

**Amphitheatre Saragossa, Spain, 1989, Schlaich Bergermann and Partners**
The bull-fighting arena in Saragossa, which could previously only be opened in summer, was partly covered with a retractable roof for year-round use for other events.
The roof covering of translucent PVC-coated polyester has been permanently
installed as sun protection over the stands. The roof opening at the centre of the
arena can be automatically closed if the weather is bad.
Amphitheater Saragossa, Spanien, 1989, **Schlaich Bergermann und Partner**
Um das zuvor nur im Sommer als Stierkampfarena genutzte Amphitheater in Saragossa ganzjährig auch für andere Veranstaltungen nutzen zu können, wurde es mit
einem teilweise wandelbaren Dach versehen. Die Überdachung aus transluzentem
PVC-beschichteten Polyester ist als Sonnenschutz im Bereich der Tribünen fest
installiert. Die Dachöffnung in der Mitte der Arena kann bei ungünstigen Witterungs-
verhältnissen vollautomatisch geschlossen werden.

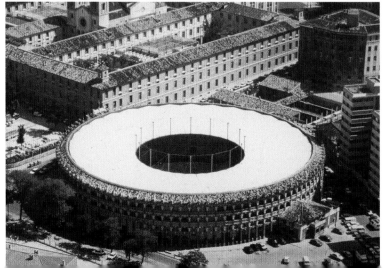

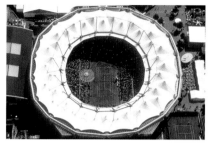

Retractable roof for the Centre Court at Rothenbaum, Hamburg, Germany, 1995–1997, **Schweger and Partners;
Roof construction: Werner Sobek**

The roof covering of translucent white PVC-coated polyester fabric spans the stands and also the playing area if required. The roof construction with a span width of approximately 102 metres is based on the construction principle of the spoked wheel. It has an outer permanent part and an adjustable interior roof with a diameter of approximately sixty-three metres.

Bewegliches Dach für den Center Court am Rothenbaum, Hamburg, Deutschland, 1995–1997, **Schweger und Partner;
Dachkonstruktion: Werner Sobek**

Die Überdachung aus transluzentem weißen PVC-beschichteten Polyestergewebe überspannt die Tribünen und bei Bedarf auch die Spielfläche. Die Dachkonstruktion mit einer freien Spannweite von etwa 102 Metern, die vom Konstruktionsprinzip des Speichenrads abgeleitet wurde, besitzt einen äußeren, permanent bedachten Teil und ein wandelbares Innendach mit etwa 63 Metern Durchmesser.

Retractable roof over the Stiftsruine, Bad Hersfeld, Germany, 1968–1969, **Institute for Lightweight Structures and Conceptual Design under Frei Otto**
Wandelbares Dach über der Stiftsruine, Bad Hersfeld, Deutschland, 1968–1969, **Institut für leichte Flächentragwerke unter der Leitung von Frei Otto**

Horizontal Space Definer
*Horizontal Raumabschluss*

 UMBRELLA
*SCHIRM*

Umbrella *The structural principle of the umbrella has remained unchanged for many centuries: a spoked substructure around a ring moves about a central mast, allowing the umbrella to be put up and down – a textile membrane is spanned over the top. As they are both convertible and mobile, portable umbrellas are the most flexible textile structures around. Apart from providing sun and rain protection, they used to serve as the identification for prominent persons. Although umbrellas are no longer mobile above a certain size, they can still be used temporarily, for example as shading at market stands, at beaches, or cafés. Electrically-powered large umbrellas can span considerable areas, thus providing weather protection to several hundred people at once. In contrast to classical synclastic umbrellas in which a textile membrane spans over a rod structure in dome-like fashion, large umbrellas are anticlastic, such that a membrane spans under the rods in funnel-like fashion.*

Schirm *Seit vielen Jahrhunderten hat sich am Konstruktionsprinzip des Schirms nichts geändert: ein Mittelmast, an dem die speichenförmige Unterkonstruktion mittels eines Rings bewegt und somit der Schirm auf- und abgespannt wird. Darüber ist die textile Membran befestigt. Der tragbare Schirm ist die flexibelste textile Konstruktion, da er wandelbar und zugleich mobil ist. Neben dem Schutz vor Sonne oder Regen wurde er früher auch als Kennzeichnung herausragender Persönlichkeiten verwendet. Ab einer gewissen Größe ist der Schirm nicht mehr mobil, aber temporär nutzbar, um etwa bei Märkten, am Strand oder im Café Schatten zu spenden. Elektrisch betriebene Großschirme können beträchtliche Flächen überdecken und somit mehrere hundert Personen vor der Witterung schützen. Bei ihnen sind – im Gegensatz zu der klassischen Form der synklastisch geformten Schirme, bei der die textile Membran sich kuppelartig über ein Gestänge spannt – die Schirme antiklastisch geformt, das heißt die Membran wird trichterförmig unter dem Gestänge gespannt.*

ondon Roof, London, Great Britain, 2002,
**sa – Karsten Huneck and Bernd Truempler**
*ondon Roof, London, Großbritannien, 2002,*
**sa – *Karsten Huneck und Bernd Truempler***

# UMBRELLA / portable
*SCHIRM / tragbar*

Japan, end of the nineteenth century
Japan, Ende des 19. Jahrhunderts

London Roof, London, Great Britain, 2002, **osa – Karsten Huneck and Bernd Truempler**
In this temporary installation, osa questioned the significance of permanent architecture, exploring the possibilities of creating a space for a brief period of time that would also involve the public. The act of opening an umbrella epitomises the concept of a temporary roof over the bearer's head in the simplest way possible. A fluent, temporary roof of approximately 200 open umbrellas was therefore set up in the middle of Trafalgar Square.

London Roof, London, Großbritannien, 2002, **osa – Karsten Huneck und Bernd Truempler**
Mit der temporären Installation stellte osa die Bedeutung von permanenter Architektur infrage und suchte unter Teilnahme der Öffentlichkeit nach Möglichkeiten, zeitlich begrenzt Raum zu erschaffen. Der Regenschirm verkörperte durch den Akt des Öffnens eines temporären Daches über dem eigenen Kopf das Konzept auf einfache Art und Weise. So entstand mitten auf dem Trafalgar Square ein fließendes, temporäres Dach aus etwa 200 aufgespannten Schirmen.

Procession on Waisak
Day, Candi Mendut, Java,
Indonesia, 2008
Prozession am Wesak-
Tag, Candi Mendut, Java,
Indonesien, 2008

Procession, Siem Reap, Cambodia, 2008
Prozession, Siem Reap, Kambodscha, 2008

117

## UMBRELLA / temporary
### *SCHIRM / temporär*

Sun shades in India, early twentieth century
Sonnenschirme in Indien, Anfang des 20. Jahrhunderts

Sun shades on the beach at Monterosso al Mare, Italy, 2007
Sonnenschirme am Strand von Monterosso al Mare, Italien, 2007

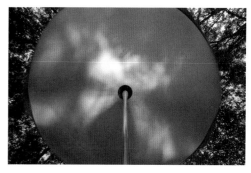

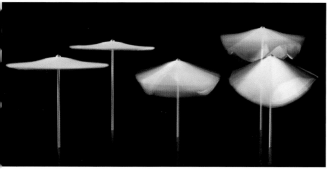

Rotation umbrella, Stuttgart, Germany, 2003,
**Werner Sobek with Transsolar**
This strutless textile umbrella roof rotates around its shaft,
driven by a motor. The centrifugal force resulting from the
rotation stretches the membrane from its resting position,
hanging limply around the shaft, into a largely horizontal
position.
Rotationsschirm, Stuttgart, Deutschland, 2003,
**Werner Sobek mit Transsolar**
Das spantenlose textile Schirmdach rotiert – angetrieben
von einem Motor – um den Schaft. Durch die aus der
Rotation resultierenden Fliehkräfte wird die Membran aus
einer schlaff um den Schaft hängenden Ruhelage in eine
im Wesentlichen horizontale Lage aufgespannt.

Lake Walchen, Germany, 2008
Walchensee, Deutschland, 2008

Schwägalp, Switzerland, 2007
Schwägalp, Schweiz, 2007

UMBRELLA / fixed
*SCHIRM / ortsfest*

Shanghai International Circuit, China, 2004,
**Wilke GmbH and Taiyo Kogyo Corporation**
Shanghai International Circuit, China, 2004,
**Wilke GmbH und Taiyo Kogyo Corporation**

"Drei Pilze" (Three Mushrooms),
BUGA 1955, Kassel, Germany,
**Frei Otto**
„Drei Pilze", BUGA 1955, Kassel,
Deutschland, **Frei Otto**

Pneumatic umbrellas, Expo 1970, Osaka, Japan, **Tanero Oki**
Pneumatische Schirme, Expo 1970, Osaka, Japan, **Tanero Oki**

Convertible umbrellas for the inner courtyards of the Prophet's Holy Mosque, Madinah, Saudi Arabia, 1993, **SL-Rasch GmbH**
To improve the climatic conditions in the mosque's two inner courtyards and reduce energy consumption, without however destroying their character, twelve convertible umbrellas were erected there. Their white Teflon membranes create a roof covering with an area of 17 x 18 metres that is 14 metres high when opened. The precise times of their opening and closing are calculated daily by computer, based on weather reports.
Wandelbare Schirme für die Innenhöfe der Moschee des Heiligen Propheten in Medina, Saudi-Arabien, 1993, **SL-Rasch GmbH**
Um die klimatischen Bedingungen innerhalb der beiden Innenhöfe zu verbessern und den Energieverbrauch zu senken, ohne jedoch den Charakter der Höfe zu zerstören, wurden dort zwölf wandelbare Schirme aufgestellt. Deren weiße Membran aus Teflon überdeckt jeweils eine Fläche von 17 x 18 Metern und ist in geöffneter Position 14 Meter hoch. Aufgrund von Wettermessungen werden die genauen Zeitpunkte des Öffnens und Schließens täglich mittels Computer berechnet und gesteuert.

Horizontal Space Definer
*Horizontaler Raumabschluss*

CURRENT PROJECTS
*AKTUELLE PROJEKTE*

RONAN & ERWAN BOUROULLEC,
J. MAYER H. ARCHITECTS,
LACATON & VASSAL,
LITTMANN KULTURPROJEKTE,
2B ARCHITECTES,
SNØHETTA,
VON GERKAN, MARG AND PARTNERS.

## RONAN & ERWAN BOUROULLEC

Textile Pavilion, MUDAM, Luxembourg, 2006
*Textiler Pavillon, MUDAM, Luxemburg, 2006*

The restaurant of the Musée d'Art Moderne Grand-Duc Jean (MUDAM), designed by Pei Cobb Freed & Partners, is located directly below a glass roof. Ronan & Erwan Bouroullec developed a textile pavilion as autonomous architecture to break the vertical geometry of the space and thus establish a protected place in more human scale amidst the monumental architecture. Their greatest challenge was to counteract the strong solar radiation under the glass roof. A curved roof made of textile tiles ("North Tiles"), and supported by a wooden skeleton provides shade to the guests, also creating an acoustically pleasant, soft atmosphere.

Das Restaurant des von Pei Cobb Freed & Partners erbauten Musée d'Art Moderne Grand-Duc Jean (MUDAM) befindet sich direkt unter einem Glasdach. Ronan & Erwan Bouroullec entwickelten einen textilen Pavillon als autonome Architektur, um die vertikale Geometrie des Raums zu brechen und somit einen geschützten, auf das menschliche Maß begrenzten Ort inmitten der monumentalen Architektur zu schaffen. Die größte Herausforderung war es, der starken Sonneneinstrahlung unter dem Glasdach entgegenzuwirken. Ein gekrümmtes Dach aus textilen Ziegeln („North Tiles"), das von einem Holzgerüst getragen wird, spendet den Gästen Schatten und schafft eine akustisch angenehm gedämpfte Atmosphäre.

## J. MAYER H. ARCHITECTS

Arium, ISCID, initiated by Stylepark, realized by Nya Nordiska, Hanover, Germany, 2003
*Arium, ISCID, initiiert von Stylepark, realisiert von Nya Nordiska, Hannover, Deutschland, 2003*

A venue for events and a meeting place were established in the atrium of the Ernst-August-Carrée on the occasion of the ISCID conference. A thirty-metre-long and ten-meter-wide polyamide sail was suspended by wire cables in the atrium to form a temporary roof, providing protection from solar radiation. Sunlight could only enter through thirteen round openings. The openings in the ceiling corresponded to large seating islands on the ground. The space, covered by the sail, sewn together from different lengths of material in yellow, green, and blue tones, provided a contemplative alternative to the hectic congress.

Anlässlich der ISCID-Konferenz wurde im Atrium des Ernst-August-Carrée ein Ort für Veranstaltungen und als Treffpunkt realisiert. Ein 30 Meter langes und zehn Meter breites Segel aus Polyamid wurde mit Drahtseilen als temporäres Dach im Atrium abgehängt und bot Schutz vor Sonneneinstrahlung. Einzig 13 kreisförmige Ausschnitte ließen Sonnenlicht einfallen. Den Ausschnitten in der Decke entsprachen große Sitzinseln auf dem Boden. Der Raum, nach oben abgeschirmt durch das aus verschiedenen Stoffbahnen in Gelb-, Grün- und Blautönen zusammengenähte Segel, bot einen kontemplativen Gegenpol zum hektischen Kongresstag.

## LACATON & VASSAL

Houses in Mulhouse, France, 2002–2005
*Wohnhäuser in Mulhouse, Frankreich, 2002–2005*

The light upper floor of this housing complex rests like a greenhouse on top of the three-meter-high ground floor of prefabricated concrete components. Parts of the "greenhouse" are thermally insulated and can be heated. The other areas form conservatories that are enveloped by corrugated sheets of polycarbonate. They can be ventilated using vertical sliding elements and via an automatic mechanism in the roof. Awnings can be opened up along a horizontal cable in order to additionally regulate the room temperature when the sun is shining; they span the space like a cloudy ceiling to provide shade. Curtains behind the large glass areas in the living spaces provide protection against cold and heat. Niches can be separated by curtains if required.

Wie ein Gewächshaus ruht das lichte Obergeschoss der Wohnanlage auf dem aus Betonfertigteilen erstellten, drei Meter hohen Erdgeschoss. Teilbereiche des „Gewächshauses" sind thermisch isoliert und beheizbar. Den anderen Bereich bilden Wintergärten, die von semitransparenten, gewellten Polykarbonatplatten umschlossen sind. Sie können durch vertikale Schiebeelemente und automatisch über eine Mechanik im Dach belüftet werden. Um bei Sonneneinstrahlung die Raumtemperatur zusätzlich regulieren zu können, lassen sich entlang horizontal gespannter Seile Sonnensegel ausfahren, die wie eine wolkige Decke den Raum überspannen und ihn beschatten. Hinter den großen Glasflächen der Wohnräume schützen Vorhänge vor zu starkem Kälte- oder Hitzeeintritt. Bei Bedarf lassen sich Nischen durch Vorhänge abtrennen.

## LITTMANN KULTURPROJEKTE
Citysky, Basel, Switzerland, 2008
*Stadthimmel, Basel, Schweiz, 2008*

Subodh Gupta

Daniel Buren

In 2008, Basel was given a partial artificial sky. A city sky, designed by nine internationally renowned artists, hung between the façades of individual buildings on printed canvas made of net vinyl. In reference to the Roman vela or the sails that span Spanish pedestrian zones to provide sun protection, these horizontally-spanned sails created an upper boundary, allowing a new "roofed" city space to be experienced below the artificial sky. As an artistic intervention, and in their proximity to ceiling painting, these colourful translucent street pictures counterbalanced the increasing uniformity and alienation of public space, temporarily giving it a new identity. The visibility of the motifs and the transparency of the sails varied with changing lighting conditions. The images overlapped with the building façades in the background depending on where the observer was standing. At night, the motifs came to the fore on the then opaque sails.

Basel erhielt 2008 einen partiellen Kunsthimmel. Zwischen der Fassaden einzelner Gebäude hing ein von neun international bekannten Künstlern gestalteter Stadthimmel in Form von bedruckten Zelttüchern aus Netzvinyl. Als Referenz an die Vela der Römer und die vor Sonne schützenden Segel über spanischen Fußgängerzonen bildeten die horizontal gespannten Segel eine Begrenzung nach oben und machten unterhalb des künstlichen Himmels einen neuen „bedachten" Stadtraum erfahrbar. Als künstlerische Intervention begegneten die farbenfrohen lichtdurchlässigen Straßenbilder mit ihrer Nähe zur Kunstform der Deckenmalerei der zunehmenden Uniformierung und Entfremdung des öffentlichen Raums und verschafften ihm temporär eine neue Identität. Die Sichtbarkeit der Motive und die Transparenz der Segel variierten mit den wechselnden Lichtverhältnissen. Je nach Standpunkt des Betrachters entstand eine Überlagerung der Bilder mit den Hausfassaden im Hintergrund. Nachts traten die Motive auf den dann blickdichten Segeln in den Vordergrund.

Renate Buser

Peter Kogler

## 2B ARCHITECTES

Swiss Pavilion for Arco, Madrid, Spain, 2003
*Schweizer Pavillon für Arco, Madrid, Spanien, 2003*

On the occasion of the international Arco art fair in Madrid, 2b architectes developed an exhibition pavilion for Switzerland in the interior courtyard of the Conde Duque cultural centre, providing space for exhibitions and other art-related events. Two containers stacked on top of one another as "Swiss Boxes" formed a three-dimensional white cross. The translucency of the white outside skin, made of polycarbonate, created a closed interior space that was illuminated by softened daylight. At night-time, when the interior space was lit up, the cubes looked like huge lanterns, illuminating the whole courtyard.

Lengths of a red, UV-proof net material, which is generally used in scaffolding structures, were hung up between the white, crossing containers and the walls of the former barracks building. They formed the red area of the Swiss flag, which could only be recognised from a bird's eye view. The covering of red bands – in reference to the toldos that are hung up in the streets and squares of Spain for sun protection – created a further space that was closed to they sky in the inner courtyard.

Anlässlich der internationalen Kunstmesse Arco in
Madrid entwickelten 2b architectes für die Schweiz
einen Ausstellungspavillon im Innenhof des Kulturzen-
trums Conde Duque, der Platz für Ausstellungen und
andere kunstbezogene Veranstaltungen bieten sollte.
Zwei als „Swiss boxes" übereinander gelagerte Con-
tainer bildeten ein dreidimensionales weißes Kreuz.
Aufgrund der Transluzenz der weißen Außenhaut
aus Polycarbonat entstand ein geschlossener, durch
gedämpftes Tageslicht erhellter Innenraum. Nachts,
wenn das Innere beleuchtet wurde, erschienen die
Kuben wie große Laternen und illuminierten den
gesamten Innenhof.

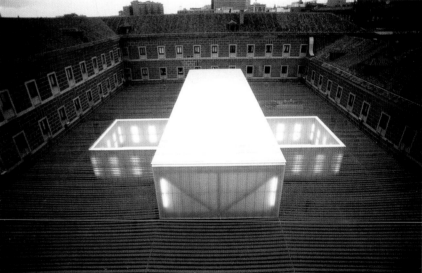

Von den weißen, übereinander gekreuzten Containern wurden rote Bahnen aus einem gewöhnlich im
Gerüstbau eingesetzten UV-beständigen Netzmaterial
waagrecht zu den Mauern des ehemaligen Kasernen-
gebäudes gespannt. Sie bildeten die rote Fläche der
Schweizer Fahne, die nur aus der Vogelperspektive
zu erkennen war. Beschattet durch die roten Bänder
- eine Reverenz an die vor Sonne schützenden
Toldos, die in Spanien seit jeher über Straßen und
Plätzen gespannt werden –, entstand im Innenhof ein
weiterer nach oben geschlossener Raum.

## SNØHETTA

The Tubaloon, Kongsberg Jazz Festival, Kongsberg,
Norway, 2006
*The Tubaloon, Kongsberg Jazz Festival, Kongsberg,*
*Norwegen, 2006*

A temporary roof covering was required to provide weather protection to the stage of this annual jazz festival in the Norwegian town of Kongsberg. The "Tubaloon" is a hybrid structure that consists of a steel skeleton spanned by a white membrane with a pneumatic air tube around its circumference. Its shape is similar to the human inner ear but it also looks like a wind instrument or a seashell. The membrane spans an area of approximately 1000 square meters and is guyed by wire tethers. "Tubaloon," a combination of the words "tuba" and "balloon," is designed to be assembled and disassembled and is erected for three weeks each time. It is stored in containers for the rest of the year.

Für das alljährlich stattfindende Jazzfestival im norwegischen Kongsberg wurde eine temporäre Bühnenüberdachung als Schutz vor Witterungseinflüssen benötigt. Der Tubaloon ist eine Misch struktur und besteht aus einem Stahlskelett, das mit einer weißen Membran überzogen und im Randbereich von einem pneumatischen Luftschlauch umgeben ist. Seine Form ähnelt der des menschlichen Innenohrs, aber auch der eines Blasinstruments oder einer Muschelschale. Die Membran überspannt eine Fläche von rund 1000 Quadratmetern und wird mit Seilen im Boden verankert. Tubaloon – zusammengesetzt aus „Tuba" und „Baloon" – ist für den mehrmaligen Auf- und Abbau konzipiert und wird jeweils für drei Wochen aufgestellt. Den Rest des Jahres wird er in Containern verstaut. Aufgrund seiner schützenden Form wird bei kleinen Veranstaltungen die Intimität gewahrt. Da die Membrankonstruktion nahezu komplett durchlässig ist, eignet sie sich auch für größere Veranstaltungen. Die elegante weiße Form, die bei Nacht in wechselnden Farbtönen beleuchtet wird, hat aufgrund der PVDF-beschichteten PVC-Membran eine besondere Brillanz.

## GMP VON GERKAN, MARG AND PARTNERS ARCHITECTS

Commerzbank Arena, Frankfurt on Main, Germany, 2002–2005
*Commerzbank Arena, Frankfurt am Main, Deutschland, 2002–2005*

Retractable interior roof
Wandelbares Innendach

A membrane of PVC-coated woven polyester was installed in this stadium for the 2006 World Football Championships, allowing it to be covered over quickly if required. The material-saving principle of the "purse-string" roof was developed by Schlaich Bergermann and Partners engineers. A video cube is attached to a central node over the middle of the playing field; the folded roof membrane is stored there. The roof unfolds from the centre along radial cables to form a closed roof surface in conjunction with the fixed stand roof made of a prestressed cable structure covered with translucent PTFE glass. The steel cable membrane roof spans up to 240 meters and covers an area of approximately 9,000 square-meters.

Anlässlich der Fußballweltmeisterschaft 2006 wurde das Stadion mit einer Membran aus PVC-beschichtetem Polyestergewebe ausgestattet, um es bei Bedarf in kurzer Zeit überdachen zu können. Das materialsparende Prinzip dieses „Raffdaches" wurde vom Ingenieurbüro Schlaich Bergermann und Partner entwickelt. An einem Zentralknoten mittig über dem Spielfeld ist ein Videowürfel befestigt, der die zusammengefaltete Dachmembran aufnimmt. Von der Mitte heraus entfaltet sich das Dach entlang der radialen Seilbinder und bildet zusammen mit der festen Tribünenüberdachung, einer mit transluzentem PTFE-Glas überdeckten vorgespannten Seilkonstruktion, bei Bedarf eine geschlossene Dachfläche. Das Stahlseil-Membrandach hat eine Spannweite von bis zu 240 Metern und überdeckt eine Fläche von rund 9000 Quadratmetern.

Permanent tribune roof
Feste Tribünenüberdachung

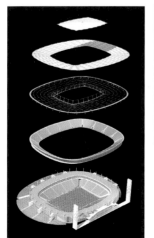

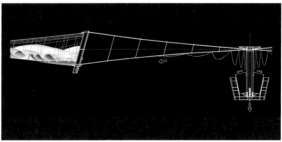

Operation procedure, interior roof
Fahrvorgang Innendach

## GMP VON GERKAN, MARG AND PARTNERS ARCHITECTS

Century Lotus Sports Park, Foshan, China, 2004–2006
*Century-Lotus-Sportpark, Foshan, China, 2004–2006*

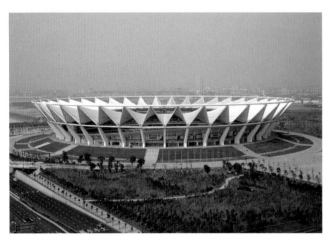

Stadium
Stadion

The Century Lotus Sports Park in Foshan consists of a multi-functional stadium and an indoor swimming pool. This round stadium with its gigantic white membrane roof rises above the sports park like a lotus blossom. The spoke wheel construction of the translucent stadium roof, with a folded PVC membrane covering, measures 350 metres in diameter and covers both the stands and the outer galleries. It can be opened out over the playing field within twelve minutes, transforming the open stadium into a closed arena and temporarily providing the whole interior area with weather protection. When not in use, the entire interior roof disappears into a huge video cube which floats over the centre of the playing field.

The roof covering of the indoor swimming pool consists of a triple-layered translucent PVC membrane and, as weather and heat protection, is part of the thermal building envelope. The spacing between the membranes is filled with conditioned compressed air.

Indoor swimmimng pool
Schwimmhalle

Ein Multifunktionsstadion und eine Schwimmhalle bilden den Century-Lotus-Sportpark in Foshan. Gleich einer Lotusblüte überragt das runde Stadion mit seinem riesigen, weißen Membrandach den Sportpark. Die Speichenradkonstruktion des transluzenten Stadiondaches mit der gefalteten Membrandeckung aus PVC misst 350 Meter im Durchmesser und überdeckt sowohl die Tribünen als auch die äußeren Umgänge. Über dem Spielfeld lässt sich das Faltdach je nach Bedarf innerhalb von zwölf Minuten schließen und das offene Stadion in eine geschlossene Arena verwandeln, die temporär im gesamten Innenbereich Schutz vor der Witterung bietet. Solange es nicht benötigt wird, verschwindet das gesamte Innendach in einem großen, über dem Zentrum des Spielfeldes schwebenden Videokubus.

Die Überdachung der Schwimmhalle besteht aus einer dreilagigen transluzenten Membran aus PVC und ist als Witterungs- und Wärmeschutz Bestandteil der thermischen Gebäudehülle. Der Membranzwischenraum ist mit konditionierter Druckluft gefüllt.

Interior view of the stadium
Innenansicht des Stadions

THREE-DIMENSIONAL SPACE DEFINER
*DREIDIMENSIONALER RAUMABSCHLUSS*

# HISTORICAL OVERVIEW
## *HISTORISCHER ÜBERBLICK*

## Tent

The traditional tent consists of the basic elements of a frame and a cover. It allows its user to quickly construct a protective covering against the weather with few materials and little effort and shields its inhabitants from view. Because the materials used are so perishable, it is hardly possible to date the origins of the tent as human housing. Excavations in Siberia have uncovered 30,000 year-old camps of Palaeolithic hunters in the tundra. Their tent coverings were made of branches, leaves and bark, and later of animal furs and skins.

Reconstruction of a Palaeolithic hunter's tent in Siberia approx. 30,000 years ago / *Rekonstruktion eines Zeltes paläolithischer Jäger Sibiriens vor ca. 30.000 Jahren* [38]

Today, the tents of nomads still provide an impression of the origins of human housing and its development. In the following section, the black tent, yurt, and tipi – the "classic" nomad tent forms – will be described. Because they have to be constantly on the move due to their way of life, always searching for pasture for their herds, nomads' tents are simple to put up and take down and easy to transport. These tents are also characterised by great adaptability to changing climatic and varying weather conditions.[1]
"The 'Black Tent' is the tent of the Arabian Bedouins, but has spread over time into western North Africa and into Afghanistan."[2] Due to the lack of wood there, it is constructed to require only a minimum of wooden poles. The tent covering, with its guy ropes, is stretched over tent poles arranged in three longitudinal rows, making the construction stable, and it consists of several lengths of sewn together black goat hair fabric, which is of great tensile strength. Goat hair provides perfect protection against rain, because it contracts as soon as it becomes damp and is then waterproof. Its naturally smooth, oily surface gives it additional water-resistant

qualities. In summer, the black tent offers both protection from direct sun and shade and its lighter weave prevents air from being trapped inside the tent. It is erected with its back side to the prevailing wind direction and additionally screened on that side by the erection of a side wall. In the event of high winds, the roof profile can be adapted by lowering or completely removing the outer poles. In winter, the tent is insulated against the cold by the addition of further side walls. Curtains separate the tent into the reception and men's sections and the women's section.[3]
The description of the tabernacle in the Book of Exodus is regarded as the oldest instance of the black tent in writing. Its frame was covered with ten ornately-embroidered lengths of tent material sewn together. For added protection, a tent roof of goat hair was laid over that and this was again reinforced by the skin of a ram that was dyed red.[4]

Berber tent at the edge of the Sahara, Tunisia, 2007 / *Berberzelt am Rand der Sahara, Tunesien, 2007* [39]

"The yurt is the Central Asian tent of the Turkic peoples and Mongols native to that part of the world and was brought by the advancing nomads into Asia Minor."[5] A yurt's walls consist of a mobile, foldable frame of wooden poles, which is erected in cylindrical form and stabilised with a tie, above which a spoked-frame domed roof arches. There is a door in the outer wall. The domed tent's diameter is about five metres and it is approximately three metres high at the highest point in the middle, where there is an opening to provide light and an outlet for smoke from the fireplace. The wooden frame covered with felt has little tensile strength, which is however not necessary for the yurt as its frame stands alone. The tent's felt coverings are laid to overlap so that the connecting edges are waterproof. Its top cover-

ing is usually oiled so that water runs off it.
Temperatures inside the yurt can be adjusted to the exterior climate by opening and closing individual parts of the covering. In summer, the felt side walls can be rolled up to let in light and air. To protect against the cold in winter, yurt walls can consist of up to eight felt coverings.[6]

Yurt, Bulunkul, Tadzhikistan, 2008 / *Jurte, Bulunkul, Tadschikistan, 2008*

The traditional housing of the North American Indian, the tipi, is a well-designed conical tent. Its supporting structure of several wooden poles in a cone shape is slanted more steeply at the rear to withstand wind. Over this was stretched a tent skin, originally made of several bison or buffalo skins sewn together, which was however replaced by a canvas tarpaulin over time. An average tipi had a diameter of about six metres and a pole height of about eight metres. The entrance was on the side away from the wind, so a fireplace could be placed inside the tent. An adjustable smoke flap at the tent's highest point acted as a necessary flue, keeping the inside of the tent smoke-free. The lining attached to the interior kept out draughts and provided protection from the rain, while also ensuring that the tent was ventilated.

Tents of the Mescaleros, around 1900 / *Zelte der Mescaleros, um 1900*

While the black tent and the yurt are still in use today, North American Indians no longer use the tipi as a mobile dwelling place because they no longer live a nomads, but on reservations in settled housing.

Many modifications and mixed forms of these tent constructions were widespread among indigenous peoples such as the Eskimos, Sami, or Siberian pastoral peoples well into early twentieth century.[7]

While a tent was the usual home of nomads, their use among settled peoples from the antiquity up into nineteenth century was reduced to courtly and military applications.[8] A series of reliefs and mosaics connected with antique writings give a good idea of the art of tent construction in the classical civilisations of the antiquity. Historical finds, such as the metal fittings found in the tomb of Hetepheres I (around 2,550 BC) also attest to the early use of tents. A framework of wooden poles that can be easily dismantled, on the exterior of which were grommets for attaching a fabric covering, could be reconstructed.[9]

Descriptions of the audience tent and marriage tent of Alexander the Great (356–323 BC) demonstrate the extravagant use of ostentatious festival tents during the antiquity. Athenaeus described Alexander the Great's marriage tent as follows: "Moreover, the construction was costly and magnificent, adorned with extensive draperies and fine linen and lined with purple and crimson carpets, which were interwoven with gold."[10]

Alexander the Great's audience tent was embellished with precious embroidery and supported by fifty golden poles. In the middle of the tent stood a golden throne. The festival tent of Ptolemy II (around 275 BC) was said to cover an area of about 1,200 square metres. It was supported by wooden columns, on which rested a horizontal wooden frame covered with scarlet fabric. A corridor surrounding the interior on three sides was separated from the interior by richly decorated curtains, also scarlet.[11]

Tents were used for festive occasions and military purposes. A relief showing an Assyrian tent from the army camp of Sennacherib (705–681 BC) portrays a forked support with the tent covering stretched over it.

Assyrian tent, Relief in Nineveh, Assyria (modern Iraq), 705–681 BC / Assyrisches Zelt, Relief in Ninive, Assyrien (heutiger Irak), 705–681 v. Chr.

The Roman Empire, with its huge missions of military conquest, had an immense demand for tents. So-called frame tents and ridge tents with a saddleback roof and fabric coverings were used.

Another important civilisation in regard to the art of tent construction developed in the Ottoman Empire and extended from Persia into India. Miniatures from the Turkish and Ottoman Empires have bequeathed many representations of their typical domed tents to us.[12]

Throne tent of Suleiman with a domed roof, Turkish miniature, 1566 / Thronzelt Suleimans mit kuppelförmiger Spitze, türkische Miniatur, 1566

"So far no origin or independent development of tent construction in Central Europe has been demonstrated."[13] The Persian Wars resulted in the Persians' magnificent tents reaching Greece, where they influenced theatre construction in the form of the skene and, by way of Rome, also influenced the festival and military tents of the European Middle Ages.[14] Moorish tent constructions arrived in Europe via Spain in the first century AD and also influenced developments there.

Fresco of the re-conquest of Palma de Majorca, Spain, thirteenth century / Fresko der Rückeroberung Palma de Mallorcas, Spanien, 13. Jahrhundert

Countless variants of this form of round tent with a peak were in use in the Middle Ages and many drawings portray the splendid tents of commanders as well as the simplest of tents for the soldiers.

A military camp of very special dimensions was the "Camp du Drap d'Or," which was built near Calais for a meeting between the King of France, Francis I, and the King of England, Henry VIII, for three weeks in 1520. The magnificent appearance of the tents and luxurious gold-embroidered costumes gave this encounter the name of the "Field of the Cloth of Gold." 5,000 people and 3,000 horses were housed in over 400 tents, the biggest of which resembled palaces, containing magnificent banqueting halls, many rooms, and a chapel.[15]

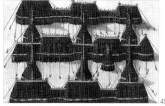

Camp du Drap d'Or, 1520 / Camp du Drap d'Or, 1520

Since the end of the eighteenth century, permanent military tent camps have been built increasingly rarely. One consequence of Napoleon's military tactic of total mobility, was the minimisation of baggage for easier transport, so small tents were carried. Large, central tent camps were no longer used.[16]

Industrialisation in the nineteenth century and the accompanying mass production in Europe and the USA made the purchase of a tent affordable for a wider section of the population. While tents had been used mainly for courtly and military purposes until the beginning of the nineteenth century, the newly-emerging middle-class leisure activities, resulting from social change, required adequate accommodation.[17] Various textile structures, ranging from one-man tents to very large tents, were offered in catalogues. Large tent halls were constructed for temporary events such as fairs, trade shows and festivals. These were not only self-supporting membrane constructions, but also of the classic frame tent type, covered with tarpaulin.

Festival tent at one of the first Oktoberfests in Munich, Germany, mid-nineteenth century / Festzelt auf einem der ersten Oktoberfeste in München, Deutschland, Mitte des 19. Jahrhunderts

While circuses initially gave guest performances in massive circus halls in Europe, the boom years of the travelling circus, which demanded tents that could quickly be put up and taken down, began in America in the eighteen-sixties. The first circus tents were round, had a central mast from which the tarpaulin was hung, and a diameter of approximately fifteen to twenty-seven metres.

Circus tent of the Stromeyer company, 1890 / Zirkuszelt der Firma Stromeyer, 1890

Over the years, the tents grew larger and so could seat a growing number of spectators. In 1850, the "Phineas Taylor Barnum Circus" could accommodate an audience of up to 12,000 people. Because a round tent with a central mast cannot not be expanded indefinitely for structural reasons, the multiple peak tent, to which any number of central elements could be added, was developed. The classic large circus tent, the Chapiteau, which could vary in size up to a diameter of about fifty-five metres and incorporate three arenas, was developed around 1900. This form of round tent with interior masts, from the tops of which the central apex of the whole tent hangs, is still in use today.[18]

Apollo Circus, 1930 / Zirkus Apollo, 1930

Today the construction of large festival tents, exhibition tents, circus tents, and small tents remains largely unchanged. Increasingly large spans, greater safety and weather resistance, and longer durability have been achieved due to continuous improvements in tent materials and the use of synthetic-fibre textile membranes. Small frame tents are now mainly used for leisure activities and on expeditions. Entire tent cities are set up every year in Muna and Arafat near Mecca for pilgrims to the Muslim *hajj*. Refugees arc also housed in tent camps and tents are used as mobile accommodation during military actions.

Tent construction and the materials used underwent a fundamental change in the mid-nineteen-fifties. Frei Otto's groundbreaking work transformed the construction of tents made of nets and membranes, transferring the idea of tensile membrane structures to large structures. It became possible to cover broad areas with less material.[19]

The first structures of this kind were large roof coverings in the form of shade cloths and pole marquees for open-air events, temporary cafés, and exhibitions. So-called cable net constructions were also adopted in the search for ways to span larger areas. It was already known in Roman times that hemp rope could be used to reinforce cotton canvas. Some circus tents also already had cable net reinforcement, which was necessary because normal tent fabric was no longer sufficient to span their large areas. Frei Otto and Rolf Gutbrod used a combination of a cable net construction made of steel cables and a translucent, flame-resistant membrane of PVC-coated polyester fabric in the construction of the German Pavilion at the 1967 Montreal World Fair. The pavilion featured the world's first large tensile cable net and was therefore a real, self-supporting textile membrane construction. It consisted of eight peaks of varying heights supported by fourteen to thirty-eight-metre-high masts and three low points lying within the area. The result was a support-free roof covering a gigantic space (approximately 8,000 square metres). This great span was achieved by applying the "Addition Principle."

German Pavilion at Expo 1967, Montreal, Canada, Frei Otto and Rolf Gutbrod / Deutscher Pavillon auf der Expo 1967, Montreal, Kanada, Frei Otto und Rolf Gutbrod

A further development of the cable net construction used for the German Pavilion at Montreal were the tent roofs of the Olympiapark in Munich, built for the Summer Olympics in 1972 by the architectural firm of Behnisch & Partner, under the expert consultation of Frei Otto. This was a construction of much bigger proportions than the one in Montreal, so

there were initial doubts as to the practicability of the design. The continuous roof, which covers three sports halls (Olympic Hall, Swim Hall and half of the Olympic Stadium) as well as the paths between them, continued the landscaping concept with its very special topography. The 74,800 square-metre roof is a cable net construction of steel cables hanging on fifty-eight steel masts, which are clad in approximately 3 x 3 metre acrylic glass panels.[20] The acrylic glass panels lasted thirty years before they had to be replaced.

Cable net construction in the Olympiapark Munich, Germany, 1972, Behnisch & Partner, Frei Otto, Leonhardt + Andrä / Seilnetzkonstruktion im Olympiapark München, Deutschland, 1972, Behnisch & Partner, Frei Otto, Leonhardt + Andrä

With the development of large tent architectures, the originally mobile tent was transformed into a permanent structure. In recent years, reinforced tensile membrane structures have been constructed to roof over sports stadiums, exhibition halls, and industrial buildings. New developments have also continuously been emerging in the area of materials, such as PTFE-coated fibreglass, for example, which is not flammable, can be recycled, and has a high self-cleaning effect.[21]

**Zelt**

Das traditionelle Zelt besteht aus den Grundelementen Tragegerüst und Hülle. Es ermöglicht dem Benutzer, mit wenig Material und Aufwand schnell eine vor der Witterung schützende Hülle zu errichten und bietet ihm zusätzlich Schutz vor Einblick. Aufgrund der Vergänglichkeit des Materials sind die Ursprünge des Zeltes als menschliche Behausung kaum datierbar. Grabungen in Sibirien brachten über 30.000 Jahre alte Lagerstätten paläolithischer Jäger in der Tundra zutage. Die Zelthaut wurde aus Zweigen, Blättern und Rinden, später aus Fellen und Häuten erlegter Tiere gefertigt.

Die Zelte der Nomaden vermitteln noch heute einen Eindruck der Ursprünge menschlicher Behausungen und deren Entwicklung. Im Folgenden werden das schwarze Zelt, die Jurte und das Tipi als die „klassischen" Zeltformen der Nomaden beschrieben. Da sie aufgrund ihrer

Lebensform ständig mobil sein müssen – stets auf der Suche nach Weideplätzen für ihre Herden – sind die Zelte der Nomaden einfach auf- und abbaubar und leicht zu transportieren. Des Weiteren zeichnen sie sich durch eine hohe Anpassungsfähigkeit an wechselndes Klima und verschiedene Witterung aus.[1]
„Das ‚Schwarze Zelt' ist das Zelt der arabischen Beduinen, hat sich aber im Laufe der Zeit bis in das westliche Nordafrika und bis Afghanistan verbreitet."[2] Es ist so konstruiert, dass es – aufgrund der dort herrschenden Holzknappheit – mit einem Minimum an Holzstangen auskommt. Über die in drei Längsreihen angeordneten Zeltstangen wird die Zelthaut mit Halteseilen abgespannt, was der Konstruktion ihre Standfestigkeit gibt. Die Zelthaut besteht aus mehreren aneinander genähten Bahnen aus schwarzem Ziegenhaargewebe, das sich durch eine große Zugfestigkeit auszeichnet. Das Ziegenhaar ist ein perfekter Schutz gegen Regen, da es sich bei der ersten Nässe zusammenzieht und dann wasserundurchlässig ist. Aufgrund seiner von Natur aus öligen und glatten Oberfläche besitzt es zusätzlich wasserabweisende Eigenschaften. Im Sommer schützt das schwarze Zelt vor direkter Sonneneinstrahlung und spendet Schatten. Die lockere Webart des Sommerzeltes verhindert, dass sich die Luft im Inneren staut. Es wird mit der Rückseite zur Windrichtung aufgestellt und auf dieser Seite durch das Anstecken einer Seitenwand noch zusätzlich abgeschirmt. Bei aufkommendem Wind kann das Dachprofil angepasst werden, indem die äußeren Stangen tiefer gesetzt oder ganz entfernt werden. Im Winter wird das Zelt durch Anbringung weiterer Seitenwände gegen Kälte isoliert. Vorhänge trennen das Zelt in Abteilungen, um den Empfangs- und Männerbereich vom Frauenbereich zu trennen.[3]
Als wohl ältestes schriftliches Beispiel des schwarzen Zeltes gilt die Beschreibung der Stiftshütte aus dem 2. Buch Mose. Ein Tragegerüst wurde mit zehn kostbar bestickten, aneinander genähten Zeltbahnen bedeckt. Zum Schutz wurde darüber ein Zeltdach aus Ziegenhaar gelegt, was nochmals durch ein rot gefärbtes Widderfell verstärkt wurde.[4]
„Die Jurte ist das innerasiatische Zelt der dort beheimateten Turkvölker und Mongolen, das mit den vordringenden Nomaden auch nach Kleinasien gebracht wurde."[5] Die Wände der Jurte bestehen aus einem beweglichen Scherengitter aus Holzstäben, welches in Form eines Zylinders aufgestellt und mit einem Zug-

band stabilisiert wird. Darüber wölbt sich ein speichenförmiges Kuppeldach. In der Außenwand befindet sich eine Tür. Der Durchmesser des Kuppelzeltes beträgt etwa fünf Meter. An der höchsten Stelle in der Mitte ist es etwa drei Meter hoch. Dort befindet sich eine Öffnung zur Belichtung und für den Rauchabzug der Feuerstelle. Bedeckt ist das Holzgestell mit Filz, der jedoch kaum Zugkräfte aufnehmen kann, was bei der Jurte allerdings nicht nötig ist, da das Gestell eigenständig steht. Die Filzdecken der Zelthaut sind überlappend verlegt, so dass die Anschlüsse wasserdicht sind. Die oberste Schicht wird meist eingeölt, damit das Wasser daran ablaufen kann. Durch Öffnen und Schließen einzelner Teile der Hülle wird die Temperatur innerhalb der Jurte dem Außenklima angepasst. Im Sommer lassen sich die Seitenwände aus Filz nach oben rollen, sodass Licht und Luft einströmen können. Zum Schutz gegen die Kälte bestehen die Wände der Jurte im Winter aus bis zu acht Filzschichten.[6]
Als traditionelle Behausung der nordamerikanischen Indianer ist das Tipi ein klug durchdachtes Kegelzelt. Die Tragekonstruktion aus mehreren kegelförmig aufgestellten Holzstangen ist auf der Rückseite steiler geneigt, um dem Wind standzuhalten. Darüber wurde ursprünglich eine Zelthaut aus mehreren aneinander genähten Bison- oder Büffelhäuten befestigt, die jedoch im Laufe der Zeit durch Segeltuchplane ersetzt wurden. Ein durchschnittliches Tipi hat einen Durchmesser von etwa sechs Metern und eine Gestängehöhe von etwa acht Metern. Der Eingang liegt auf der dem Wind abgewandten Seite. Somit kann im Inneren des Zeltes eine Feuerstelle platziert werden. Durch eine verstellbare Rauchklappe am höchsten Punkt des Zeltes wird für den erforderlichen Abzug gesorgt und das Zeltinnere bleibt rauchfrei. Das im Inneren angebrachte sogenannte Taukleid hält einerseits die Zugluft ab und schützt vor Regen, andererseits sorgt es für die Durchlüftung des Zeltes. Während das schwarze Zelt und die Jurte noch heute zum Einsatz kommen, verwenden die nordamerikanischen Indianer das Tipi nicht mehr als mobile Wohnstätte, da sie nicht mehr als Nomaden, sondern in Reservaten als feste Behausungen leben.
Bis ins frühe 20. Jahrhundert waren zahlreiche Abwandlungen und Mischformen dieser Zeltkonstruktionen bei Naturvölkern wie den Eskimos, Samen oder den sibirischen Hirtenvölkern verbreitet.[7]

Während bei den Nomaden das Zelt die ständige Wohnung darstellt, reduzierte sich bei den siedelnden Völkern von der Antike bis ins 19. Jahrhundert die Nutzung auf den höfischen und militärischen Gebrauch.[8] Eine Reihe von Reliefs und Mosaiken in Verbindung mit anriken Schriften vermitteln ein gutes Bild der Zeltbaukunst der klassischen Hochkulturen der Antike. Aber auch historische Fundstücke wie zum Beispiel Metallbeschläge im Grab von Hetepheres I. (um 2550 v. Chr.) belegen die frühe Verwendung von Zelten. Es konnte ein leicht verlegbares Gerüst aus Holzstangen konstruiert werden, an dessen Außenseite sich Ösen zur Befestigung eines Stoffüberzugs befanden.[9]

Die Beschreibungen des Audienzzeltes und des Hochzeitszeltes Alexanders des Großen (356–323 v. Chr.) demonstrieren den verschwenderischen Gebrauch prunkvoller, antiker Festzelte. Das Hochzeitszelt Alexanders des Großen beschrieb Athenaios folgendermaßen: „Darüber hinaus war die Konstruktion kostspielig und herrlich mit teuren Draperien und feinen Leinen geschmückt und unterfüttert mit purpurnen und karmesinroten Teppichen, die mit Gold verwoben waren."[10]

Das Audienzzelt Alexanders des Großen war mit kostbaren Stickereien versehen und wurde von 50 goldenen Stützen getragen. Im Zentrum des Zeltes stand sein goldener Thron.

Das Festzelt des Ptolemäus II. (um 275 v. Chr.) soll eine Grundfläche von etwa 3200 Quadratmetern überdeckt haben. Getragen wurde das Zelt von Holzsäulen, auf denen ein mit scharlachrotem Stoff gespannter, horizontaler Holzrahmen auflag. Der Innenraum war durch reich verzierte, ebenfalls scharlachrote Vorhänge von einem Gang getrennt, der an drei Seiten den Innenraum umschloss.[11]

Neben der Verwendung bei festlichen Anlässen wurden Zelte ebenfalls für militärische Zwecke eingesetzt. Die Darstellung eines assyrischen Zeltes aus dem Heerlager des Sinachirib (705–681 v. Chr.) zeigt eine gegabelte Zeltstütze mit der darüber gespannten Zelthaut.

Das römische Imperium mit seinen ausgedehnten Eroberungszügen hatte einen immensen Bedarf an Zelten. Es wurden sogenannte Gerüst- und Stangenzelte in Satteldachform mit Tuchbespannungen verwendet.

Eine weitere bedeutende Hochkultur der Zeltbaukunst entwickelte sich im osmanischen Reich sowie von Persien bis nach Indien. Durch Miniaturen des türkisch-osmanischen Reiches sind zahl-

reiche Darstellungen der typischen Kuppelzelte überliefert.[12]

„In Mitteleuropa konnte bislang kein Ursprung, keine eigenständige Entwicklung des Zeltbaus, nachgewiesen werden."[13] Durch die Perserkriege gelangten ihre Prunkzelte nach Griechenland, wo sie als „skene" den Theaterbau beeinflussten und via Rom auch die Fest- und Militärzelte des europäischen Mittelalters.[14] Maurische Zeltkonstruktionen gelangten über Spanien im 1. Jahrtausend n. Chr. nach Europa und beeinflussten ebenfalls die dortige Entwicklung.

Die Form des runden Zeltes mit der aufgesetzten Spitze wurde im Mittelalter variantenreich verwendet. Zahlreiche Zeichnungen zeigen prachtvolle Feldherrenzelte neben einfachsten Zelten für die Soldaten.

Ein Heerlager besonderen Ausmaßes war das „Camp du Drap d'Or", was aufgrund eines Treffens zwischen dem König von Frankreich, Franz I., und dem König von England, Heinrich VIII., 1520 in der Nähe von Calais für drei Wochen aufgebaut wurde. Die prunkvolle Gestaltung der Zeltunterkünfte und die luxuriösen, goldbestickten Kostüme gaben der Zusammenkunft den Namen „Goldtuchtreffen". In über 400 Zelten wurden 5000 Personen und 3000 Pferde untergebracht. Die größten Zelte waren von schlossähnlichem Aussehen und enthielten prunkvolle Bankettsäle, viele Zimmer und eine Kapelle.[15]

Seit dem Ende des 18. Jahrhunderts wurden immer seltener dauerhafte militärische Zeltlager errichtet. Eine Folge der Kriegstaktik Napoleons – die der totalen Beweglichkeit – war die Minimierung des Gepäcks für einen einfachen Transport, bei dem kleine Zelte mitgenommen wurden. Große, zentrale Zeltlager kamen außer Gebrauch.[16]

Mit der Industrialisierung im 19. Jahrhundert und der damit einhergehenden Massenproduktion in Europa und in den USA wurde der Erwerb von Zelten für eine breitere Bevölkerungsschicht erschwinglich. Waren bis zum Anfang des 19. Jahrhunderts Zelte überwiegend im höfischen und militärischen Gebrauch, erforderten durch den gesellschaftlichen Wandel neu entstehende bürgerliche Freizeitaktivitäten adäquate Behausungen.[17] Unterschiedlichste textile Bauten vom Einmannzelt bis zu Großzelten wurden mittels Katalogen angeboten. Für temporäre Veranstaltungen wie Jahrmärkte, Fachausstellungen oder Feste wurden große Zelthallen konstruiert. Es handelt sich hier nicht um frei gespannte Membrankonstruk-

tionen, sondern um den Typus des klassischen Gestellzeltes, das mit einer Zeltplane bekleidet wird.

Während in Europa Zirkusunternehmen zunächst in massiven Zirkusbauten gastierten, begann in den sechziger Jahren des 19. Jahrhunderts in Amerika die große Blüte des reisenden Zirkus, wofür schnell auf- und abbaubare Zelte benötigt wurden. Die ersten Zirkuszelte waren rund und besaßen einen Zentralmast, von dem die Zeltplane abgespannt wurde. Ihr Durchmesser betrug etwa 15 bis 27 Meter.

Im Laufe der Jahre wurden die Zelte größer und konnten somit eine steigende Anzahl an Zuschauern aufnehmen. Schon 1850 bot der „Phineas Taylor Barnum Circus" bis zu 12.000 Zuschauern Platz. Da das Rundzelt mit einem Zentralmast aus Konstruktionsgründen nicht unbegrenzt erweiterbar war, entstand das Reihenmastzelt, bei dem beliebig viele Mittelstückelemente addiert werden konnten. Um 1900 wurde das klassische Zirkusgroßzelt, das Chapiteau, mit verschiedenen Größen bis zu einem Durchmesser von etwa 55 Metern und drei Manegen entwickelt. Diese Form des Rundzeltes mit Innenmasten, von deren Spitzen der zentrale Hochpunkt des gesamten Zeltes abgespannt ist, ist noch heute in Gebrauch.[18]

Die Konstruktion der großen Fest- und Ausstellungs- sowie der Zirkus- und Kleinzelte hat sich bis heute nicht wesentlich verändert. Durch eine stetige Verbesserung der Zeltbaumaterialien und der textilen Membranen aus Kunstfasern werden zunehmend größere Spannweiten, eine höhere Sicherheit und Wetterbeständigkeit sowie eine längere Lebensdauer erreicht.

Diese Gestellzelte werden in ihrer kleinen Variante heute hauptsächlich in der Freizeit und auf Expeditionen genutzt. Für die Pilger der muslimischen Hadsch werden jedes Jahr nahe Mekka in Muna und Arafat ganze Zeltstädte errichtet. Ebenso werden Flüchtlinge in Zeltlagern untergebracht und Mannschaftszelte als mobile Unterkunft bei Militäraktionen benutzt.

Mitte der fünfziger Jahre des 20. Jahrhunderts kam es zu einem grundsätzlichen Wandel in der Zeltkonstruktion und der verwendeten Materialien. Die grundlegenden Arbeiten Frei Ottos veränderten den Zeltbau aus Netzen und Membranen, indem er die Idee vorgespannter Membranstrukturen auf Großbauten übertrug. So entstand die Möglichkeit, mit geringem Materialaufwand

weite Flächen zu überspannen.[19]

Die ersten Bauten dieser Art waren größere Überdachungen in Form von Segeln und Wellenzelten für Veranstaltungen im Freien, temporäre Cafés und Ausstellungen. Auf der Suche nach Möglichkeiten, größere Spannweiten zu erlangen, griff man auf die sogenannten Seilnetzkonstruktionen zurück. Schon bei den Römern war bekannt, dass man mit Hanfseilen Baumwollsegeltuch verstärken kann. Auch hatten bereits einige Zirkuszelte netzartige Seilverstärkungen. Dies war notwendig, da bei großen Spannweiten normales Zelttuch nicht mehr ausreichte. Diese Kombination aus einer Seilnetzkonstruktion aus Stahlseilen mit einer lichtdurchlässigen, schwer entflammbaren Membran aus PVC-beschichtetem Polyestergewebe verwendeten Frei Otto und Rolf Gutbrod für die Konstruktion des Deutschen Pavillons auf der Weltausstellung 1967 in Montreal. Dieser Pavillon war das erste große vorgespannte Seilnetz der Welt und somit eine echte, frei gespannte textile Membrankonstruktion. Sie bestand aus acht unterschiedlich hohen Zeltspitzen, die von 14 bis 38 Meter hohen Masten unterstützt wurden, und drei innerhalb der Fläche liegenden Tiefpunkten. Dadurch entstand eine stützenfreie Überdachung in einem Raum von gigantischen Ausmaßen (ca. 8000 Quadratmeter). Diese großen Spannweiten wurden durch das Prinzip der Addition erreicht.

Eine Weiterentwicklung der Seilnetzkonstruktion des Deutschen Pavillons von Montreal sind die Zeltdächer des Olympiaparks in München, die 1972 vom Architekturbüro Behnisch & Partner unter Beratung von Frei Otto für die Olympischen Sommerspiele errichtet wurden. Die Ausmaße der Konstruktion waren allerdings weit größer als in Montreal, weshalb es anfänglich Zweifel an der Realisierbarkeit des Entwurfes gab. Das durchgehende Dach, das neben drei Sportbauten (Olympiahalle, Schwimmhalle und das halbe Olympiastadion) auch die Wege zwischen ihnen überspannt, setzt das Konzept der Landschaftsarchitektur mit ihrer sehr speziellen Topografie fort. Das 74.800 Quadratmeter messende Dach besteht aus einer an 58 Stahlmasten hängenden Seilnetzkonstruktion aus Stahlseilen, die mit ca. 3 x 3 Meter großen Acrylglastafeln verkleidet ist.[20] Die Acrylglastafeln wurden erstmals 30 Jahre später ausgetauscht.

Mit der Entwicklung hin zu großen Zeltarchitekturen wandelte sich das ursprünglich mobile Zelt zu einem permanenten

Bau. In den letzten Jahren wurden verstärkt vorgespannte Membranstrukturen für die Überdachung von Sportstadien, Ausstellungshallen und Industriebauten eingesetzt. Auf dem Gebiet der Materialien entstehen fortlaufend Neuentwicklungen, wie beispielsweise das PTFE-beschichtete Glasgewebe, das nicht brennbar oder recycelbar ist und einen hohen Selbstreinigungseffekt besitzt.[21]

## Pneumatic Structure

"That a limp membrane grows taut under wind load, changing its form, and that certain forces come into play at its edge, is one of humanity's oldest technical experiences."[22] Sailing ships, sand yachts, and parachutes, but also kites function on this principle. Free and captive balloons, which were used in initial flight experiments in the seventeenth and eighteenth centuries, are regarded as the direct forerunners of today's pneumatic constructions. The invention of the first hydrogen balloon by French physicist Alexandre César Charles was of great importance for ballooning. In its basic construction it is still the paradigm of all gas balloons today. English engineer Frederick William Lanchester had the idea of using the pneumatic principle in architecture too, for which he was awarded a patent in 1918.[23]

A lively series of developments in the area of "air-supported structures" as temporary or permanent roofing for sports centres, exhibition halls and storage depots began in the mid-twentieth century.

"Structures in which differences in pressure form the shape and ensure stabilisation or make a major contribution to these aspects are described as 'pneumatic.'[24] A compressor ensures constant pressure inside the structure. To avoid a drop in pressure, access is organised via an airlock.

Walter Bird was one of the first in the USA to construct many pneumatic domes, mainly in conical and cylindrical forms,

and he initiated the American development of pneumatic domes for radar stations, the Radomes. The highly-sensitive radar devices inside the domes could transmit radar and radio waves almost completely without resistance, due to their light skins.[25]

Radar dome, USA, 1948, Walter Bird / Radarkuppel, USA, 1948, Walter Bird

In the sixties and seventies, visions of a future life in an artificial environment with a self-sufficient climate developed. Richard Buckminster Fuller's dome for roofing over part of New York is one of the most famous utopias of pneumatic construction in architecture.[26]

Dome over Manhattan, New York, USA, Utopia, 1962, Richard Buckminster Fuller / Kuppel über Manhattan, New York, USA, Utopie, 1962, Richard Buckminster Fuller

In 1971, Frei Otto and Ewald Bubner developed the idea in a pre-investment study of a pneumatically stabilised, climate-regulating envelope with a diameter of 2,000 metres and a height of 240 metres for a city of 15,000 to 45,000 inhabitants. The transparent membrane was to be supported by a network of interlocking cables.

At the same time, countless experiments in the area of pneumatic construction by groups of architects such as Archigram, Haus-Rucker-Co and Coop Himmelb(l)au within and on the periphery of the Pop scene were attracting widespread attention. Their interest was less scientifically-

oriented than attracted by the possibility of creating "environments" themselves, using a minimum of materials and within a brief period of time.[27] Actions and Happenings designed to be "mind expanding objects" were initially held in transparent skins. These activities aimed to activate the individual's experiential abilities and trigger processes of perception and consciousness through involvement in art projects. However, these optimistic visions of the future changed at the beginning of the nineteen-seventies and architects became increasingly preoccupied with environmental problems in the context of utopian theories. The thin synthetic membrane now separated humanity from a poisoned environment, serving as a protective "skin."[28]

A pneumatic residential cell, "Oasis No. 7" – a skin of transparent PVC foil with a diameter of eight metres – was attached to the façade of the Fridericianeum in Kassel. It was entered via a gangway leading out of a window and kept in shape by an air compressor. This project by Haus-Rucker-Co for Documenta 5 posed the question of whether it would one day be necessary to keep nature preserved in a pneumatic bubble.

Oasis No. 7, Documenta 5, Kassel, Germany, 1972, Haus-Rucker-Co / Oase Nr. 7, Documenta 5, Kassel, Deutschland, 1972, Haus-Rucker-Co

Expo 1970 in Osaka, at which many pneumatic buildings were shown, was a high point in these developments. One spectacular example was the Fuji Pavilion by Yutaka Murata. Its multimembrane construction comprised sixteen curved tubes with a diameter of four metres and

a length of seventy-eight metres each whose base point described a circle with a diameter of fifty metres. The construction was held together by horizontal belts. These tubes were made of a very light tear-resistant, coated PVA-fabric and were connected to a powerful central turbo air compressor, which could react immediately to strong wind. Projections brought to life the insides of the tubes.[29]

Fuji Pavilion, Expo 1970, Osaka, Japan, Yutaka Murata / Fuji-Pavilion, Expo 1970, Osaka, Japan, Yutaka Murata

During the euphoric, forward-looking phase of those years, many firms began to experiment in the area of air-supported membranes and launched products onto the market. Air-supported halls allowed roofs costing very little per square metre to be manufactured. These developments were however partly not technically perfected, so tensions and deformations in the skin due to the internal pressure, wind, and snow loads, as well as the high amount of energy required to maintain internal pressure, led to a decrease in the implementation of this technology.[30] Pneumatic constructions are still in use as a special form of architecture to provide temporary events with a protective skin.

In recent years there have been interesting developments in the area of pneumatic cushion constructions as permanent roof or façade elements or climatic envelopes for buildings. The transparent ETFE-foil used can replace glass as a construction material for many applications, such as indoor swimming pools, recreation centres and greenhouses, due to its high levels of translucency and UV-transparency, excellent durability over time, and lightness.[31]

Notes / Anmerkungen

[1] Cp. Burkhardt, Berthold: "Zur Geschichte der Zeltarchitektur". In: Zelte. Basel 1986, p. 13, and Faegre, Torvald: Zelte. Die Architektur der Nomaden. Hamburg 1980, p. 5

[2] Bammer, Anton: Wohnen im Vergänglichen. Traditionelle Wohnformen in der Türkei und in Griechenland. Graz 1982, p. 97

[3] Cp. Andrews, A. Peter: "Schwarze Zelte und Filz-Zelte". In: Zelte. Basel 1986, pp. 26–30; Faegre, Torvald: Zelte. Die Architektur der Nomaden, pp. 13–17; Bammer, Anton: Wohnen im Vergänglichen, pp. 98–101

[4] Cp. Seiler-Baldinger, Annemarie: "Le confort sauvage. Die Vielfalt des Wohnens". In: Stoffe und Räume. Eine textile Wohngeschichte der Schweiz. Langenthal 1986, p. 11, and Old Testament, Book of Exodus, Moses, 26, 1–14

[5] Bammer, Anton: Wohnen im Vergänglichen, p. 98

[6] Cp. Andrews, A. Peter: "Schwarze Zelte und Filz-Zelte", pp. 32–35; Faegre, Torvald: Zelte. Die Architektur der Nomaden, pp. 85–91; Bammer, Anton: Wohnen im Vergänglichen, pp. 98–99

[7] Cp. Faegre, Torvald: Zelte. Die Architektur der Nomaden, pp. 103–151 and pp. 153–162,

and Bunn, Stephanie: "Mobilität und Flexibilität volkstümlicher Behausungen". In: Living in Motion. Design und Architektur für flexibles Wohnen. Ditzingen 2002, pp. 134–136 and p. 151

[8] Cp. Burkhardt, Berthold: "Zur Geschichte der Zeltarchitektur", p. 14

[9] Cp. Propyläen Kunstgeschichte. Das alte Ägypten. Frankfurt on Main 1975, p. 366

[10] Athenaios 12, 538d, according to Bammer, Anton: Wohnen im Vergänglichen, p. 97

[11] Cp. Athenaios 12, 539d–e and Athenaios 5, 196a–197c, according to Bammer, Anton: Wohnen im Vergänglichen, p. 96–97, and Burkhardt, Berthold: "Zur Geschichte der Zeltarchitektur", p. 15

[12] Cp. Burkhardt, Berthold: "Zur Geschichte der Zeltarchitektur", pp. 14–15, and Bammer, Anton: Wohnen im Vergänglichen, p. 104

[13] Burkhardt, Berthold: "Zur Geschichte der Zeltarchitektur", p. 15

[14] Cp. Seiler-Baldinger, Annemarie: "Le confort sauvage. Die Vielfalt des Wohnens", p. 11

One famous example of this is the "Eden Project" by Nicholas Grimshaw. The geodesic dome of the world's biggest greenhouse is made of highly-transparent, double-walled ETFE foil cushions. Its high levels of translucency and UV transmission of over ninety per cent are prerequisites for natural plant growth.

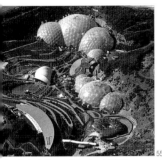

Eden Project, Cornwall, England, 1998–2001, Nicholas Grimshaw & Partners / Eden Project, Cornwall, England, 1998–2001, Nicholas Grimshaw & Partners

## Pneumatische Konstruktion

"Daß sich eine schlaffe Membran bei Windbelastung spannt, dabei ihre Form ändert und an ihrem Rand bestimmte Kräfte auftreten, dies gehört zu den ältesten technischen Erfahrungen des Menschen."[22] Segelschiffe, Segelwagen, Fallschirme, aber auch Drachen funktionieren nach diesem Prinzip. Als direkte Vorläufer heutiger pneumatischer Konstruktionen gelten Frei- und Fesselballone, mit denen im 17. und 18. Jahrhundert erste Flugversuche durchgeführt wurden. Die Erfindung des ersten Wasserstoffballons durch den französischen Physiker Alexandre César Charles war von großer Bedeutung für die Ballonfahrt. In seinem grundsätzlichen Aufbau ist er bis heute Vorbild aller Gasballons. Der englische Ingenieur Frederick William Lanchester hatte die Idee, das pneumatische Prinzip auch in der Architektur anzuwenden, worauf er 1918 ein Patent erhielt.[23]

Eine rege Entwicklung „luftgetragener Bauten" als temporäre oder dauerhafte Überdeckung von Sportzentren, Ausstellungs- oder Lagerhallen setzte Mitte des 20. Jahrhunderts ein.

„Als ‚pneumatisch' gelten solche Konstruktionen, bei denen Druckunterschiede die Formgebung und die Stabilisierung bewirken oder wesentlich dazu beitragen."[24] Für konstante Druckverhältnisse innerhalb der Konstruktion sorgt ein Gebläse. Um einen Druckabfall zu vermeiden, ist der Zugang über eine Schleuse organisiert.

In den USA konstruierte Walter Bird als einer der ersten zahlreiche pneumatische Kuppeln, hauptsächlich in Kugel- und Zylinderform. Er war der Initiator der amerikanischen Entwicklung von pneumatischen Kuppeln für Radarstationen, den Radomes. Die innerhalb der Kuppeln befindlichen hochempfindlichen Funkmessgeräte konnten aufgrund der leichten Hülle fast widerstandslos Funkstrahlen senden.[25]

In den 60er und 70er Jahren entstanden Visionen von zukünftigem Leben in künstlicher Umgebung mit autarkem Klima. Richard Buckminster Fullers Kuppel zur Überdachung eines Teils von New York gehört zu den bekanntesten Utopien pneumatischer Konstruktionen in der Architektur.[26]

1971 entwickelten Frei Otto und Ewald Bubner innerhalb einer Projektstudie die Idee einer pneumatisch stabilisierten, klimaregulierenden Hülle mit einem Durchmesser von 2000 Metern und einer Höhe von 240 Metern für eine Stadt mit 15.000 bis 45.000 Einwohnern. Die durchsichtige Membran sollte durch ein Netz sich kreuzender Seile unterstützt werden.

Zur gleichen Zeit erweckten einige Architekturgruppierungen wie Archigram, Haus-Rucker-Co und Coop Himmelb(l)au innerhalb und an der Peripherie der Popszene mit ihren zahlreichen Experimenten im Bereich der pneumatischen Konstruktionen große Aufmerksamkeit. Ihr Interesse war weniger wissenschaftlich orientiert, vielmehr begeisterte sie die Möglichkeit,

„Environments" bei minimalem Materialaufwand in kurzer Zeit selbst zu erzeugen.[27] Zunächst waren die Aktionen und Happenings in transparenten Hüllen als „mind expanding objects" angelegt. Absicht war es, die Erlebnisfähigkeit des Menschen zu aktivieren sowie Wahrnehmungs- und Bewusstseinsvorgänge durch die Teilnahme an Kunstprojekten auszulösen. Doch zu Anfang der 70er Jahre änderten sich die optimistischen Zukunftsvisionen: Nun beschäftigten sich Architekten innerhalb utopischer Theorien zunehmend mit der Umweltproblematik. Die dünne Kunststoffhülle trennte nun den Menschen von einer vergifteten Umwelt und diente als Schutzhaut.[28]

Als pneumatische Wohnzelle war die „Oase Nr. 7" – eine Hülle aus transparenter PVC-Folie mit einem Durchmesser von acht Metern – an der Außenfassade des Fridericianums in Kassel angebracht. Sie war über einen Steg von einem Fenster aus begehbar und wurde mit einem Tragluftgebläse in Form gebracht. Mit diesem Projekt stellte Haus-Rucker-Co auf der Documenta 5 die Frage, ob es eines Tages notwendig sein würde, die Natur als Konserve in einer pneumatischen Blase aufzubewahren.

Einen Höhepunkt der Entwicklung stellte die Expo 1970 in Osaka dar, auf der zahlreiche pneumatische Gebäude gezeigt wurden. Ein spektakuläres Beispiel war der Fuji-Pavillon von Yutaka Murata. Die Mehrfachmembrankonstruktion bestand aus 16 gebogenen Schläuchen mit einem Durchmesser von jeweils vier Metern und einer Länge von 78 Metern, deren Fußpunkte einen Kreis mit einem Durchmesser von 50 Metern beschrieben. Zusammengehalten wurde die Konstruktion durch horizontal verlaufende Gürtel. Die Schläuche bestanden aus einem sehr leichten und reißfesten, beschichteten PVA-Gewebe und waren an ein zentrales leistungsstarkes Turbogebläse angeschlossen, das bei

starkem Wind sofort reagieren konnte. Im Inneren wurden die Schläuche mit Projektionen bespielt.[29]

In der euphorischen, zukunftsorientierten Phase dieser Jahre begannen zahlreiche Firmen, im Bereich der luftgestützten Membranen zu experimentieren und Produkte auf den Markt zu bringen. Luftgestützte Hallen ermöglichten die Herstellung von sehr kostengünstigen Überdachungen pro Quadratmeter. Die Entwicklungen waren jedoch teilweise technisch nicht ausgereift, sodass Spannungen und Verformungen der Haut bei Innendruck, Wind und Schneebelastung sowie der hohe Energiebedarf zur Aufrechterhaltung des Innendrucks zu einem nachlassenden Einsatz dieser Technik führten.[30] Als Sonderform der Architektur werden pneumatische Konstruktionen weiterhin verwendet, um temporären Veranstaltungen eine schützende Hülle zu bieten.

In den letzten Jahren kam es zu einer interessanten Entwicklung im Bereich der pneumatischen Kissenkonstruktionen als permanentes Dach- oder Fassadenelement bzw. Klimahülle von Gebäuden. Die hierfür verwendete durchsichtige ETFE-Folie ersetzt infolge ihrer hohen Licht- und UV-Durchlässigkeit, der hervorragenden Altersbeständigkeit und Leichtigkeit bei Anwendungsbereichen wie Schwimmhallen, Erholungszentren und Gewächshäusern vielfach Glas als Baustoff.[31]

Ein bekanntes Beispiel hierfür ist das „Eden Project" von Nicholas Grimshaw. Die geodätischen Kuppeln des weltweit größten Gewächshauses wurden mit hochtransparenten, doppelwandigen ETFE-Folienkissen bestückt. Die hohe Lichtdurchlässigkeit und die UV-Transmission von über 90 Prozent sind Voraussetzung für das natürliche Pflanzenwachstum.

[15] Cp. Burkhardt, Berthold: "Zur Geschichte der Zeltarchitektur", p. 18

[16] Cp. Hoppe, Diether S.: *Freigespannte textile Membrankonstruktionen*. Vienna 2007, p. 271

[17] Cp. Burkhardt, Berthold: "Zur Geschichte der Zeltarchitektur", p. 18

[18] Cp. Burkhardt, Berthold: "Der Zeltzirkus und das IL-Zelt". In: *IL 16. Zelte*. Stuttgart 1976, and Hoppe, Diether S.: *Freigespannte textile Membrankonstruktionen.*, pp. 284–290

[19] Cp. Burkhardt, Berthold: "Zur Geschichte der Zeltarchitektur", p. 19

[20] Cp. Otto, Frei: "Mit Peter Stromeyer durch die Jahre 1953–1975". In: *IL 16. Zelte*, pp. 52–58 and pp. 60–64, and Nerdinger, Winfried (Ed.): *Frei Otto. Das Gesamtwerk. Leicht bauen, natürlich gestalten*. Basel 2005, pp. 260–269, and Hoppe, Diether S.: *Freigespannte textile Membrankonstruktionen.*, pp. 308–310

[21] Cp. Bubner, Ewald: "Der Membranbau". In: *Deutsche Bauzeitschrift*, Issue 4/2003

[22] Herzog, Thomas: *Pneumatische Konstruktionen. Bauten aus Membranen und Luft*. Stuttgart 1976, p. 30

[23] Cp. Herzog, Thomas: *Pneumatische Konstruktionen*, p. 30–36, and Otto, Frei (Ed.): *Zugbeanspruchte Konstruktionen*. Berlin 1962, pp. 10–35

[24] Otto, Frei (Ed.): *Zugbeanspruchte Konstruktionen*, p. 10

[25] Cp. Otto, Frei (Ed.): *Zugbeanspruchte Konstruktionen*, p. 10 and p. 2

[26] Cp. Hoppe, Diether S.: *Freigespannte textile Membrankonstruktionen*, p. 107

[27] Cp. Herzog, Thomas: *Pneumatische Konstruktionen*, p. 7 and p. 115

[28] Cp. Koch, Klaus-Michael (Ed.): *Bauen mit Membranen*, pp. 44–45

[29] Cp. Herzog, Thomas: *Pneumatische Konstruktionen*, p. 76 and p. 85

[30] Cp. Otto, Frei: "Mit Peter Stromeyer durch die Jahre 1953–1975", p. 44

[31] Cp. Gengnagel, Christoph: "Membranbau". In: *db deutsche bauzeitung*, Issue 2/2005, and Bubner, Ewald: "Der Membranbau"

Three-dimensional Space Definer
*Dreidimensionaler Raumabschluss*

# CONSTRUCTION & FUNCTION
## *KONSTRUKTION & FUNKTION*

Tent
*Zelt*

Pneumatic Structure
*Pneumatische Konstruktion*

Three-dimensional Space Definer
*Dreidimensionaler Raumabschluss*

TENT
*ZELT*

Tent *Its simple structural principle – a supporting structure spanned with a textile tent skin – means that there is a huge variety of tents available from dome, cone, serial, and frame tents through membrane-spanned supporting structures to self-supporting textile membrane structures. Since tents can be transported easily and can be set up and taken down with little effort, they are commonly used for temporary weather protection, accommodation, and as venues. The tents used by nomads are special; they are used for permanent yet mobile dwelling and are always taken along when their inhabitants move. Apart from mobile tents, there also exist tent constructions that, although light and flexible, are made for permanent installation in fixed places. These are tensile and membrane structures in which the membrane is guyed using masts and guy wires. Additional masts allow them to be extended to cover large arenas or exhibition areas.*

*Zelt Sein einfaches Konstruktionsprinzip – ein Tragegerüst mit einer darüber gespannten textilen Zelthaut – lässt eine enorme Bandbreite an Variationen zu – vom Kuppel-, Kegel-, Reihen- und Rahmenzelt über membranbespannte Tragegerüste bis zu freigespannten, textilen Membrankonstruktionen. Da das Zelt leicht zu transportieren und einfach auf- und abzubauen ist, wird es überall dort eingesetzt, wo als Schutz vor der Witterung temporär eine Unterkunft oder ein Veranstaltungsort benötigt wird. Eine Besonderheit sind die Zelte der Nomaden, die als permanente, aber mobile Behausung genutzt und ständig mitgenommen werden. Neben den mobilen Zelten gibt es auch Zeltkonstruktionen, denen zwar ebenfalls der Charakter des Flexiblen und Leichten innewohnt, die jedoch für den dauerhaften Einsatz an einem fixen Ort bestimmt sind. Es handelt sich dabei um Seilnetz- und Membrankonstruktionen, bei denen die Membran mittels Masten und Seilen frei abgespannt ist. Durch Addition mehrerer Masten wird die Überdachung großer Arenen oder Ausstellungsflächen erreicht.*

"Make It Right – Pink Project," New Orleans,
USA, 2007, initiated and designed by **Brad Pitt**
in collaboration with **Graft.**
*Make It Right – Pink Project", New Orleans,*
*USA 2007, initiiert und entworfen von **Brad Pitt***
*in Zusammenarbeit mit **Graft.***

TENT / temporary
*ZELT / temporär*

Fresco of the recapture of Palma de
Mallorca, Spain, thirteenth century
Fresko der Rückeroberung Palma de
Mallorcas, Spanien, 13. Jahrhundert

Yurt, Sarytash, Kyrgyzstan, 2008
Jurte, Sarytash, Kirgistan, 2008

"Tent Village," 2001/"The Tent Village Revisited," 2007,
**Studio Dré Wapenaar**
Individual modules with public and private areas have been
combined on different levels to form a tent village, thus creat-
ing their own microcosm. One of the "Tent Villages" built
in 2001 was remodelled in 2007 to become a "Tent Village
Revisited" and can be rented for temporary events.
„Tentvillage", 2001/„The Tentvillage-Revisited", 2007,
**Studio Dré Wapenaar**
Auf verschiedenen Ebenen werden einzelne Module mit öffentlichen und privaten Bereichen zu einem Zeltdorf zusammen-
gefügt und bilden einen eigenen Mikrokosmos. Eins der 2001
entstandenen „Tentvillages" wurde 2007 zu einem „Tentvillage-
Revisited" umgebaut und kann für temporäre Veranstaltungen
gemietet werden.

"Yurta," Canada, 2005, **Bakerygroup/Padlewski Szeto Inc.**
"Yurta" is an easily transportable and erectable tent that provides accommodation in the Canadian wilderness during the tourist season. Its role model was the yurt of the Asian nomads whose structure was reinterpreted and reduced to an absolute minimum to make it portable. A "Yurta" can be erected by two people without extra tools within thirty minutes. The supporting structure of ash wood is furnished with a waterproof outside skin of acrylic-coated polyester and an insulation layer of flame-resistant wool felt, as well as a side covering of air-permeable cotton canvas.

„Yurta", Kanada, 2005, **Bakerygroup/Padlewski Szeto Inc.**
„Yurta" ist ein leicht zu transportierendes und aufzubauendes Zelt, das während der Touristensaison eine Herberge in der kanadischen Wildnis bietet. Vorbild war die Jurte der asiatischen Nomaden, deren Struktur neu interpretiert und bis auf das Notwendigste reduziert wurde, um sie wirklich tragbar zu machen. „Yurta" lässt sich von zwei Personen ohne zusätzliche Hilfsmittel innerhalb von 30 Minuten aufstellen. Das Tragegerüst aus Eschenholz wird mit einer Kuppel aus Acryl-beschichtetem Polyester als wasserdichte Außenhaut und mit einer Isolierung aus schwer entflammbarem Wollfilz sowie einer seitlichen Abdeckung aus luftdurchlässigem Baumwollzelttuch versehen.

TENT / temporary
ZELT / temporär

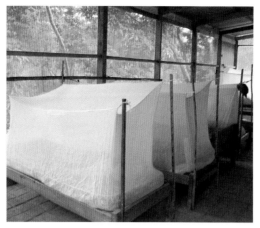

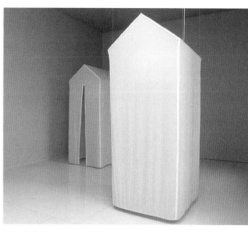

Mosquito nets, near Rurrenabaque, Bolivia, 2004
Moskitonetze, in der Nähe von Rurrenabaque, Bolivien, 2004

"Stille Örtchen" (Quiet Little Places), exhibition projects, 2001–2006, **Fremdkörper Designstudio – Andrea Mehlhose & Martin Wellner**
„Stille Örtchen", Ausstellungsprojekt 2001–2006, **Fremdkörper Designstudio – Andrea Mehlhose & Martin Wellner.**

"The Stitch Room," Installation in the collective exhibition "MyHome," Vitra Design Museum, Weil am Rhein, Germany, 2007, **Ronan & Erwan Bouroullec**
„The Stitch Room", Installation in der Gemeinschaftsausstellung „MyHome", Vitra Design Museum, Weil am Rhein, Deutschland, 2007, **Ronan & Erwan Bouroullec**

Military tent, Ladakh, India, 2007
Militärzelt, Ladakh, Indien, 2007

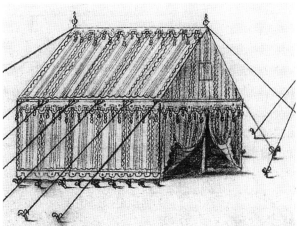

Long tent from the *Décoration intérieure et jardins de Versailles* album, eighteenth century
Langzelt aus dem Album *Décoration intérieure et jardins de Versailles*, 18. Jahrhundert

Accommodation for homeless people, Tokyo, Japan, 2002
Obdachlosenunterkunft, Tokio, Japan, 2002

TENT / temporary
*ZELT / temporär*

"The Pink Project – Make It Right", New Orleans, USA, 2007–2008, initiated and designed by **Brad Pitt** – in conjunction with **Graft**
"The Pink Project" by Brad Pitt in collaboration with Graft was launched as the kick-off event to the "Make It Right" initiative to collect donations for the reconstruction of living spaces destroyed by Hurricane Katrina in New Orleans. The five-week installation extended over fourteen blocks and demonstrated the devastation of Lower Ninth Ward through 427 apparently randomly scattered elements. The individual elements served as placeholders for later construction. As soon as enough donations had been collected to erect a house, some of the elements were combined to form a symbolic house. The success of the fund-raising campaign could thus be read from the houses erected.
„The Pink Project – Make It Right", New Orleans, USA, 2007–2008, initiiert und entworfen von **Brad Pitt** – in Zusammenarbeit mit **Graft**
Als Auftaktveranstaltung der „Make It Right"-Initiative wurde „The Pink Project" von Brad Pitt zusammen mit Graft ins Leben gerufen, um Spenden für den Wiederaufbau des durch den Hurrikan Katrina zerstörten Wohnraums in New Orleans zu sammeln. Die fünfwöchige Installation erstreckte sich über 14 Blocks und führte durch 427 scheinbar willkürlich verstreute Elemente die Verwüstung des Lower Ninth Ward vor Augen. Die einzelnen Elemente dienten als Platzhalter für eine spätere Bebauung. Sobald genug Spenden zur Errichtung eines Gebäudes zusammengekommen waren, wurden einige der Elemente zu einem symbolischen Haus zusammengesetzt. So konnte der Erfolg der Spendenaktion an den errichteten Häusern abgelesen werden.

"Treetents," The Netherlands, 1998 – Remake 2005, **Studio Dré Wapenaar**
The "Treetents" were originally developed as a fictive project for a group of English environmental activists who chained themselves to trees that were to fall victim to motorway construction. The tents were intended to give the activists, who lived in the treetops, a pleasant sanctuary over the forest floor. Three "Treetents" have been hanging as holiday accommodation in the trees of a campsite in The Netherlands since 1998. Since 2005, Dré Wapenaar has been producing a new series of tents for use at temporary events.
„Treetents", Niederlande, 1998 – Neuauflage 2005, **Studio Dré Wapenaar**
Als fiktives Projekt wurden die „Treetents" ursprünglich für eine Gruppe englischer Umweltaktivisten entwickelt, die sich an Bäume ketteten, die dem Bau von Autobahnen zum Opfer fallen sollten. Die Zelte sollten für die in den Baumkronen lebenden Aktivisten einen angenehmen Unterschlupf über dem Waldboden ermöglichen. Als Urlaubsdomizil hängen drei „Treetents" seit 1998 an den Bäumen eines Campingplatzes in den Niederlanden. Seit 2005 produziert Dré Wapenaar eine neue Serie von Zelten, die bei temporären Veranstaltungen zum Einsatz kommen.

"Dream House," Huesca, Spain, 2004, **ex.studio.**
**Patricia Meneses + Iván Juárez**
The glowing cocoon "Dream House" hangs from a
treetop as a sanctuary for self-reflection.
„Dream House", Huesca, Spanien, 2004, **ex.studio.**
**Patricia Meneses + Iván Juárez**
Als Zufluchtsort zur Selbstreflexion hängt der leuch-
tende Kokon „Dream House" in einer Baumkrone.

"CampingFlat," various places in The Netherlands and in
Belgium, 2003, **Kevin van Braak**
"CampingFlat" – a campsite on four floors of a scaffolding, veiled in green netting – seems like an all-inclusive
package for the spoiled camper. However, it is all an
illusion: synthetic lawn, plastic fire, and the singing of the
birds comes from loudspeakers. Danger is reduced to a
minimum as is the adventure of the camper.
„CampingFlat", verschiedene Orte in den Niederlanden
und in Belgien, 2003, **Kevin van Braak**
„CampingFlat" – ein Campingplatz auf vier Etagen eines
mit grünem Netz verhüllten Baugerüstes – erscheint wie
ein Komplettpaket für den verwöhnten Camper. Jedoch ist
alles nur Illusion: künstlicher Rasen, Plastikfeuer und das
Vogelzwitschern kommt aus Lautsprechern. Die Gefahr
ist bis auf ein Minimum reduziert und somit auch das
Abenteuer des Campers.

TENT / temporary
ZELT / temporär

Ford "Model-T," USA, Early twentieth century
Ford „T-Model", USA, Anfang 20. Jahrhundert

"Soft Clinic," 2002, **Bakerygroup/Padlewski Szeto Inc.**
When closed, this plywood trailer harbours a foldable structure
made of bamboo poles and a skin of polyethylene foil. Two
sides of the trailer can simply be folded out to form the floor of
the rooms above it.
„Soft Clinic", 2002, **Bakerygroup/Padlewski Szeto Inc.**
Im geschlossenen Zustand beherbergt der Anhänger aus
Sperrholz die faltbare Konstruktion aus Bambusstangen und
einer Hülle aus Polyethylenfolie. Zwei Seiten des Anhängers
lassen sich einfach herunterklappen und bilden so den Boden
der darüber liegenden Räume.

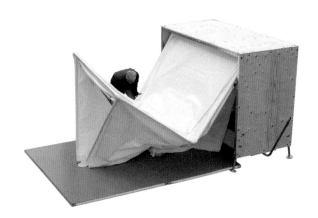

"Markies," 1986–1995, **Eduard Böhtlingk**

Once the destination has been reached, this mobile holiday home unfolds automatically, trebling in floor area. The living area is enclosed by a PVC awning which can be rolled in if the weather is good, so that the area can also be used as a terrace. The sleeping area is created by rolling down an opaque awning made of polyester/cotton fabric. The kitchen, dining room and bathroom are located inside the main mobile home.

„Markies", 1986–1995, **Eduard Böhtlingk**

Am Reiseziel angekommen, entfaltet sich das mobile Ferienhaus automatisch und verdreifacht seine Grundfläche. Der Wohnzimmerbereich ist von einer transparenten Markise aus PVC umgeben, die bei gutem Wetter hochgefahren werden kann, sodass dieser Teil auch als Terrasse nutzbar ist. Der Schlafbereich entsteht durch das Herunterfahren einer blickdichten Markise aus einem Polyester-/Baumwollgewebe. Die Küche, das Esszimmer und das Bad befinden sich im Inneren des zentralen Wohnwagens.

TENT / temporary
ZELT / temporär

"ideal house cologne," International Furniture Fair, Cologne, Germany, 2005, **Patricia Urquiola**
A textile skin of a sort of macro-macramé forms the outer limits of the frame of the "ideal house cologne."
„ideal house cologne", Internationale Möbelmesse, Köln, Deutschland, 2005, **Patricia Urquiola**
Eine textile Haut aus einer Art Makro-Makramee bekleidete als äußere Begrenzung das Gerüst des „ideal house cologne".

"1001 mètres," workshop by Sevil Peach 2008, sponsored by Kvadrat, Boisbuchet, France
„1001 mètres", Workshop von Sevil Peach 2008, gefördert durch Kvadrat, Boisbuchet, Frankreich

"Bar in the Academy Garden," Munich, 1999, **für alle gestaltung, Frédérique Desvaux** in collaboration with **Matthias Gindhart**
A pavilion comprising a construction of scaffolding components and plastic foil was erected in the garden of the Akademie der Bildenden Künste for the duration of its annual exhibition. The bar activity inside could be distinguished from outside at night due to the translucent skin.

„Bar im Akademiegarten", München, 1999, **für alle gestaltung, Frédérique Desvaux** in Zusammenarbeit mit **Matthias Gindhart**
Im Garten der Akademie der Bildenden Künste wurde für die Dauer der Jahresausstellung ein Pavillon, bestehend aus einer Konstruktion aus Gerüstbauteilen und Kunststofffolie, aufgestellt. Nachts war der im Innenraum stattfindende Barbetrieb aufgrund der transluzenten Haut von außen ablesbar.

TENT / temporary

ZELT / temporär

"Aux arbres, citoyens," Nantes, France, 2003–2006,
**Tetrarc and Concept Plastique**
The mobile tent provided weather protection at various
citizen's meetings in different districts of Nantes. Its
mobility was guaranteed by the supporting structure
– a giant oak – which could be disassembled into individual parts. A circular metal structure lay on top of it;
was covered by an inflatable lens made of transparent
PVC. The sides of the tent were closed by a film.
"Aux arbres, citoyens", Nantes, Frankreich, 2003–
2006, **Tetrarc und Concept Plastique**
Während diverser Bürgerzusammenkünfte in verschie
denen Stadtteilen von Nantes bot das Wanderzelt
Schutz vor der Witterung. Die Mobilität wurde durch
eine in Einzelteile zerlegbare Tragkonstruktion – eine
riesige Eiche – gewährleistet. Darauf lagerte eine
kreisförmige Metallkonstruktion, die horizontal mit eine
aufblasbaren Linse aus transparentem PVC bedeckt
war. Die Seiten des Zeltes wurden durch eine Folie
geschlossen.

Temporary building at the graduation festival
of the Faculty of Architecture of the **RWTH
Aachen**, Germany, 2004
Temporäre Bauten auf dem Diplomfest der
Fakultät für Architektur der **RWTH Aachen**,
Deutschland, 2004

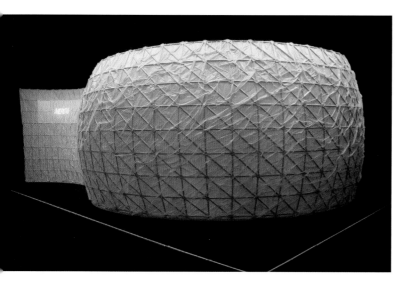

"Nautilus" fair stand of the Mero company, Euroshop
2002, Dusseldorf, Germany, **Werner Sobek**
The existing pole/node system by Werner Sobek
Design was further developed to form a single-layered
shell structure of arbitrary spatial curvature. A plastic
foil was applied to the wall shell on both sides and
then made shape-retaining by creating a vacuum.
The folds that were intentionally created during that
process characterise the texture of its translucent
surface.
Messestand „Nautilus" der Firma Mero, Euroshop
2002, Düsseldorf, Deutschland, **Werner Sobek**
Für den Messeauftritt wurde das bestehende Stab-/
Knotensystem durch Werner Sobek Design zu
einer einlagigen Schalenkonstruktion mit beliebiger
räumlicher Krümmung weiterentwickelt. Über die
Wandschale wurde beidseitig eine Kunststofffolie
aufgebracht, die anschließend durch Erzeugung eines
Vakuums formstabilisiert wurde. Die dabei gezielt
erzeugten Falten prägen die spezifische Textur der
transluzenten Oberfläche.

TENT / permanent
*ZELT / permanent*

Wolfgang Meyer Sports Complex, Hamburg, Germany, 1994,
**Schlaich Bergermann and Partners**
A tensile membrane construction was chosen for the roof
covering of an existing ice-skating and racing bike track. The
delicate supporting structure made of four main masts and
eight flying struts, which are tensioned by interior cables, is
ultimately spanned by a thin membrane made of polyester
fabric anchored to the foundations by cables from the edges.
Apart from acting as a space-closing skin, the membrane is
also part of the primary load-bearing structure.
Wolfgang-Meyer-Sportanlage, Hamburg, Deutschland, 1994,
**Schlaich Bergermann und Partner**
Für die Überdachung der bestehenden Kunsteis- und Rad-
rennbahn wurde eine vorgespannte Membrankonstruktion
gewählt. Die zierliche Tragstruktur aus vier Hauptstützen
und acht seilunterspannten Luftstützen wird lediglich von
einer dünnen Membran aus transluzentem Polyestergewebe
überspannt, die zum Rand hin mit Seilen an Fundamenten
verankert ist. Die Membran ist nicht nur raumabschließende
Hülle, sondern Teil der tragenden Primärstruktur.

Campus Centre, University of La Verne, USA,
1974, **The Shaver Partnership**
A 5,600 square-metre space for use as a sports
hall has been roofed over by combining four cone
tents, each with a central mast, and a ring suspension. Teflon-coated fibreglass fabric was used
as a membrane for the first time ever here.
Campus Center, University of La Verne, USA,
1974, **The Shaver Partnership**
Durch die Addition von vier Kegelzelten mit jeweils
einem Zentralmast und einer Ringabhängung
wurde ein Raum von 5600 Quadratmetern für die
Nutzung als Sporthalle überdeckt. Als Membran
wurde erstmals teflonbeschichtetes Glasfasergewebe verwendet.

German pavilion at the 1967 World Fair, Montreal, Canada, **Frei Otto and Rolf Gutbrod**
Deutscher Pavillon auf der Weltausstellung 1967, Montreal, Kanada, **Frei Otto und Rolf Gutbrod**

Olympic Stadium, Olympic Park Munich, Germany, 1972, **Behnisch & Partners, Frei Otto, Leonhardt + Andrä**
Olympiastadion, Olympiapark München, Deutschland, 1972, **Behnisch & Partner, Frei Otto, Leonhardt + Andrä**

King Fahd International Stadium, Riad, Saudi Arabia, 1984, **Ian Fraser Associates with John Roberts and Schlaich Bergermann and Partners**
PTFE fibre-glass membrane roof suspended from cables and cable masts
King Fahd Internationales Stadion, Riad, Saudi-Arabien, 1984, **Ian Fraser Associates mit John Roberts und Schlaich Bergermann und Partner**
An Seilen und Seilmasten aufgehängtes PTFE-Glasfaser-Membrandach

Three-dimensional Space Definer
*Dreidimensionaler Raumabschluss*

PNEUMATIC STRUCTURE
*PNEUMATISCHE KONSTRUKTION*

Pneumatic Structure *Spherical shapes, domes, double domes, cylinders, ring tubes, and more; pneumatic structures come in a wide variety of shapes and sizes. They are based on the tyre principle such that the membrane covering is also the supporting element. Differences in pressure between inside and outside stabilise the structure. A fan ensures that the inside pressure remains constant while the entrance usually incorporates a mantrap to avoid drops in pressure. From the nineteen-fifties to the nineteen-seventies, pneumatic structures were* *increasingly used to temporarily or permanently cover sports centres, exhibition halls and warehouses. These days, they often function as temporary envelopes for public events. Permanent buildings with façades made of inflatable foil panels represent a special application of pneumatics. They have a membrane double-skin façade, which, as a thermal buffer zone, can react to changing outside temperatures, thus contributing to energy savings.*

Pneumatische Konstruktion *Kugelformen, Kuppeln, Doppelkuppeln, Zylinder, Ringschläuche und mehr: Die pneumatische Konstruktion erlaubt eine große Formenvielfalt. Sie basiert auf dem Prinzip des Pneus, wobei die Membranhülle gleichzeitig Trageelement ist. Die Druckunterschiede zwischen innen und außen bewirken die Stabilisierung der Form. Für konstante Druckverhältnisse innerhalb der Konstruktion sorgt ein Gebläse. Um einen Druckabfall zu vermeiden, ist der Zugang über eine Schleuse organisiert. In den fünfziger bis siebziger Jahren* *des 20. Jahrhunderts wurden pneumatische Konstruktionen vermehrt als temporäre oder dauerhafte Überdachung von Sportzentren, Ausstellungs- oder Lagerhallen verwendet. Heute werden sie oftmals als temporäre Hülle von Veranstaltungen im öffentlichen Raum eingesetzt. Eine Sonderform sind die Fassaden dauerhafter Gebäude aus aufblasbaren Folienkissen, die als Membran-Doppelfassade konstruiert sind um als thermische Pufferzone auf wechselndes Außenklima reagieren und dazu beitragen zu können, Energiekosten einzusparen.*

"Küchenmonument," (Kitchen Monument),
2006–2007, **raumlaborberlin and
Plastique Fantastique**
*"Küchenmonument", 2006–2007,
raumlaborberlin und Plastique Fantastique*

PNEUMATIC STRUCTURE / temporary
PNEUMATISCHE KONSTRUKTION / temporär

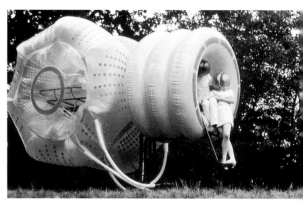

"Gelbes Herz" (Yellow Heart), Vienna, Austria, 1968,
**Haus-Rucker-Co**
The pneumatic construction consisting of a PVC foil rhythmically
increased and decreased in size as a result of the corresponding
control of a ventilation unit.
„Gelbes Herz", Wien, Österreich, 1968, **Haus-Rucker-Co**
Die aus einer PVC-Folie bestehende pneumatische Konstruktion
vergrößerte und verkleinerte sich in rhythmischer Form durch eine
entsprechende Steuerung des Luftaggregats.

"Ballon für Zwei" (Balloon for Two), Vienna, Austria, 1967,
**Haus-Rucker-Co**
A large, shapeless, crumpled plastic skin was pushed
out of a window of the building at Apollogasse 3 during
an action by Haus-Rucker-Co. It unfolded through the
window opening onto the street into a walk-in balloon with
a diameter of approximately 3.5 metres.
„Ballon für Zwei", Wien, Österreich, 1967, **Haus-Rucker-Co**
Während einer Aktion von Haus-Rucker-Co schob sich
eine große, unförmig zerknitterte Kunststoffhülle aus
einem Fenster des Hauses Apollogasse 3. Durch die
Fensteröffnung hindurch entfaltete sie sich im Straßenraum zu einem begehbaren Ballon von etwa 3,5 Metern
Durchmesser.

Tor Strasse 166 – "Space Invaders," Berlin, Germany, 2008,
**Plastique Fantastique & Sound and Experience Design**
An empty building in Berlin-Mitte – Tor Strasse 166: new
volumes were inflated by pressure and sound waves.
Torstraße 166 – „Space Invaders", Berlin, Deutschland, 2008,
**Plastique Fantastique & Sound and Experience Design**
Ein leeres Haus in Berlin-Mitte – die Torstraße 166: mit Druck-
und Soundwellen wurden neue Volumina aufgeblasen.

"paraSITE," long-term project, USA, since 1998,
**Michael Rakowitz**
"paraSITE" is an ongoing project that offers individual inflatable accommodation made of provisional materials such as plastic bags and sticky tape to homeless people in various cities in the USA. The pneumatic structures are attached via a tube to extractor air ducts of air conditioning systems, which inflate and heat the double-membrane structures. This temporary accommodation also attracts public attention to the problem of homelessness.

„paraSITE", Langzeitprojekt, USA, seit 1998,
**Michael Rakowitz**
„paraSITE" ist ein fortlaufendes Projekt, das Obdachlosen in verschiedenen Städten der USA individuelle, aufblasbare Behausungen aus provisorischen Materialien wie Plastiktüten und Klebeband anbietet. Die pneumatischen Strukturen werden jeweils mit einem Schlauch an Abluftdurchlässen von Klimaanlagen angebracht, wodurch sie sich aufrichten und die Doppelmembranstrukturen erwärmt werden. Gleichzeitig machen die temporären Unterkünfte in der öffentlichen Wahrnehmung auf das Problem der Obdachlosigkeit aufmerksam.

PNEUMATIC STRUCTURE / temporary
PNEUMATISCHE KONSTRUKTION / temporär

Fuji Pavilion, Expo 1970, Osaka, Japan,
**Yutaka Murata**
Fuji-Pavillon, Expo 1970, Osaka, Japan,
**Yutaka Murata**

Tea House for the Museum of Applied Art Frankfurt, Germany, 2007–ongoing, **Kengo Kuma**
On special occasions the skin of the teahouse is filled with air by a compressor system. The double-walled membrane of a semi-transparent PTFE fibre fabric creates a golf-ball-like texture, and makes an air lock unnecessary. Integrated LED technology makes the teahouse glow in the dark. The outer skin can be heated by warm air when outside temperatures drop.
Teehaus für das Museum für Angewandte Kunst, Frankfurt, Deutschland, 2007–jetzt, **Kengo Kuma**
Zu besonderen Anlässen wird die Hülle des Teehauses durch ein Kompressorsystem mit Luft gefüllt. Die doppelwandige Membran aus einem semitransparenten PTFE-Fasergewebe erzeugt eine golfballähnliche Textur und macht zudem eine Luftschleuse überflüssig. Eine integrierte LED-Technik lässt das Teehaus im Dunklen sanft erstrahlen. Bei kalten Temperaturen ist eine Beheizung der Außenhülle mit Warmluft möglich.

Castilla, Castilla-La Mancha, Spain, 2007,
**Plastique Fantastique**
The "Castilla" pneumatic structure was conceived for the
"New Technologies" mobile exhibition. Two bubbles made of
polyethylene and aluminium compound foil were connected
by two parallel tunnels. The entrance was located in one of the
tunnels. Axial high-performance ventilators created overpres-
sure inside within a very short period of time, thus stabilising
the shape of this spatial object.

Castilla, Kastilien-La Mancha, Spanien, 2007,
**Plastique Fantastique**
Konzipiert wurde die pneumatische Struktur „Castilla" für die
Wanderausstellung „Neue Technologie". Zwei Blasen aus
Polyethylen- und Aluverbundfolie wurden durch zwei parallele
Tunnel verbunden, wobei sich in einem dieser Verbindungstun-
nel der Eingang befand. Axial-Hochleistungsventilatoren, die
innerhalb kürzester Zeit einen Überdruck im Inneren erzeugten,
sorgten für die Formstabilität der Raumobjekte.

"Karl Marx Bonsai – Der Blumentopf" (Karl Marx Bonsai – The
Flower Pot), Berlin, Germany, 2008, **Plastique Fantastique &
Sound and Experience Design**
As an intervention in public space, the area around the trunk of a
tree was temporarily livened up with a walk-in pneumatic structure
made of plastic foil. Loud sounds made the skin vibrate and thus
acted as an airy loudspeaker.

„Karl Marx Bonsai – Der Blumentopf", Berlin, Deutschland, 2008,
**Plastique Fantastique & Sound and Experience Design**
Als Eingriff in den öffentlichen Raum wurde der Platz um einen
Baumstamm temporär mit einer begehbaren pneumatischen
Struktur aus Kunststofffolie bespielt. Von Geräuschen beschallt,
wurde die Hülle zum Vibrieren gebracht und fungierte wie eine
luftige Lautsprecherbox.

PNEUMATIC STRUCTURE / temporary
*PNEUMATISCHE KONSTRUKTION / temporär*

SPD advertising pavilion, Berlin, Germany, 1962,
**L. Stromeyer & Co. GmbH**
Werbepavillon der SPD, Berlin, Deutschland, 1962,
**L. Stromeyer & Co. GmbH**

"Küchenmonument" (Kitchen Monument), 2006–
2007, **raumlaborberlin and Plastique Fantastique**
The "Küchenmonument" travelled to various European cities to create a place for temporary collectives.
A box harboured the pneumatic structure and the technology required to blow it up, also functioning as the entrance to the bubble. A skin of translucent fibre-reinforced PE foil unfolded from the box. A ventilator inflated the structure and then continued to supply air to it. The bubble nestled into the already existing objects and created a space that permitted dialogue between inside and outside as a result of its transparency.
"Küchenmonument", 2006–2007, **raumlaborberlin und Plastique Fantastique**
Um im öffentlichen Raum einen Ort für temporäre Gemeinschaften zu schaffen, reiste das „Küchenmonument" in verschiedene europäische Städte. Eine Box beherbergte die pneumatische Struktur sowie die Technik zum Aufblasen und fungierte als Eingangsraum in die Blase. Aus dieser Box heraus entfaltete sich eine Hülle aus einer transluzenten, faserverstärkten PE-Folie. Ein Ventilator blies zunächst die Struktur vollständig auf und führte danach kontinuierlich Luft zu. Die Blase schmiegte sich an das Vorhandene an und stellte einen Raum dar, der durch seine Transparenz den Dialog zwischen innen und außen zuließ.

"Sternenschleifer," "Steirischer Herbst 2006," Austria,
**raumlaborberlin**
As a mobile planetarium, the "Sternenschleifer" took part
in an international art festival. Star constellations were
projected into the silver pneumatic dome made of double-
layered vapour barrier foil.
„Sternenschleifer", „Steirischer Herbst 2006", Österreich,
**raumlaborberlin**
Als mobiles Planetarium nahm der „Sternenschleifer"
an dem internationalen Kunstfestival teil. In die silberne,
pneumatische Kuppel aus zweischichtiger Dampfsperrfolie
wurden Sternenkonstellationen projiziert.

American Pavilion, World Fair in Osaka, Japan, 1970,
**Davis – Brody; de Harak, Chermayeff & Geismar**
A 142-metre-long and eighty-three-metre-wide oval
shape was spanned with an air-supported, stepped
membrane of fibre glass fabric which was fixed by a
net of diagonally spanned cables.
Amerikanischer Pavillon, Weltausstellung in
Osaka, Japan, 1970, **Davis – Brody; de Harak,
Chermayeff & Geismar**
Ein Oval von 142 Metern Länge und 83 Metern Breite
wurde mit einer luftgestützten, steppdeckenartig
strukturierten Membran aus Glasfasergewebe über-
spannt, die durch ein Netz aus diagonal gespannten
Seilen gesichert wurde.

Roofing over Swimming Pool, Cannes, France, 1965, **Roger Taillibert**
The Montfleury Hotel swimming pool was the first pool in Europe to be
covered by a pneumatic roof. The membrane, made of white PVC-coated
polyester fabric, covered an area of 24 x 48 metres.
Schwimmbadüberdachung, Cannes, Frankreich, 1965, **Roger Taillibert**
Das Hotelschwimmbad Montfleury war das erste Bad in Europa unter
einem Pneu. Die Membran aus weißem Polyestergewebe mit PVC-Beschichtung überdachte eine Fläche von 24 x 48 Metern.

First air-supported Radome, Cornell University Aerospace
Laboratory, Buffalo, USA, 1948, **Walter Bird**
Erster luftgestützter Radome, Raumfahrtlabor der Cornell-
Universität, Buffalo, USA, 1948, **Walter Bird**

# PNEUMATIC STRUCTURE / permanent
*PNEUMATISCHE KONSTRUKTION / permanent*

"Eden Project," Cornwall, England, 1998–2001,
**Nicholas Grimshaw & Partners**
The intersecting geodetic domes of this climatic skin for plants
is equipped with highly-transparent, double-walled ETFE foil
cushions. They are kept under constant pressure by ventilators that also keep them in shape. The high UV-permeability
of the recyclable ETFE foil is not only of advantage to plant
growth, it also reduces heating costs for the climatic zone that
must be heated to reach tropical temperatures.
„Eden Project", Cornwall, England, 1998–2001,
**Nicholas Grimshaw & Partners**
Die miteinander verschnittenen, geodätischen Kuppeln der Klimahülle für Pflanzen sind mit hochtransparenten, doppelwandigen ETFE-Folienkissen bestückt. Durch Ventilatoren werden
sie unter konstantem Druck und somit formstabil gehalten.
Die hohe Durchlässigkeit der recycelbaren ETFE-Folie für UV-
Strahlung kommt nicht nur dem Pflanzenwachstum zugute,
sondern reduziert auch die Heizkosten für die auf Tropentem-
peraturen erwärmten Klimazonen.

Allianz Arena, Munich, Germany, 2001–2005,
**Herzog & de Meuron**
As a transformable glowing volume, this football
stadium is a landmark of the area to the north of
Munich. Its skin is made of approximately 2,800
shimmering, diamond-shaped ETFE cushions.
Their translucency means that the playing field is
not overshadowed, allowing the grass to grow
better. The colour of the foil cushions can be
changed using a computer-controlled lighting
circuit so that the identity of the home team
always remains legible, in correspondence to the
current match situation. The cushion façade is
supported by a steel roof structure that is barely
visible from the outside.

Allianz Arena, München, Deutschland, 2001–
2005, **Herzog & de Meuron**
Als wandlungsfähiger Leuchtkörper markiert
das Fußballstadion den Ort im Norden von
München. Seine Haut besteht aus etwa 2800
weiß schimmernden, rautenförmigen ETFE-Kis-
sen. Dank ihrer Lichtdurchlässigkeit führen sie
zu einer geringen Verschattung des Spielfelds
und damit zu einem guten Rasenwachstum.
Die Folienkissen können mittels einer computer-
gesteuerten Lichtschaltung ihre Farbe ändern.
Auf diese Weise ist je nach Spielsituation die
Identität der Heimmannschaft von außen ablesbar. Gehalten wird die Kissenfassade von einem
Dachtragwerk aus Stahl, das äußerlich kaum
sichtbar ist.

Three-dimensional Space Definer
*Dreidimensionaler Raumabschluss*

CURRENT PROJECTS
*AKTUELLE PROJEKTE*

MICHAEL RAKOWITZ,
STUDIO DRÉ WAPENAAR,
PLEINMUSEUM FOUNDATION,
AMO,
R & SIE(N),
FAR,
RAUMLABORBERLIN,
REM KOOLHAAS AND CECIL BALMOND,
CSCEC + PTW + CCDI AND ARUP.

MICHAEL RAKOWITZ
(P)LOT: Propositions I, 2004–ongoing
(P)LOT: Propositions I, 2004–jetzt

(P)LOT questions the occupation and assignment of public space in different cities, encouraging active participation in urban life. Rather than parking cars in the spaces along streets, (P)LOT suggests renting those places for alternative uses. By buying a resident's permit or throwing coins into a parking metre, residents can establish a temporary encampment or they can use such spaces for diverse activities like making a temporary garden or dining out of doors. A first initiative for the appropriation of public space was the transformation of normal car bodies into portable tents that could be used as living or leisure space. Weatherproof "vehicle protective coverings" made of PVC tarpaulin and tent poles could be made to look like a mid-range or luxury car as desired.

(P)LOT hinterfragt in verschiedenen Städten die Besetzung und Überlassung des öffentlichen Raums und regt zu einer aktiven Teilnahme am Stadtleben an. Anstelle der üblichen Benutzung von Parkplätzen am Straßenrand als Aufbewahrungsort für Fahrzeuge schlägt (P)LOT vor, diese Parzellen für eine alternative Nutzung zu mieten. Durch den Kauf von Anwohnerparkausweisen bzw. den Münzeinwurf in Parkuhren haben die Anwohner die Möglichkeit, temporäre Lager zu errichten oder den Platz für verschiedene Aktivitäten – wie die Installation temporärer Gärten oder „Outdoor-Dining" – zu nutzen. Eine erste Initiative für die Aneignung öffentlichen Raums wurde durch die Transformation gewöhnlicher Autoabdeckungen in tragbare Zelte zur Nutzung als Wohn- oder Freizeitraum realisiert. Je nach Wunsch hat die wetterfeste „Fahrzeugschutzhülle" aus PVC-Plane und Zeltstangen das Aussehen eines Mittelklassewagens oder einer Luxuslimousine.

STUDIO DRÉ WAPENAAR
The FourGrandPianoPavilion, The Netherlands, 2004–ongoing
The FourGrandPianoPavilion, Niederlande, 2004–jetzt

Originally developed for piano pieces by the Dutch composer
Simeon ten Holt, the FourGrandPianoPavilion has been used
as a mobile tent venue at various music festivals. The structure, consisting of a steel frame and a PVC-coated polyester
membrane, can hold up to 250 people and eight pianos that
are positioned in the four "corners" of the pavilion while the
audience gathers in the centre. Each piano is individually
audible and locatable. Projections of the musicians' faces on
large round screens allow them to communicate with each
other. The interior of this pavilion communicates with the outside world as a result of the membrane's optical and acoustic
permeability.

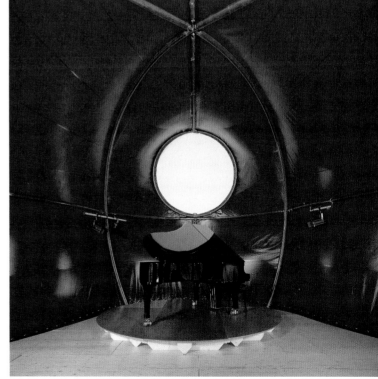

Ursprünglich für die Klavierstücke des niederländischen Komponisten
Simeon ten Holt entwickelt, wurde der FourGrandPianoPavilion
als mobiles Veranstaltungszelt auf verschiedenen Musikfestivals
eingesetzt. Die Konstruktion aus einem Stahlrahmen und einer PVC-
beschichteten Polyestermembran kann bis zu 250 Personen und acht
Klaviere aufnehmen. Sie sind in den vier „Ecken" des Pavillons aufgestellt, während sich das Publikum in der Raummitte befindet. Dadurch
ist jedes Klavier einzeln hör- und lokalisierbar. Die Musiker können dank
der Projektion ihrer Gesichter auf große runde Schirme miteinander
kommunizieren. Die optische und auch akustische Durchlässigkeit
der Membran lässt das Innere des Pavillons in Kommunikation mit der
Außenwelt treten.

## PLEINMUSEUM FOUNDATION AMSTERDAM

Mobile exhibition pavilion, different cities in Europe, from 2004–ongoing
*Mobiler Ausstellungspavillon, verschiedene Städte in Europa, seit 2004–jetzt*

"Pleinmuseum" is a mobile exhibition pavilion that is erected on main squares – at the centre of public life – in different cities. Since 2004, the museum has presented its digital collection in ten cities in The Netherlands, Belgium, France, and Italy. Integrated into the life of the city, this is an open, flexible museum that is easily accessible to everyone. It remains closed during the daytime in reference to the "white cube," the exemplary model of a modernistic museum. After sunset, the cube opens hydraulically to form a dynamic architectural installation of steel poles and canvas. Its walls become projection surfaces, whose appearances continually change, like the skin of a chameleon. As a temporary platform for visual communications, this fifteen-metre-long and five-metre-high pavilion activates public space, allowing artists and designers to communicate with a broad audience.

„Pleinmuseum" ist ein mobiler Ausstellungspavillon, der auf zentralen Plätzen verschiedener Städte – inmitten des öffentlichen Lebens – aufgestellt wird. Seit 2004 hat das Museum seine digitale Sammlung in bislang zehn Städten in den Niederlanden, Belgien, Frankreich und Italien präsentiert. In das städtische Leben integriert, ist es ein offenes und flexibles Museum, das für jeden leicht zugänglich ist. Tagsüber bleibt der Pavillon geschlossen und bezieht sich symbolisch auf den „White Cube", das beispielhafte Modell des modernistischen Museums. Nach Sonnenuntergang öffnet sich der Würfel hydraulisch und formt eine dynamische architektonische Installation aus Stahlstangen und Segeltuch. Die Wände werden zu Projektionsflächen, deren Erscheinung sich wie die Haut eines Chamäleons kontinuierlich ändert. Als temporäre Plattform für visuelle Kommunikation aktiviert der 15 Meter lange und fünf Meter hohe Pavillon den öffentlichen Raum, in dem Künstler und Designer mit einem breiten Publikum kommunizieren können.

AMO

Prada Transformer, Seoul, South Korea, 2009
*Prada Transformer, Seoul, Südkorea, 2009*

A rotatable pavilion whose shape was derived from a tetrahedron was developed to accommodate a fashion exhibition, a film festival, and art exhibition and a fashion show over a period of a view months. It consisted of a steel structure that was composed of four different basic shapes: a circle, a square, a hexagon, and a cross. Each surface was perfectly adapted to its function as the floor of an exhibition hall, a cinema, or a catwalk. The twenty-metre-high structure had no clearly defined ceiling or exterior wall, and no fixed floor. Each of its four basic shapes could alternately be a wall, ceiling, or floor. The structure was tipped into a different position for each event. An elastic, translucent white membrane was spanned over the frames, made of PVC.

Um für einige Monate nacheinander eine Modeausstellung, ein Filmfestival, eine Kunstausstellung oder eine Modenschau beherbergen zu können, wurde ein drehbarer Pavillon entwickelt, dessen Form von einem Tetraeder abgeleitet ist. Er bestand aus einer Stahlkonstruktion, die aus vier verschiedenen Grundformen zusammengesetzt wurde: einem Kreis, einem Rechteck, einem Sechseck und einem Kreuz. Jede Fläche war perfekt an ihre Bestimmung als Boden einer Ausstellungshalle, eines Kinos oder auch als Laufsteg angepasst. Der 20 Meter hohe Bau hatte keine eindeutig definierte Decke oder Außenwand und keinen fixierten Boden. Denn jede der vier Grundformen konnte mal Wand, mal Decke und mal Boden sein. Wie ein dynamischer Organismus wurde die Konstruktion für jede Veranstaltung in eine neue Position gekippt. Überzogen waren die Rahmen mit einer elastischen und transluzenten, weißen Membran aus PVC.

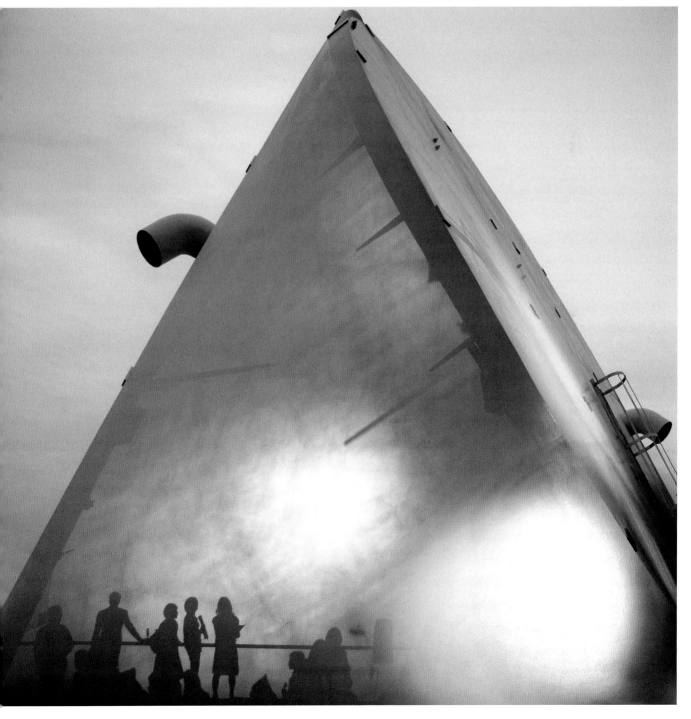

## R & SIE(N) – FRANÇOIS ROCHE AND STÉPHANIE LAVAUX

Spidernethewood, Nîmes, France, 2007
*Spidernethewood, Nîmes, Frankreich, 2007*

Inmitten wildwachsender Vegetation befindet sich das zweigeschossige Gebäude, von dem man über verschiebbare Glastüren in die umgebende „Spinnennetzstruktur" gelangt. Mit einer Innenfläche von 400 Quadratmetern und einem durch Polypropylennetze definierten Außenbereich von 2000 Quadratmetern gleicht es einer Lichtung im Wald. Im Inneren des Betonblocks sind die Wände und Decken größtenteils mit Polyurethanfolie überzogen. Vorhänge aus transluzenten Kunststoffstreifen dienen als flexible Türverschlüsse. Die Wegeführung im Gebäude wird außen durch ein Labyrinth aus Netzstrukturen fortgesetzt, innerhalb dessen sich Wege, Freiflächen und ein Schwimmbad befinden. Die äußerst widerstandsfähige und haltbare Netzstruktur „bändigt" einerseits die umgebende Vegetation, schafft aber gleichzeitig einen Rahmen, der von Bäumen, Büschen und rankendem Wein im Laufe der Zeit in einer Art „lost game" überwuchert wird. Permanent „under construction" ändert die Struktur ständig ihr Aussehen. Die Grenzen von Innen und Außen werden aufgrund der Durchlässigkeit der Netze aufgehoben.

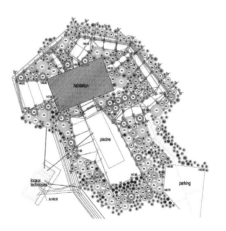

This two-storey building is positioned at the heart of wild vegetation; a surrounding "spider web structure" is accessed from it via sliding glass doors. With an interior area of 400 square-metres and an exterior area, defined by 2,000 square metres of polypropylene nets, it resembles a clearing in a forest. The walls and ceilings inside the concrete block have mostly been lined with polyurethane film. Curtains of translucent plastic strips serve as flexible door closures. The paths inside the building extend outside into a labyrinth of net structures within which paths, open spaces, and a swimming pool are positioned. This extremely resistant and durable net structure "tames" the surrounding vegetation while also creating a frame that will in time become overgrown by trees, bushes and vine creepers to form a kind of "lost game." Permanently "under construction," the structure continually changes its appearance. Boundaries between inside and outside disappear as a result of the permeable net structure.

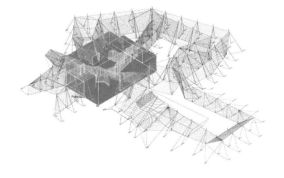

## FAR – FROHN & ROJAS

Wall House, Santiago de Chile, Chile, 2004–2007
*Wall House, Santiago de Chile, Chile, 2004–2007*

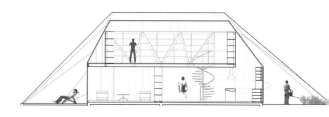

The composition of the "Wall House" is based on four building envelopes between which a series of spaces and climatic zones forms. The house gradually dissolves towards the outside space beginning with a concrete core inside through space-defining shelves and a translucent envelope of insulating polycarbonate sheets to a thin textile outside skin. The outer skin consists of an energy screen and insect fabric. The fabric of the energy screen is made of reflecting aluminium bands that are woven with polymer threads. Different weave densities are used, depending on orientation to the sun, in order to reflect between fifty and seventy-five per cent of the sunlight. This creates diffused light inside the building and a pleasant spatial climate. Energy-savings of up to thirty-five per cent can be made. A continuous protected outside space is created by the fact that the outer fabric remains up to 4.5 metres away from the polycarbonate envelope on the ground floor. Three zips have been sewn into the membrane, through which one can enter the garden.

Der Aufbau des „Wall House" basiert auf vier Gebäudehüllen, zwischen denen sich eine Serie von Räumen und Klimazonen bildet. Ausgehend von einem Betonkern im Inneren über raumbildende Regale und eine transluzente Hülle aus isolierenden Polycarbonatplatten bis hin zu einer dünnen textilen Außenhaut löst sich das Haus schrittweise zum Außenraum hin auf. Die äußerste Hülle besteht aus einem Energieschirm und einem Insektengewebe. Das Gewebe des Energieschirms besteht aus reflektierenden Aluminiumbändchen, die mit Polymerfäden verwoben sind. Je nach Himmelsrichtung werden verschiedene Gewebedichten eingesetzt, um etwa 50–75 Prozent des Sonnenlichts zu reflektieren. Dadurch entsteht im Gebäudeinneren diffuses Licht und ein angenehmes Raumklima. Eine Energieeinsparung von bis zu 35 Prozent wird ermöglicht. Indem sich das Gewebe im Erdgeschoss bis zu ca. 4,5 Meter von der Polycarbonathülle entfernt, entsteht ein kontinuierlich geschützter Außenraum. In die Membran sind drei Reißverschlüsse eingenäht, durch die man in den Garten gelangt.

R & SIE(N) – FRANÇOIS ROCHE AND STÉPHANIE LAVAUX

Barak House, Sommières, France, 2001
*Haus Barak, Sommières, Frankreich, 2001*

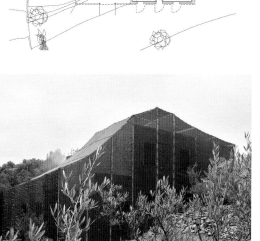

located in a protected area around Sommières Castle, a prerequisite for planning permission for this residential home was its almost complete invisibility. The contours of its tent-like exterior follow those of the landscape, emulating the lines of a nearby old stonewall. Its apparently fragile and temporary envelope consists of polyurethane net panels that are held together by carbon fibre cables and plastic clips. A seven-room concrete block structure is located underneath. There is enough room for a future invisible extension to be built under the protective covering of the outside envelope.

As well as providing storm protection, the shade given to the concrete block by the polyurethane net – a material usually used as an agricultural textile – helps to regulate inside temperatures. A curtain of translucent plastic strips has been installed inside the building for mosquito protection and it also serves as a flexible spatial partition between the kitchen and other living spaces.

Voraussetzung für die Baugenehmigung des Wohnhauses war seine fast vollständige Unsichtbarkeit, da es sich in einer Schutzzone des Schlosses Sommières befindet. Mit seinem zeltartigen Äußeren folgt das Gebäude den Konturen der Landschaft und ahmt den Verlauf einer nahen alten Steinmauer nach. Die scheinbar fragile und temporäre Hülle besteht aus Polyure-

thannetz-Paneelen, die mit Carbonfaserseilen und Kunststoffklammern zusammengehalten werden. Darunter befindet sich eine Betonblock-Struktur mit sieben Zimmern. Im Schutz der Außenhülle ist ausreichend Raum für eine zukünftige, von außen unsichtbare Erweiterung vorhanden.

Die Beschattung des Betonblocks durch das Polyurethannetz, das gewöhnlich im Bereich der Agrartextilien eingesetzt wird, trägt dazu bei, die Temperatur im Inneren zu regulieren; zudem dient es als Schutz bei Sturm. Im Inneren ist ein Vorhang aus transluzenten Kunststoffstreifen als Mückenschutz angebracht, der auch als flexible Raumtrennung zwischen der Küche und den anderen Wohnräumen dient.

RAUMLABORBERLIN
Hovercraft – lifting modernism, Paris, France, 2008
Hovercraft – lifting modernism, Paris, Frankreich, 2008

On the occasion of the seventy-fifth anniversary of the "Fondation Suisse" Swiss student residence located in the "Cité Universitaire de Paris," raumlaborberlin was commissioned to temporarily remedy one of the building's problem points – the lack of a space for large-scale festivities. Its terrace – a semi-public space that can only be used in the summer months – was made winter-proof using a translucent membrane made of PE film, thus transforming it into a semi-private space. Diverse events took place in the pneumatic hall over a three-day period. The building's entrance was shifted to properly integrate the semi-permeable public space into it – as a conservatory rather than a large porch. For three days, the "Salon Curbe" became the entrée, while the foyer served as an air lock.

Zum 75-jährigen Jubiläum des 1933 von Le Corbusier gebauten Schweizer Studentenwohnheims „Fondation Suisse" in der „Cité Universitaire de Paris" wurde raumlaborberlin beauftragt, ein Problem des Gebäudes – das Fehlen eines Raums für größere Feierlichkeiten – temporär zu beheben. Mittels einer transluzenten Membran aus PE-Folie wurde die Terrasse – ein halböffentlicher Raum, der aber nur im Sommerhalbjahr nutzbar ist – wintertauglich gemacht und damit in einen halbprivaten Raum transformiert. An drei Tagen fanden in der pneumatischen Halle diverse Veranstaltungen statt. Um diesen semipermeablen öffentlichen Raum richtig in das Gebäude zu integrieren – nicht als vergrößerten Windfang, sondern eher als Wintergarten – wurde der Eingang des Gebäudes verlegt. Drei Tage lang wandelte sich der „Salon Curbe" zum Entrée und das Foyer zur Luftschleuse.

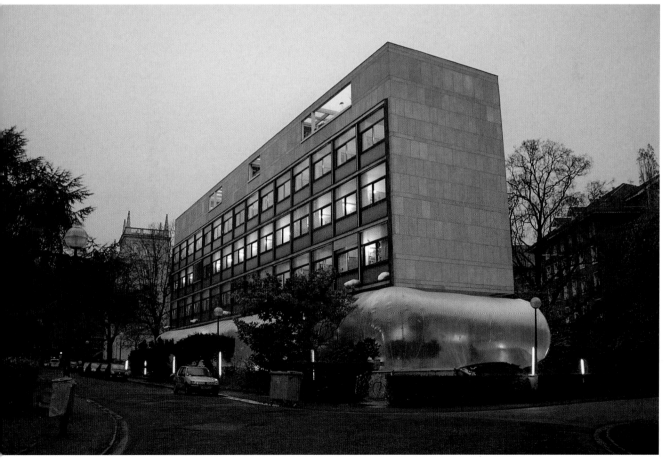

REM KOOLHAAS AND CECIL BALMOND

In 2006, having been invited by the Serpentine Gallery, Rem Koolhaas and Cecil Balmond designed a temporary pavilion to be erected for three months in the garden of the gallery. An inflatable egg-shaped roof covering hovered over translucent polycarbonate slabs arranged in circular formation. The top part provided shading as well as protection from wind and rain. This semi-transparent structure was illuminated from inside at night while the space below it served as a café and a forum for daily events. The balloon was horizontally divided into two parts by a so-called balloon-net membrane: its upper half was filled with helium and its lower with compressed air. The balloon-net membrane transferred the pressure of the air into the helium-filled part, thus stabilising the whole structure. Depending on the weather, the balloon, made of PVC-coated polyester membrane and held in position by cables anchored to the ground, could be raised to reach a total height of twenty-four meters. In open-roof position, it hovered four metres above the walls of the frame.

Eingeladen von der Serpentine Gallery, gestalteten Rem Koolhaas und Cecil Balmond 2006 einen temporären Pavillon, der für drei Monate im Garten der Galerie errichtet wurde. Über kreisförmig angeordneten transluzenten Polycarbonatplatten schwebte eine aufblasbare eiförmige Überdachung, die Schatten spendete und vor Regen sowie Wind schützte. Nachts wurde die semitransparente Struktur von innen beleuchtet. Der darunterliegende Raum diente als Café sowie als Forum für tägliche Veranstaltungen. Der Ballon war horizontal durch eine sogenannte Ballonnetz-Membran in zwei Bereiche geteilt: Die obere Hälfte war mit Helium, die untere mit Druckluft gefüllt. Die Ballonnetz-Membran übertrug den Druck der Luft in die mit Helium gefüllte Hälfte und stabilisierte auf diese Weise die gesamte Struktur. Je nach Wetterlage konnte der Ballon aus PVC-beschichteter Polyestermembran, der durch im Boden verankerte Seile sicher in Position gehalten wurde, bis zu einer Gesamthöhe von 24 Metern angehoben werden. In geöffneter Dachposition schwebte er vier Meter über den Wänden des Gehäuses.

## CSCEC + PTW + CCDI AND ARUP

Watercube – National Swimming Centre, Beijing, China, 2003–2008
Watercube – Nationales Schwimmzentrum, Peking, China, 2003–2008

The bluish shimmering cube of the National Swimming Centre takes water as its structural and topical leitmotiv – in conjunction with the rectangle shape, an important motif of Chinese tradition and mythology. The natural shape of soap bubbles has been translated into an architectural form. This filigree skin of cushions of ETFE film has been constructed as a double-layer façade, which, as a thermal buffer zone, reacts to the changing outside climate. The film, oriented towards the cavity of the façade, is printed with a silver, barely visible dotted pattern. Depending on the amount of sun protection required, the degree of printing varies from ten to sixty-five per cent. Ninety per cent of the solar energy entering the building is used to heat the pool and interior spaces, thus decreasing the energy required by thirty per cent. Its transparent façade allows natural daylight to enter to the core of this building, meaning that artificial lighting is not required during the day. At night the façade lights up, attracting attention to activities taking place inside.

Der bläulich schimmernde Kubus des Nationalen Schwimmzentrums assoziiert Wasser als strukturelles und thematisches Leitmotiv – verbunden mit der Form des Rechtecks, das ein wichtiges Motiv in der chinesischen Tradition und Mythologie ist. Die natürliche Struktur von Seifenblasen ist in eine architektonische Form übersetzt. Die filigrane Hülle aus ETFE-Folienkissen ist als Membran-Doppelfassade konstruiert, die als thermische Pufferzone auf das wechselnde Außenklima reagiert. Die zum Fassadenzwischenraum orientierten Folien sind mit einem silbernen, kaum sichtbaren Punktmuster bedruckt; je nach erforderlichem Sonnenschutz variiert der Bedruckungsgrad von zehn bis 65 Prozent. 90 Prozent der einfallenden Sonnenenergie wird zum Aufheizen der Becken und der Innenräume genutzt, womit der Energieverbrauch um bis zu 30 Prozent herabgesetzt wird. Die transparente Fassade erlaubt den Einfall von natürlichem Tageslicht ins Gebäudeinnere. Somit kann tagsüber auf künstliches Licht verzichtet werden. Nachts leuchtet die Fassade, um auf die Aktivitäten im Inneren aufmerksam zu machen.

## GEWEBE

### Natürliche Fasern

#### Cotton

Cotton is heat-resistant to the temperatures experienced in building practice and is resistant to normal amounts of chemical exposure. It has a moisture absorption of up to thirty-two per cent of its own weight without feeling wet. Its tendency to crease can be reduced by incorporating synthetic resin into it. Cotton weaves are usually impregnated rather than coated. Impregnation gives the weave a temporary flame-retardant surface, which is also fungicidal and water resistant. Cotton is not suited for permanent application to outside situations as a result of its low strength, low elasticity and – despite impregnation – a life span of only five years under the influence of weathering. It is limited to interior spaces or to low-strain temporary outdoor uses.

#### Wool

Wool has a high moisture absorption of up to thirty per cent of its own weight without feeling wet. Its natural moisture content impedes wool from becoming electrostati-cally charged. It has adequate strength and high elasticity, giving it good crease recovery values. Wool is naturally flame resistant. It is a classical material for use as furniture or decoration fabric and it is also used for carpets in interior spaces.

#### Linen

Linen absorbs moisture quickly and also releases it quickly. It has a high wet strength. Its very high tear resistance is between two and three times greater than that of cotton. However, its elasticity is lower than cotton meaning that it tends to crease easily. Linen has a smooth, high-grade shiny texture, high luminosity and is brilliant in colour. It is used as furniture or decoration fabric in interior spaces.

#### Baumwolle

Baumwolle ist im baupraktischen Temperaturbereich hitzebeständig und widerstandsfähig gegenüber üblichen Konzentrationen chemischer Belastung. Sie verfügt über eine Feuchtigkeitsaufnahme von bis zu 32 Prozent des Eigengewichts, ohne sich nass anzufühlen. Die Knitteranfälligkeit kann durch Einlagerung von Kunstharzen vermindert werden. Baumwollgewebe wird üblicherweise nicht beschichtet, sondern imprägniert. Die Imprägnierung verleiht dem Gewebe eine zeitlich begrenzte flammhemmende, fungizide und Wasser abweisende Oberfläche. Für den permanenten Gebrauch im Außenbereich eignet sich Baumwolle nicht, da sie eine geringe Festigkeit, eine geringe Elastizität und – trotz Imprägnierung – unter Einfluss von Witterung nur eine Lebensdauer von bis zu fünf Jahren hat. Ihr Einsatzgebiet begrenzt sich auf den Innenraum oder wenig belastete, temporäre Anwendungen im Außenbereich.

#### Wolle

Wolle verfügt über eine hohe Feuchtigkeitsaufnahme von bis zu 30 Prozent des Eigengewichts, ohne sich nass anzufühlen. Durch ihren natürlichen Feuchtigkeitsgehalt wird die elektrostatische Aufladung der Wolle erschwert. Sie besitzt eine ausreichende Festigkeit und eine hohe Elastizität und verfügt somit über gute Knittererholungswerte. Wolle ist von Natur aus schwer entflammbar. Sie ist ein klassisches Material für die Anwendung als Möbel- oder Dekorationsstoff sowie als Teppichboden im Innenraum.

#### Leinen

Leinen nimmt Feuchtigkeit schnell auf und gibt sie auch schnell wieder ab. Es hat eine hohe Nassfestigkeit. Die sehr hohe Reißfestigkeit ist etwa zwei- bis dreimal so groß wie bei Baumwolle. Die Elastizität ist jedoch geringer als die der Baumwolle und daher ist Leinen knitteranfällig. Leinen hat eine glatte, edel glänzende Oberfläche und eine hohe Leuchtkraft sowie Farbbrillanz. Es wird als Möbel- oder Dekorationsstoff im Innenraum verwendet.

### Synthetische Fasern

#### PA – Polyamide

PA is characterised by good tear resistance and rigidity, it is very abrasion-proof and extremely stretchable. Its mechanical characteristics are minimised by the effects of UV light, moisture, and oxygen. PA melts at approximately 220 degrees Celsius. PA fibres are usually combined with other fibres for use as furniture and decoration fabrics and in carpets.

#### PES – Polyester

Uncoated PES fabric is not rainproof and can therefore only be used in interior spaces. It has good UV-resistance and a light translucency of between thirty and thirty-five per cent. It is highly creaseesistant due to its elasticity. Its moisture absorption is low. PES fabric is hard-wearing, rot-resistant and resistant to chemicals. Polyester melts at approximately 260 degrees Celsius and is flammable, however it can be made flame retardant. It has a lifespan of between ten and twenty years. Special PES acoustic textiles have a sound-absorbing effect. They reduce the reverberation period in space and absorb background noises thus minimising sound pollution.

### PES coated with Aluminium or Steel

Polyester weaves are lined with a thin layer of aluminium on the rear side to produce optimum glare, visual and sun protection, and to provide efficient heat protection, thus regulating the spatial climate. The textile retains a certain degree of transparency depending on the layer thickness. Its high reflection of solar radiation reduces the amount of light entering and creates dimmer, glare-free light; irradiation is also reduced. Alternatively, a thin layer of steel can be applied in a vacuum. Tiny particles of steel are projected onto the textile using cathode sputtering. Since steel is darker than aluminium, these textiles reflect solar irradiation less. Steel-coated textiles are washable and have a lower tendency to kink and rupture.

### PES coated with PVC

When coated with PVC, PES weaves become rainproof and can then be used for weather protection in outdoor areas. They have good UV resistance and a light-translucency of between zero and twenty-five per cent. PVC-coated polyester weaves are flame resistant and–like all membranes–their low mass per unit area and low material thickness give them an extremely low fire load. Such weaves melt in case of fire, thus allowing heat and fumes to burn off directly. Their potentially high strength and tear resistance and high material expansion make them suitable membranes for wide spanning surface structures. They are often used for convertible or mobile structures as a result of their high kink resistance. PVC coating provides permanent protection from soiling and premature aging, giving PES weaves a life-span of between fifteen and twenty years. This material is well suited to printing.

### PTFE – Polytetrafluoroethylene, uncoated

Uncoated PTFE weave is not rainproof. It is fireproof and has good UV resistance. Its light-translucency is between fifteen and forty per cent. Its anti-adhesive characteristics make it very resistant to soiling and chemicals. Its permanent kink resistance and abrasion resistance are excellent so that it is often used in foldable membranes for sun protection. It has a lifespan of at least twenty-five years.

### Coated Fluoropolymer Weave

A coating can be needed to make this weave waterproof. Coated fluoropolymer weaves such as THV-coated PTFE or ETFE or PVDF-coated PVDF can consist of the same or different fluoropolymer compounds for the weave and coating. Their low rupture strength and low weld seam strength mean that coated fluoropolymer weaves can only be used for small spans for example in interior spaces. This material allows diffused and thus low-glare light within the daylight colour spectrum to pass through it; an effect that is perceived to be very pleasant. The light permeability of fluoropolymer weaves can reach up to ninety per cent. No other fully coated weaves can currently reach such a high value.

### Aramid Weave, coated with PVC

Aramid is the short name for aromatic polyamide. This fibre is relatively rigid and chemically and thermally resistant. Aramid fibre weave is the most highly resilient of all synthetically manufactured textile membranes. However, since it is not UV resistant, aramid weave must be sheathed in an opaque PVC (or PTFE) coating. It can be made flame resistant or fireproof depending on the type and mass of coating. Its application is limited to special uses that require high strength but do not need high elasticity and translucency.

### PA – Polyamid

PA zeichnet sich durch eine gute Reißfestigkeit und Steifigkeit aus, ist sehr abriebfest und äußerst dehnbar. Durch den Einfluss von UV-Licht, Feuchtigkeit und Sauerstoff werden die mechanischen Eigenschaften herabgesetzt. PA schmilzt bei ca. 220 Grad Celsius. Meist in Mischung mit anderen Fasern werden PA-Fasern zu Möbel- und Dekorationsstoffen sowie zu Teppichböden verarbeitet.

### PES – Polyester

Unbeschichtetes PES-Gewebe ist nicht regendicht und daher nur für die Anwendung im Innenbereich geeignet. Es hat eine gute UV-Beständigkeit und eine Lichttransluzenz von 30–35 Prozent. Aufgrund seiner Elastizität hat es eine hohe Knitterfestigkeit. Die Feuchtigkeitsaufnahme ist gering. PES-Gewebe ist strapazierfähig, verrottungsbeständig und chemisch beständig. Polyester schmilzt bei ca. 260 Grad Celsius und ist entflammbar, kann jedoch flammhemmend ausgerüstet werden. Die Lebensdauer beträgt 10–20 Jahre.

Spezielle Akustiktextilien aus PES haben schallabsorbierende Wirkung. Sie reduzieren die Nachhallzeit im Raum und dämpfen die Hintergrundgeräusche. Die Lärmbelästigung wird minimiert.

### PES mit Aluminium- oder Stahlbeschichtung

Um einen optimalen Blend-, Sicht- und Sonnenschutz sowie einen effizienten Wärmeschutz zur Regulierung des Raumklimas zu erhalten, werden Polyestergewebe auf der Rückseite mit einer dünnen Aluminiumschicht versehen. Das Textil behält dabei je nach Dichte der Schicht eine gewisse Transparenz. Die hohe Reflexion der Sonnenstrahlung reduziert den Lichteinfall und schafft ein gedämpftes Licht ohne Blendung, gleichzeitig wird die Wärmeeinstrahlung verringert. Ebenso kann eine dünne Stahlschicht in einem Vakuumverfahren aufgebracht werden. Dabei werden winzige Stahlpartikel mithilfe von Kathodenzerstäubung auf das Textil geschossen. Da Stahl dunkler als Aluminium ist, reflektieren diese Textilien die Sonneneinstrahlung weniger stark. Die stahlbeschichteten Textilien sind waschbar und weisen eine geringe Anfälligkeit gegenüber Knicken und Brüchen auf.

### PES mit PVC-Beschichtung

Mit einer Beschichtung aus PVC ist das PES-Gewebe regendicht und deshalb auch im Außenbereich als Wetterschutz einsetzbar. Es hat eine gute UV-Beständigkeit und eine Lichttransluzenz von 0–25 Prozent. PVC-beschichtetes Polyestergewebe ist schwer entflammbar und bildet – wie alle Membranen – aufgrund seines geringen Flächengewichts und seiner geringen Materialstärke eine extrem geringe Brandlast. Im Brandfall schmilzt das Gewebe und schafft somit die Möglichkeit des direkten Rauch- und Wärmeabzugs. Die hohe erreichbare Festigkeit und Weiterreißfestigkeit bei gleichzeitig hoher Materialdehnung erlauben den Einsatz als Membran für weit gespannte Flächentragwerke. Aufgrund seiner sehr guten Knickbeständigkeit wird das Gewebe häufig für wandelbare oder mobile Konstruktionen eingesetzt. Die PVC-Beschichtung sorgt für einen dauerhaften Schutz vor Anschmutzen und vorzeitiger Alterung, sodass die Lebensdauer 15–20 Jahre beträgt. Das Material lässt sich sehr gut bedrucken.

## PTFE – Polytetrafluorethylen, unbeschichtet

Unbeschichtet hat das PTFE-Gewebe keine Regendichtigkeit. Es ist unbrennbar und hat eine sehr gute UV-Beständigkeit. Die Lichttransluzenz beträgt 15–40 Prozent. Aufgrund der antiadhäsiven Eigenschaften ist das Anschmutzverhalten und die Beständigkeit gegen Chemikalien sehr gut. Die Dauerknickbeständigkeit und Abriebfestigkeit sind hervorragend, sodass PTFE-Gewebe häufig als Faltmembranen zum Schutz vor der Sonne eingesetzt werden. Die Lebensdauer beträgt mindestens 25 Jahre.

## Fluorpolymergewebe, beschichtet

Zur Erreichung der Wasserundurchlässigkeit kann ggf. eine Beschichtung notwendig werden. Beschichtete Fluorpolymergewebe, wie beispielsweise THV-beschichtete PTFE- oder ETFE-Gewebe oder auch PVDF-beschichtete PVDF-Gewebe, können aus gleichen oder unterschiedlichen Fluorpolymerverbindungen für Gewebe und Beschichtung bestehen. Wegen ihrer geringen Bruchfestigkeiten sowie aufgrund der geringen Schweißnahtfestigkeiten beschränkt sich

das Anwendungsspektrum der beschichteten Fluorpolymergewebe bislang auf kleine Spannweiten bzw. auf Innenanwendungen. Das Material lässt ausschließlich diffuses, also blendungsarmes Licht im Farbspektrum des Tageslichts hindurch, was als sehr angenehm wahrgenommen wird. Die Lichtdurchlässigkeit der Fluorpolymergewebe kann bis zu 90 Prozent betragen. Ein solch hoher Wert ist mit anderen vollflächig beschichteten Gewebearten zurzeit nicht erreichbar.

## Aramidgewebe, mit PVC-Beschichtung

Aramid ist die Kurzbezeichnung für aromatische Polyamide. Die Faser ist relativ steif, chemisch und thermisch widerstandsfähig. Das Aramidfasergewebe ist der am stärksten belastbare Werkstoff unter den synthetisch hergestellten textilen Membranen. Da es jedoch nicht UV-beständig ist, muss das Aramidgewebe von einer opaken Beschichtung aus PVC (oder auch PTFE) ummantelt werden. Je nach Beschichtungsart und -masse kann es schwer entflammbar oder unbrennbar sein. Das Einsatzgebiet beschränkt sich auf spezielle Anwendungen mit hohen erforderlichen Festigkeiten, bei denen große Elastizität und Transluzenz nicht erforderlich ist.

## Anorganische Fasern

### Fibreglass Weave

This weave consists of threads of glass filament of varying diameter that are of high tensile strength and rigidity. They behave neutrally in regard to environmental influences and chemicals. The material expansion and tear resistance are quite low as a result of the relatively brittle glass weave. This material is categorised

as fireproof. Its quite low kink resistance means that it cannot be used for convertible membrane structures.

### Fibreglass Weave, coated with PTFE

Fibreglass weave coated in PTFE can be used as weather protection for large spans and large-sized modules as a result of its rain impermeability. It has very high UV resistance and a light-translucency of approximately thirteen per cent. It is also characterised by its very high durability, resistance to fire, and good chemical resistance. Its surface is anti-adhesive and therefore self-cleaning. It has a minimum life span of between twenty-five and thirty years.

### Fibreglass Weave, coated with Silicon

Silicon-coated fibreglass weave has similar characteristics to a coating with PTFE, however its behaviour in outside areas as far as soiling is concerned is not satisfactory. Its light-translucency is twenty per cent higher than if coated with PTFE. Improvements have been made with regard to soiling in recent years. Silicon coating is less expensive than PTFE coating thus making it a potentially interesting membrane material.

### Metal Weave

Metal weave consists of an open-pored weave usually made of round, flat wires, litz wires or cables made of metallic materials such as stainless steel, titanium steel, chrome steel or chromium-nickel steel or of non-ferrous metal. Round wires normally have a diameter of between eighteen micro-metres and sixteen millimetres. Metal weaves are usually easy to maintain and have a high sturdiness and longevity. Many different surfaces can be created through staining, anodising,

varnishing, etc. Metal weaves are used as façade cladding and sun protection, as well as for interior roofs and partitions in inside spaces due to their alternating transparency according to the position of the observer and lighting conditions.

## Glasfasergewebe

Das Gewebe besteht aus Glasfilamentgarnen unterschiedlicher Durchmesser. Diese besitzen eine sehr hohe Zugfestigkeit und Steifigkeit. Gegenüber Umwelteinflüssen und Chemikalien verhalten sie sich neutral. Die Materialdehnung und die Weiterreißfestigkeit sind aufgrund des relativ spröden Glasgewebes gering. Das Material ist als nicht brennbar eingestuft. Aufgrund der relativ geringen Knickbeständigkeit eignet es sich nicht für den Einsatz als wandelbare Membrankonstruktion.

## Glasfasergewebe, mit PVC-Beschichtung

Aufgrund seiner Regendichtigkeit ist das Glasfasergewebe mit PTFE-Beschichtung im Wetterschutz für große Spannweiten und Modulgrößen einsetzbar. Es hat eine sehr hohe UV-Beständigkeit und eine Lichttransluzenz von bis ca. 13 Prozent. Weiter zeichnet es sich durch eine sehr hohe Haltbarkeit, Unbrennbarkeit sowie eine sehr gute chemische Beständigkeit aus. Die Oberfläche ist antiadhäsiv und somit selbstreinigend. Die Lebensdauer beträgt mindestens 25–30 Jahre.

## Glasfasergewebe, mit Silikon-Beschichtung

Das Glasfasergewebe mit Silikon-Beschichtung hat ähnliche Eigenschaften wie das mit PTFE-Beschichtung, jedoch ist das Anschmutzverhalten im Außenbereich nicht zufriedenstellend. Jedoch ist die Lichttransluzenz mit über 20

Prozent höher als bei Glasfasergewebe mit PTFE-Beschichtung. In den letzten Jahren wurden Verbesserungen im Anschmutzverhalten erreicht. Die Silikon-Beschichtung ist kostengünstiger als die PTFE-Beschichtung und somit interessant für den Einsatz als Membranmaterial.

## Metallgewebe

Metallgewebe bestehen aus einem offenporigen Gewebe aus zumeist runden, flachen Drähten, Litzen oder Seilen metallischer Werkstoffe wie Edelstahl, Titan-, Chrom- oder Chromnickelstahl oder auch Nichteisenmetall. Runddrähte haben standardmäßig einen Durchmesser zwischen 18 Mikrometer und 6 Millimeter. Metallgewebe haben einen geringen Pflegeaufwand sowie eine große Robustheit und Langlebigkeit. Durch Beizen, Eloxieren, Lackieren etc. wird eine Vielzahl an Oberflächen erreicht. Aufgrund der wechselnden Transparenz je nach Betrachterstandpunkt und Lichtsituation werden Metallgewebe als Fassadenverkleidung und Sonnenschutz, aber auch im Innenbereich als Innendecke oder Raumteiler verwendet.

## FOLIEN

### PES and PC – Polyester and Polycarbonate

Translucent acoustic films of polyester and polycarbonate are micro-perforated. The perforations capture incident sound waves thus having a noise-absorbing effect. The reverberation period in space is reduced and background noises are absorbed. Speech intelligibility is increased.

### PVC – Polyvinylchloride

PVC film is suitable for indoor use over medium to low spans and for temporary application in outdoor areas. Its temperature-dependent expansion behaviour as well as its low strength make it unsuitable for permanent outdoor use. It is rain proof and fire resistant, however it is not UV resistant. As a transparent film it is characterised by its very high light translucency of up to ninety-five per cent. It can be manufactured in colour or milky matte with a light-permeability of approximately seventy-nine per cent. It can be used as a projection surface in fair and exhibition structures or as a suspended luminous ceiling or rear-lit wall.

### ETFE – Ethylene-Tetrafluoroethylene

ETFE film is normally used as a transparent material in double- or multilayered pneumatic structures both inside and outside. Its light weight of under 1 kg/m2 has advantages over other plastics and glass, allowing filigree load-bearing structures to be erected. It has a high UV resistance and UV light-permeability. ETFE film systems are therefore increasingly used as permanent roof surfaces over greenhouses, swimming pools, and animal pens. ETFE film has excellent mechanical characteristics and good fire performance. The surface is self-cleaning and multifariously printable. Furthermore, it is almost totally recyclable. It has a minimum life span of between twenty-five and thirty years. Its relatively low tear resistance compared to the high rupture strength of a PVC-coated polyester weave makes the maximum span of an outdoor load-dissipating film structure much smaller that a corresponding structure made of a coated weave.

### THV – Tetraflouroethylene-Hexafluoropropylene-Vinylidene Fluoride Copolymer

THV film is chemically related to ETFE film. It has an extremely high transparency, is more elastic and easier to handle than ETFE film, however it is much less tear resistant and is thus only suited to small spans. It can be used to span point-fixed cable nets or projecting roofs.

### PES und PC – Polyester und Polycarbonat

Transluzente Akustikfolien aus Polyester oder Polycarbonat sind mikroperforiert. Die Lochungen fangen auftreffende. Die Nachhallzeit im Raum wird reduziert und die Hintergrundgeräusche gedämpft. Die Sprachverständlichkeit wird erhöht.

### PVC – Polyvinylchlorid

PVC-Folie eignet sich für Innenanwendungen bei mittleren und geringen Spannweiten und für temporäre Anwendungen im Außenbereich. Das stark temperaturabhängige Dehnungsverhalten ist neben ihrer geringen Festigkeit ein Ausschlusskriterium für dauerhafte Außenanwendungen. Sie ist regendicht und schwer entflammbar, jedoch nicht UV-beständig. Als transparente Folie zeichnet sie sich durch eine sehr hohe Lichttransluzenz bis zu 95 Prozent aus. Sie kann auch farbig oder milchig matt mit einer Lichtdurchlässigkeit von ca. 79 Prozent hergestellt werden. Als Projektionsfläche im Messe- oder Ausstellungsbau, als abgehängte Lichtdecke oder hinterleuchtete Wand ist sie vielfältig einsetzbar.

### ETFE – Ethylen-Tetrafluorethylen

ETFE-Folie wird überwiegend als transparentes Material in zwei- oder mehrlagigen pneumatischen Konstruktionen im Innen- wie Außenbereich verwendet. Ihr geringes Gewicht von unter 1 kg/m² bietet gegenüber anderen Kunststoffen und Glas Vorteile und lässt den Bau filigraner Tragekonstruktionen zu. Sie hat eine sehr hohe UV-Beständigkeit und UV-Lichtdurchlässigkeit. Deshalb finden ETFE-Foliensysteme zunehmend Anwendung als permanente Dachflächen von Gewächshäusern, Schwimmbädern und Tiergehegen. ETFE-Folie hat ausgezeichnete mechanische Eigenschaften und ein gutes Brandverhalten. Die Oberfläche ist selbstreinigend und vielfältig bedruckbar. Zudem ist sie nahezu vollständig recyclebar. Die Lebensdauer beträgt mindestens 25–30 Jahre. Aufgrund der relativ geringen Reißfestigkeit im Gegensatz zu der Bruchfestigkeit eines PVC-beschichteten Polyestergewebes ist die maximale Spannweite einer Last abtragenden Folienkonstruktion im Außenbereich deutlich geringer als eine entsprechende Konstruktion aus einem beschichteten Gewebe.

### THV – Tetraflourethylen-Hexafluorpropylen-Vinylidenfluorid-Coploymer

THV-Folie ist eine chemische Verwandte der ETFE-Folie. Sie hat eine extrem hohe Transparenz, ist elastischer und leichter verarbeitbar, aber deutlich weniger reißfest als ETFE-Folie und daher nur für sehr kleine Spannweiten geeignet. Sie eignet sich als Bespannung von Seilnetzen mit Punktbefestigern oder Vordächern.

1 Cp. Kaltenbach, Frank (Ed.): Detail Praxis. Transluzente Materialien. Glas, Kunststoff, Metall. Munich 2003, pp. 58–98 and Koch, Klaus-Michael (Ed.): Bauen mit Membranen. Munich 2004, pp. 48–65 and Hoppe, Diether S.: Freigespannte textile Membrankonstruktionen. Vienna 2007, pp. 53–65 and Tritthardt, Jörg: "Textiles Bauen". In: Deutsches Architektenblatt, Issues 1/2000 and 3/2000 and www.creationbaumann.com/press_detail_de,5501,72877,detail.html (26.06.09)

# Index of Materials and Manufacturers
## Material- und Herstellernachweis

## Projekt und Material

## Textilhersteller

HOUSE 47°40'48"N/13°8'12"E (p. 68–69)
Polyethylene raschel fabric/Polyethylen Raschelgewirk

*Textile processing/Textilverarbeitung:*
**Europlan Wassermair GmbH**
www.wassermair.com
T: +43 (0)7732 46090

ZENITH MUSIC HALL (p. 70–71)
Silicon-reinforced fibre-glass fabric/Silikonverstärktes Glasfasergewebe

Canobbio S.p.A.

LUNA ROSSA TEAM BASE (p. 72–73)
Coated sail/Beschichtete Segel

*Construction and mounting/Konstruktion und Montage:*
Tensoforma Trading srl

CASA DA MÚSICA (p. 74-75)
VOILE CS
100 % Trevira CS
g/sqm/g/m²: 50
Translucency/Transluzenz: 60%
Fire Resistance/Feuerbeständigkeit: Permanently flame resistant DIN 4102 B/Permanent schwer entflammbar DIN 4102 B
and/und
CLIVIA 600
Pure cotton/Reine Baumwolle
g/sqm/g/m²: 600
Translucency/Transluzenz: no/nein
Fire resistance/Feuerbeständigkeit: DIN 4102 B1

**Gerriets GmbH**
www.gerriets.com
T: +49 (0) 7665 960-0

SHOWROOM KVADRAT (p. 76–77)
North Tiles
Core: flameproof polyethylene foam/Kern: feuerbeständiger Polyethylenschaum
Covering material/Bezugsstoff: Divina and/und Divina Melange: wool/ Wolle
or/oder
Tempo
Trevira CS
Fire resistance/Feuerbeständigkeit: yes/ja
Acoustic-improving characteristics/Akustik-verbessernde Eigenschaften

**Kvadrat A/S**
www.kvadrat.dk
T: +45 8953 1866

PRESENTATION OF SWITZERLAND AT THE FRANKFURT BOOK FAIR (p. 78–79)
Dekomolton (Decorative molleton)
Pure cotton/Reine Baumwolle
g/sqm/g/m²: 165
Translucency/Transluzenz: no/nein
Fire resistance/Feuerbeständigkeit: DIN 4102 B1

**Gerriets GmbH**
www.gerriets.com
T: +49 (0) 7665 960-0

MERCEDES BENZ MUSEUM (p. 80–81)
VOILE CS
100 % Trevira CS
g/sqm/g/m²: 50
Translucency/Transluzenz: 60%
Fire Resistance/Feuerbeständigkeit: Permanently flame resistant DIN 4102 B/Permanent schwer entflammbar DIN 4102 B
and/und
CONTRA H FEIN
Viscose filament yarn/Viskosefilamentgarn
g/sqm/g/m²: 200
Fire resistance/Feuerbeständigkeit: DIN 4102 B1
and/und
Glattglanzfolie (Smooth glossy film)
PVC
g/sqm/g/m²: 230
Fire resistance/Feuerbeständigkeit: DIN 4102 B1

**Gerriets GmbH**
www.gerriets.com
T: +49 (0) 7665 960-0

EXTENSION TO SCHOOL COMPLEX HIRZENBACH (p. 82–83)
PES, equipped with flame retardant/PES, schwer entflammbar ausgerüstet

Christian Fischbacher Co. AG

CONCERT HALL (p. 84–85)

*Prime contractor/Generalunternehmer:*
**Stahl & Traumfabrik AG**
www.stahlundtraum.ch
T: +41 44 485 41 71

ROC AVENTUS APELDOORN (p. 86–87)
Transparent flag fabric and lorry tarpaulin/Transparenter Flaggenstoff und Lastwagenplane

TEXTILE PAVILION MUDAM (p. 124–125)
North Tiles
Core: flameproof polyethylene foam/Kern: feuerbeständiger Polyethylenschaum
Covering material/Bezugsstoff: Divina and/und Divina Melange: wool/ Wolle
or/oder
Tempo
Trevira CS
Fire resistance/Feuerbeständigkeit: yes/ja
Acoustic-improving characteristics/Akustik-verbessernde Eigenschaften

**Kvadrat A/S**
www.kvadrat.dk
T: +45 8953 1866

ARIUM (p. 126–127)
Lia/ 52 pistachio
100% polyamide/100% Polyamid
g/sqm/g/m²: 80
Translucency/Transluzenz: yes/ja
UV-resistance/UV-Beständigkeit: 4–5
Acoustic characteristics/Akustische Eigenschaften: medium/mittel
Fire resistance/Feuerbeständigkeit: DIN 4102 B1

**Nya Nordiska Textiles GmbH**
www.nya.com
T: +49 5861 8090

HOUSES IN MULHOUSE (p. 128–129)
Shading umbrella made of acrylic with aluminium ribbons/Schattierschirm aus Acryl mit Alubändchen

Novavert GmbH & Co. KG

CITYSKY (p. 130–131)
PVC-coated net fabric/PVC-beschichtetes Netzgittergewebe

SWISS PAVILION FOR ARCO (p. 132–133)
HDPE ribbons/HDPE-Bändchen

Tegum AG

THE TUBALOON (p. 134–135)
PVDF-coated PVC/PVDF-beschichteter PVC

Canobbio S.p.A.

COMMERZBANK ARENA (p. 136–137)
PVC-coated PES/PVC beschichteter PES

S. Ferrari S.A.

CENTURY LOTUS SPORTS PARK (p. 138–139)
PVC

Taiyo Kogyo Corporation

(PLOT): PROPOSITIONS (p. 178–179)
PVC

THE FOURGRANDPIANOPAVILION (p. 180–181)
PVC-coated PES /PVC-beschichtetes PES

PRADA TRANSFORMER (p. 184–185)
PVC

Cocoon Holland BV

SPIDERNETHEWOOD (p. 186–187)
Polyurethane netting/Polyurethannetz

Huck Occitania

WALL HOUSE (p. 188–189)
Energy umbrella made of aluminium ribbons/Energieschirm aus Aluminiumbändchen
and/und
Insect fabric/Insektengewebe

BARAK HOUSE (p. 190–191)
Polyurethane/Polyurethan

EMIS France

HOVERCRAFT – LIFTING MODERNISM (p. 192–193)
PE film/PE-Folie

SERPENTINE GALLERY (p. 194–195)
PVC-coated PES, PVC film and ETFE film/PVC-beschichtetes PES, PVC-Folie und ETFE-Folie

Hightex GmbH

WATERCUBE – NATIONAL SWIMMING CENTRE (p. 196–197)
EFTE film/EFTE-Folie

Vector Foiltec

Picture index
*Bildverzeichnis*

## Abbildungen

## Bildnachweis

Every effort has been made to identify all rights holders before publication. We would ask any rights holders we did not manage to contact to get in touch with the author or the publisher.

Trotz intensiver Bemühungen konnten nicht alle Bildrechteinhaber ausfindig gemacht werden. Wir bitten, sich ggf. mit der Autorin oder dem Verlag in Verbindung zu setzen.

# Bibliography
## *Literaturverzeichnis*

Architekturmuseum in Basel (Ed.): *Zelte*. Basel 1986

Arcus. Architektur und Wissenschaft (Ed.): *Der umgekehrte Weg. Frei Otto zum 65. Geburtstag*. No. 10. Cologne 1990

Bammer, Anton: *Wohnen im Vergänglichen. Traditionelle Wohnformen in der Türkei und in Griechenland*. Graz 1982

Bauakademie der DDR, Institut für Städtebau und Architektur (Ed.): *Karl Friedrich Schinkel*. Berlin 1982

Brockhaus (Ed.): *Enzyklopädie*. Volume 2. Mannheim 1992

Cohen, Jean-Louis: *Ludwig Mies van der Rohe*. Paris 2007

Durm, Josef: *Die Baukunst der Etrusker. Die Baukunst der Römer*. Darmstadt 1885

Eberlein, Johann Konrad: *Apparatio regis – revelatio veritatis. Studien zur Darstellung des Vorhanges in der bildenden Kunst von der Spätantike bis zum Ende des Mittelalters*. Wiesbaden 1982

Exhibition catalogue *Stoffe und Räume. Eine textile Wohngeschichte der Schweiz*. Langenthal 1986

Faegre, Torvald: *Zelte. Die Architektur der Nomaden*. Hamburg 1980

Graefe, Rainer: *Vela erunt*. Mainz 1979

Giedion, Siegfried: *Die Herrschaft der Mechanisierung*. Frankfurt/Main, 1982

Hammer-Tugendhat, Daniela/Tegethoff, Wolf: *Ludwig Mies van der Rohe. Das Haus Tugendhat*. Vienna 1998

Harather, Karin: *Haus-Kleider. Zum Phänomen der Bekleidung in der Architektur*. Wien 1995

Heinz, Dora: *Europäische Wandteppiche I*. Braunschweig 1963

Herzog, Thomas: *Pneumatische Konstruktionen. Bauten aus Membranen und Luft*. Stuttgart 1976

Hoppe, Diether S.: *Freigespannte textile Membrankonstruktionen*. Wien 2007

Institut für Leichte Flächentragwerke, University of Stuttgart (Ed.): *IL 5. Wandelbare Dächer*. Stuttgart 1972

Institut für Leichte Flächentragwerke, University of Stuttgart (Ed.): *IL 7. Schatten in der Wüste*. Stuttgart 1972

Institut für Leichte Flächentragwerke, University of Stuttgart (Ed.): *IL 16. Zelte*. Stuttgart, 1976

Institut für Leichte Flächentragwerke, University of Stuttgart (Ed.): *IL 30. Schattenzelte – Sun and Shade. Toldos. Vela*. Stuttgart 1984

Kaltenbach, Frank (Ed.): *Detail Praxis. Transluzente Materialien. Glas, Kunststoff, Metall*. Munich 2003

Koch, Klaus-Michael (Ed.): *Bauen mit Membranen*. Munich 2004

Lang, Hans: *Gotische Bildteppiche*. Stuttgart circa 1975

Loschek, Ingrid: *Reclams Mode- & Kostümlexikon*. Stuttgart 1999

Meier-Oberist, Edmund: *Kulturgeschichte des Wohnens im abendländischen Raum*. Hamburg 1956

Nerdinger, Winfried (Ed.): *Frei Otto. Das Gesamtwerk. Leicht bauen, natürlich gestalten*. Basel 2005

Otto, Frei (Ed.): *Zugbeanspruchte Konstruktionen*. Berlin 1962

Propyläen (Ed.): *Kunstgeschichte. Das alte Ägypten*. Frankfurt/Main 1975

Reinle, Adolf: *Zeichensprache der Architektur*. Zurich 1976

Semper, Gottfried: *Der Stil in den technischen und tektonischen Künsten oder praktische Ästhetik*, Volume I. Mittenwald 1977
(Reprint of the original edition: Volume I, Frankfurt/Main 1860)

Schmidt. Heinrich J.: *Alte Seidenstoffe*. Braunschweig 1958

Schwartz-Clauss, Mathias/Vegesack, Alexander von (Ed.): *Living in Motion. Design und Architektur für flexibles Wohnen*. Ditzingen 2002

Skidmore, Owings & Merrill (Ed.): *SOM Skidmore, Owings & Merrill. Architektur und Städtebau 1973–1983*. Stuttgart 1983

Stiftung Bauhaus Dessau (Ed.): *Gunta Stölzl. Meisterin am Bauhaus Dessau. Textilien, Textilentwürfe und freie Arbeiten 1915–1983*. Ostfildern-Ruit 1997

Tegethoff, Wolf: *Mies van der Rohe. Die Villen und Landhausprojekte*. Essen 1981

### Magazines – Zeitschriften:

*db deutsche bauzeitung* No. 7, 1960

*db deutsche bauzeitung* No. 2, 2005

*Deutsches Architektenblatt* No. 1, 2000 and No. 3, 2000

*Deutsche Bauzeitschrift* No. 4, 2003

### Internet:

Création Baumann: *The citation in internet*.
www.creationbaumann.com/press_detail_de,5501,72877,detail.html/ 26.06.09

SL Rasch: *The citation in internet*.
www.sl-rasch.de/ 20.05.09

Sylvie Krüger (born in 1973) was a founding partner of Korridor (1999–2002), a multi-disciplinary design office with a focus on textile spatial partitions as well as textile product design, exhibition design, the conception and implementation of photo production, and trend consultation within the realm of textiles. From 2004–2006 she managed the home textiles studio of Wever automotive and upholstery fabric weaving mill and was responsible for the public image of the company.
From 2002–2004 and since 2007 she operates independently with a focus on textile, colour and interior design. She lives and works in Munich.

*Sylvie Krüger (geb. 1973) war Gründungspartner von Korridor (1999–2002), einem multi-disziplinären Designbüro mit den Tätigkeitsschwerpunkten textile Raumtrennungen und textiles Produktdesign, Ausstellungsdesign, Konzeption und Realisierung von Fotoproduktionen und Trendberatung im textilen Bereich. 2004–2006 Leitung des Heimtextilateliers der Automobil- und Möbelstoffweberei Wever und verantwortlich für die Außendarstellung des Unternehmens.*
*2002–2004 und seit 2007 selbstständig tätig mit dem Schwerpunkt Textil-, Farb- und Interiordesign. Sie lebt und arbeitet in München.*

**Thank you**
I would like to express my sincere thanks to the following people: Andreas Ferstl, without whose commitment this book would never have become reality. Heike Henig, Lorenz Löbermann, Helmut Reuter, Adelgud Janik, Ingrid and Peter Krüger.

Special thanks go to the architects, designers, artists, and companies that were involved and who kindly placed their pictorial and planning material at my disposal for this book. I would also like to thank the photographers who generously gave me access to their photographic material.

*Danke*
*Für ihre Unterstützung möchte ich folgenden Personen ganz ausdrücklich danken: Andreas Ferstl, ohne dessen Engagement das Buch nicht zustande gekommen wäre. Heike Henig, Lorenz Löbermann, Helmut Reuter, Adelgund Janik, Ingrid und Peter Krüger.*

*Mein besonderer Dank gilt den beteiligten Architekten, Designern, Künstlern und Firmen, die ihr Bild- und Planmaterial für dieses Buch zur Verfügung gestellt haben. Danken möchte ich auch allen Fotografen, die mir großzügig ihr Bildmaterial zur Verfügung gestellt haben.*